2

CANADIAN PUBLIC OPINION ON THE AMERICAN CIVIL WAR

STUDIES IN HISTORY, ECONOMICS AND PUBLIC LAW

EDITED BY THE FACULTY OF POLITICAL SCIENCE OF
COLUMBIA UNIVERSITY

Volume CXXIV]   [Number 2

Whole Number 273

CANADIAN PUBLIC OPINION ON THE AMERICAN CIVIL WAR

BY

HELEN G. MACDONALD, Ph.D.

New York
COLUMBIA UNIVERSITY
NEW YORK: COLUMBIA UNIVERSITY PRESS, 2960 BROADWAY
LONDON: P. S. KING & SON
1926

To

CANADA AND THE UNITED STATES
MAY BROTHERHOOD PREVAIL

PREFACE

A study of the American Civil War, in as far as it affected the British North American Provinces, is of special interest to Canadians. Believing that is a field of Canadian history in which comparatively little has been done, moreover one of much importance, I have endeavored to picture the trend of opinion in all parts of Canada at that stirring time.

From my study of the period, I believe that the American Civil War left its imprint upon the political institutions of British North America to a greater extent than has been generally recognized. A survey of the newspapers of British America seems to prove that the people generally were divided in accordance with party lines, the Liberals sympathized with the North, and the Conservatives with the South. The British North American Provinces realized that in the event of war between Great Britain and the United States, Canada must necessarily be the battlefield. Hence to Canadians the preservation of amicable relations became a matter of utmost importance. The American struggle, moreover, emphasized the need of a closer union of all the British provinces, and hastened confederation. An examination of the government correspondence convinces one that much of the credit for averting war must be given to the sanity of leadership on both sides of the line which divides Canada and the United States.

Much of the material for this study was obtained at the Public Archives, and Library of Parliament, Ottawa, Canada. The author gratefully acknowledges the kindness of the librarians; in particular, Miss Smillie of the Dominion

Archives and Mr. McCormac of the Library of Parliament. The author also gratefully acknowledges her indebtedness to Mrs. T. S. McMorran and Mrs. Kennedy of Ottawa who verified data for her. A special debt of gratitude is due Dr. O. D. Skelton, Canadian historian, now of the Department of External Affairs of Canada, Dr. R. L. Schuyler of Columbia, and also Mr. J. B. Brebner of the same institution, who have read the entire manuscript and offered helpful suggestions. Especially does the author express her appreciation to Dr. D. R. Fox for his supervision of the study, for his numerous suggestions, unfailing kindness, consideration and encouragement in the course of its preparation.

CONTENTS

CHAPTER I

BRITISH NORTH AMERICA AND THE UNITED STATES
1840-1860

Commercial Relations — Survey of Great Britain's Trade Policy — Navigation Acts—Control over Colonial Trade—Colonial Preference—Canadian Corn Act 1843—Transformation in Great Britain's Trade Policy —The Repeal of the Corn Laws in 1846—Disastrous Effect in British North America—Abolition of Colonial Preference—Protests—Advocates of Reciprocity—Advocates of Annexation—Repeal of the Navigation Acts—The Rebellion Losses Bill—Defeat of the Conservatives 1848—The British North American League 1849—Montreal Annexation Manifesto 1849—Newspaper Opinion in Canada West and Canada East—The Influence of the Manchester School of Liberals—Effect of Lord John Russell's Speech in North America—Lord Elgin's Vision of Empire—Official British Attitude Opposed to Annexation—Reciprocity Secured.

MORE deeply than has been generally recognized the American Civil War left its imprint upon the political institutions of British North America.[1] A consideration of the attitude toward that conflict adopted by the people of these provinces should, therefore, be of interest to the English-speaking world. But the full significance, or even the partial significance, of British North American opinion throughout the war period cannot be grasped by either the American or the Canadian of the twentieth century without a pre-

[1] Included within the term British North America were Canada West, Canada East, and the Maritime Provinces. From 1791 until 1841 the names *Upper Canada* and *Lower Canada* were invariably used, and then in order to meet the situation presented by two legal systems, a convention grew up of using the terms *Canada West* and *Canada East* in connection with ministerial offices. As this practice was reinforced by the usage of the postal authorities, the latter terms were in general use from 1841 until 1867. From that time the two have been called *Ontario* and *Quebec*.

liminary survey of the relations which had naturally arisen between two adjacent countries with a common language. The points of contact between the United States and British America may be considered first under the heading of commercial relations, involving a study of the questions of annexation and reciprocity. The first division of the study is largely an economic phase, but not wholly, for even here the influence of the mother land and the affection of many of the inhabitants for the British Crown cannot be ignored.

For many years the commercial policy of the colonies had been largely determined by Great Britain, whose old colonial system had involved the passage of almost one hundred parliamentary statutes.[1] Throughout the seventeenth and eighteenth century, the restrictions that Great Britain, in accordance with the mercantilistic doctrines then prevalent, imposed upon her colonies in an attempt to control their trade, were light in comparison with those enforced by other European countries throughout their dependencies.[2] Great Britain was, however, desirous of creating an empire commercially independent of any other country, a self-sufficing economic unit.[3] To further this trade policy, the early royal governors upon their appointment received instructions with regard to the various trade statutes with which they must be familiar.[4] So far was Great Britain successful in accomplishing her purpose that the period from 1650 to 1830 has been called " the period

[1] George Louis Beer, *British Colonial Policy 1754-65*, chap. x, p. 193.

[2] *Political Science Quarterly*, 1917, R. L. Schuyler, " Preference and Sir Robert Peel," p. 430.

[3] Herbert L. Osgood, *The American Colonies in the Seventeenth Century*, vol. iii, p. 193.

[4] George Louis Beer, *British Colonial Policy 1754-65*, chap. x, footnote p. 193, Trade Instructions to John Reynolds, governor of Georgia, August 6, 1754.

of trade ascendancy ".[1] In 1651 a Navigation Act was
passed with a two-fold object in view, the encouragement
of English shipping and manufacturing. By this measure
foreigners were restricted in their commercial intercourse
with the colonies since all goods exported from the colonies
must be carried in English or colonial built ships, owned by
English subjects, and manned by a crew of whom the majority had to be English.[2] This Act was aimed directly at
the Dutch, then the sole rival of England as carriers of
goods, not as manufacturers; for in Holland, ships were
built at a lower cost than in England. At the expense, therefore, of the Dutch, England built up her merchant marine.

The Navigation Act of 1660, called by contemporary
writers the " Sea Magna Charta " [3] or " Charta Maritima ",
excluded foreign built ships also. A violation of this act
meant the loss of both ship and cargo; moreover, it provided that certain " enumerated " articles produced in the
English colonies, including sugar, tobacco, cotton, wool,
indigo, ginger, fustic or other dyeing woods, could be
shipped only to England, Ireland, and the British colonies.
The Governors of the British Colonies were instructed to
insist upon the strict enforcement of the Navigation Acts.
Three years later all foreign-built ships were declared alien.
By the Act of 1673 export duties were levied on the
enumerated articles when shipped from one colony to another. If the reply of the Massachusetts General Court in
1665 [4] to the remonstrances of the Royal Commissioners
concerning infringements of the act in which the court, after
its declaration that it had been misrepresented to the king,

[1] H. E. Egerton, *A Short History of British Colonial Policy*, bk. ii, p. 55.
[2] H. L. Osgood, *American Colonies in the Seventeenth Century*, vol.
iii, p. 205.
[3] *Ibid.*, pt. i, vol. i, chap. ii, p. 58.
[4] *Ibid.*, pt. i, vol. ii, chap. xi, p. 248.

declared that " we are not conscious that we have greatly violated the same ", may be considered indicative of the temper of the colonies, the enforcement of the Navigation Acts even in the period of trade ascendancy must have been an extremely difficult matter.

Although certain features of the Navigation Acts formed one of the grievances of the American people in 1776, the termination of the Revolutionary War did not bring their abolition, for through them Great Britain still sought to control the trade of her remaining colonies. The arguments advanced in Great Britain for their maintenance were in accordance with the old mercantilistic theory that colonies existed primarily for the benefit of the Mother Country. The prevalent conception of the Navigation Acts in the early nineteenth century in Great Britain may be found in the explanation given by Huskisson,[1] in the House of Commons, May 12, 1826: " Our Navigation laws have a two-fold object. First, to create and maintain in this country a great commercial marine; secondly (an object not less important in the eyes of statesmen) to prevent any one other nation from engrossing too largely a portion of the navigation of the rest of the world. Acting upon this system, the general rule of our policy has been to limit as much as possible the right of importing the productions of foreign countries into this country, to ships of the producing country, or to British ships." The motives for adopting that system were, first, that such portion of the carrying trade of foreign countries as did not fall to Great Britain's shipping, should be divided as equally as possible among the other Maritime States, and not enjoyed by any one of them in particular; and, secondly, that countries entertaining relations of commerce with this country, and not possessing shipping of their own, should export their produce to Eng-

[1] In 1826, Huskisson was President of the Board of Trade; in 1827, he was Colonial Secretary.

land in British ships only, instead of employing the ships of any third Power.[1]

The old colonial system from time to time extended the so-called enumerated articles until in 1840 more than eighty articles were listed.[2] Sir Robert Peel further extended the principle of colonial preference by his tariff schedule of 1842 which levied differential duties in favor of 375 colonial products.[3] In 1843 Peel's Corn Act admitted Canadian wheat and flour at a merely nominal duty. In return for this preference in the British market the Canadian legislature agreed to impose a duty of three shillings a quarter, on all American grain crossing the Canadian frontier. On this condition the British government further promised that " all grain cleared from Canadian ports, whether native grown or imported from the United States, would be admitted at fixed duty of one shilling " instead of at the existing rate, which, depending upon English prices, varied from one shilling to five shillings.[4] The natural result was the fostering, the building up, of certain industries in Canada on an unstable foundation, and especially the investment of considerable capital in Canada in the erection of flour mills and the construction of canals.[5] Much of the money went into canals, for the idea that the St. Lawrence system would drain the Middle West was an old one. It was also believed that the Welland and St. Lawrence canals largely nullified the purpose of the Erie Canal.

The following year, however, there was a relaxation in the preferential system, a foreshadowing of free trade, for

[1] *Hansard Parliamentary Debates*, 3rd ser., vol. 105, p. 103.

[2] *Political Science Quarterly*, Sept., 1917, R. L. Schuyler, " Preference and Sir Robert Peel," p. 432.

[3] *Johns Hopkins University Studies*, 1922, Tansill, Charles C., " The Canadian Reciprocity Treaty of 1854," p. 12.

[4] *Ibid.*, p. 13.

[5] *Ibid.*, p. 10.

by the customs act of 1844 the duties on foreign wool were repealed and the preference granted hitherto to colonial coffee was greatly reduced. This system was not, however, greatly relaxed until the Corn Act of 1846, which brought bankruptcy to the owners of the newly erected mills by abolishing the preference to colonial corn, and the resultant commercial depression, especially in Montreal, was acute. The Earl of Cathcart, Governor-General of Canada, in 1846, wrote a letter to Gladstone, then secretary of state for the colonies, in which he stated that "the successful operation of the newly completed canal system depended upon the continuance of colonial preference." Since the American route via the Erie Canal was shorter, and not blocked by ice for several months each year, he declared, some preference must be given to the grain shipped by the St. Lawrence route if the debt incurred in the construction of the Canadian canals was not to be repudiated.[1] In his reply of March 3, 1846, Gladstone deprecated the injury to Canadian trade, but declared that cheap food was a prime necessity for Great Britain.[2] Lord Elgin who became Governor-General of Canada, January, 1847, rightly diagnosed the cause of the distress in Canada: "It is the inconsistency of Imperial Legislation, and not the adoption of one policy rather than another, which is the bane of the colonies."[3]

By the Corn Act of June 26, 1846, colonial grain was to continue "to receive a preference until February, 1849, after which date all importations of oats, barley, and wheat wherever grown were to pay only a nominal duty of one shilling per quarter."[4] The same day a tariff act which reduced

---

[1] *Ibid.*, p. 15.

[2] *Ibid.*, p. 15.

[3] Theodore Walrond, *Letters and Journals of Lord Elgin*, August 18, 1848, p. 16.

[4] *Johns Hopkins University Studies*, 1922, Tansill, Charles C., "The Canadia Reciprocity Treaty of 1854," pp. 13-14.

the preferential duties on colonial timber was passed. Disraeli, the leader of the Conservative party in Great Britain, come to recognize that this party could no longer cling to its traditional policy of protection, for he said in 1853 that all that remained of it were the " rags and tatters " of that system.[1] The tariff acts of 1853 and 1860, therefore, sponsored by the radical free-traders to whom Disraeli gave his support, finally eliminated the few remaining duties in favor of the colonies.[2]

Full details of the bill submitted to the British parliament for the repeal of the Corn Laws were known in Canada, as early as February, 1846. At once protests which pointed out the serious consequences of the withdrawal of a preferential tariff were drawn up by the Boards of Trade of Montreal and Quebec, followed a month later by the Board of Trade of Toronto, and were transmitted to the Secretary of State for the Colonies. In its protest the Montreal Board of Trade expressed its fear that the growing commercial intercourse of British North America with the United States due to the abandonment by Great Britain of colonial preference would sooner or later lead to a political union. Professing, therefore, their devotion to the institutions of Great Britain and desire to perpetuate the connection, the petitioners laid before Queen Victoria the probable consequences of the Corn Act of 1846. The total cessation of differential duty on grain in favor of the colonies would ruin the St. Lawrence trade, for the produce of Canada West would be attracted to New York, which soon would become the port of import as well as of export. Such a diversion of trade would cement ties of interest between Canada and the United States, and would proportionately

---

[1] *Hansard Parliamentary Debates*, vol. 124, p. 1036.

[2] *Political Science Quarterly*, vol. xxxiii, 1918, R. L. Schuyler, " The Abolition of British Imperial Preference," pp. 88-91.

weaken the attachment of the colony to the mother land. Even if the contention of the economists in England that the colonies meant a pecuniary loss to Great Britain were true, the Montreal Board of Trade professed its unwillingness to accept their conclusion that the connection, therefore, should be severed; moreover, they professed their opinion that the preservation of Great Britain's political power and influence were cheaply purchased in spite of any pecuniary loss the colonies might occasion her. So far from seeking a return of the old system of protection, they claimed that they had no objection " to the utmost freedom of trade compatible with the safety of the ties subsisting between the colony and the mother country." They proposed the remedial measures, which they believed would be effective :

1st. The repeal of the navigation laws as they relate to Canada, and the throwing open of the navigation of the St. Lawrence; and

2nd. The enactment of a moderate fixed duty, say not less than five shillings per quarter on foreign wheat, colonial to be admitted free.[1]

The free-trade policy of Great Britain, with its total disregard of imperial interdependence, an interdependence, moreover, heretofore fostered by the traditional policy of the mother land, caused widespread dissatisfaction. The danger of separation, as a consequence of the substitution of free trade for a preferential tariff, was recognized by John A. Macdonald, then the Solicitor General of the Crown in Canada West, and later first Prime Minister of the Dominion of Canada. He said that he hoped that the commercial class would maturely weigh all the consequences which must result from the substitution of the United States markets for those of the mother country, for he was con-

[1] *Cf.* the Quebec *Gazette*, January 8, 1849, petition of Montreal Board of Trade.

vinced that it would be impossible for Canadians to make such a change in their commercial relations without very soon bringing about a change in all their other relations. If their interests ceased to be identified with those of the mother country, he feared their whole mental outlook would change; moreover, their customs and laws, even their institutions, would be assimilated to those of the country with whom they cultivated friendly relations. "There was a time . . . when he believed that patriotism had no connection with self interest; but he had lived long enough to change his opinion on that subject; and he did think that loyalty had some relation to pecuniary consideration." [1]

As a measure of partial relief Lord Elgin urged upon the British Government the repeal of the navigation laws. The operation of these laws, which gave to Great Britain the bulk of the carrying trade of the British North American Provinces without giving the Canadians the compensating advantages of a preference in the British market was regarded as a grievance.[2] A comparison of the rates from Montreal and New York to and from England showed that the Montreal merchant paid higher freight rates on goods than the New York merchant.. Since the continued enforcement of the navigation laws meant excess freight paid by the Canadian to the English ship owner, the Canadian merchant found that he was no longer able to compete on equal terms with the American merchant. A protest which urged upon the British Parliament the repeal was accordingly transmitted by the provincial legislature.

The transformation in the trade policy of Great Britain, the substitution of free trade for protection, had forced upon her colonies the necessity of finding new markets.

---

[1] *Hansard Parliamentary Debates*, 3rd ser., vol. 86, 1846, p. 557.

[2] H. E. Egerton, *Historical Geography of the British Colonies*, vol. v, pt. ii, p. 196. (General editor C. P. Lucas.)

The American government had been prompt to recognize its opportunity. An Act of Congress in 1847 allowed Canadian and foreign goods to pass through the United States in bond, duty free. The merchants of Canada West, in consequence of the above-mentioned act, imported and exported by way of New York, instead of Montreal.

There were not wanting liberal-minded statesmen in England ,who recognized the justice of the plea of the British North American Provinces for the repeal of the Navigation laws. Upon the adoption of free trade, Great Britain, however, did not recognize that eventually she must surrender all right to control the fiscal policy of the British North American Colonies. Indeed Earl Grey, Colonial Secretary from 1846 to 1852, explicitly stated that " when the system of Free Trade was adopted, no question had ever been raised as to its being right to maintain this authority of Parliament (though on some occasions the wisdom with which it was exercised was disputed) nor was it imagined by any one that it was to be relinquished because the new policy of relieving trade from injurious restriction was to be adopted." [1] All parties, he claimed, assumed as a matter of course that Great Britain would continue to regulate the commercial policy of the empire. Since, however, the colonies no longer received a preference in the British market, they no longer felt that it was incumbent upon them to serve the commercial interests of Great Britain. The necessity for securing new markets was apparent to all. The adoption of free trade in Great Britain practically forced fiscal independence upon the British North American Colonies.

Although the need for a repeal of the navigation laws was evident to the British Parliament, the pressure of domestic business threatened to prevent any definite action.

[1] Earl Grey, *Canadian Pamphlets 21*, " The Commercial Policy of the British Colonies and The McKinley Tariff," p. 13.

When word was received to this effect, Lord Elgin wrote a letter, June 15, 1848, to the Secretary of State for the Colonies, in which he pointed out the need for immediate action.

The Canadian farmer is a suppliant at present to the Imperial Legislature, not for favor, but for justice; strong as is his affection for the mother country and her institutions, he cannot reconcile it to his sense of right that after having been deprived of all protection for his products in her markets, he should be subjected to a hostile discriminatory duty in the guise of a law for the protection of navigation.[1]

He realized both the need and the obligation imposed upon himself, of safeguarding Canadian interests. Thus he issued a warning of the probable consequences if " provisions [were] suffered to remain on the British statute book which would seem to bring the material interests of the colonists and the promptings of duty and affection into opposition." [2]

Even before the passage of the Corn Act of 1846, the colonies had not lacked champions in the British Parliament.[3] Lord Stanley, Conservative leader in the House of Lords, declared that its passage, in view of previous legislation by the Imperial Parliament, involved a violation of faith with Canada. His protest upon the reading of the bill entered on the journals of the House stated that it would " tend to sever the strongest bond of union ", to undermine the whole colonial system, to which the British Empire owed much of its greatness.[4] Sir Howard Douglas, a former governor of New Brunswick, was likewise apprehensive.[5]

---

[1] *Hansard Parliamentary Debates*, 3rd ser., 1849, vol. 105, p. 71.

[2] *Ibid.*, p. 72.

[3] *Cf. Political Science Quarterly*, vol. xxxii, 1917, R. L. Schuyler, " Preference and Sir Robert Peel," p. 446.

[4] *Hansard Parliamentary Debates*, 3rd ser., vol. 87, " Canadian Importation Bills," no. 1, p. 962.

[5] *Political Science Quarterly*, vol. xxxiii, Schuyler, R. L., " The Abolition of British Imperial Preference," p. 86.

Recognizing that the abolition of colonial preference would involve great suffering in the British colonies, especially in Canada, he urged that Great Britain assume the colonial debt incurred for internal improvements, grant Canada West and Canada East commercial freedom, repeal all duties on Canadian produce, modify the navigation laws, and open the St. Lawrence river to foreign vessels.[1]   Lord John Russell, in connection with the British Possessions Bill introduced late in the session of 1846, said that Great Britain should not keep up any protective duty in the colonies which they might consider " unnecessary and injurious ", and on the other hand should not deprive them of those duties which they might think necessary for revenue.[2]   The Queen by order in council was empowered " to give her assent to acts of colonial legislatures reducing or repealing protective duties imposed upon their imports from foreign countries by the Imperial Parliament."   The colonial legislature was, therefore, given a right which heretofore had been reserved for the British Parliament.   This act gave the colonies power to repeal duties which were already in existence but did not grant them the power either to enact differential duties, or to impose further duties on British goods.[3]   The British North American Colonies soon availed themselves of the right to repeal all imperial duties, and to abolish preferential duties in favor of British goods.[4]

Although the protectionist Tories in Great Britain, supporters of the old worn-out mercantilistic theory, opposed the repeal of the navigation laws, the added injustice of their enforcement under free trade was eventually recognized.

[1] *Hansard Parliamentary Debates*, 3rd ser., vol. 88, p. 745.

[2] *Ibid.*, p. 683.

[3] *Hansard Parliamentary Debates*, 3rd ser., vol. 88, p. 683.

[4] *Political Science Quarterly*, 1918, vol. xxxiii, R. L. Schuyler, " The Abolition of British Imperial Preference," p. 88.

The navigation laws were repealed June 26, 1849. The bill had been, however, delayed too long to be of service to the Montreal merchants that year.[1]

Since the free-trade policy of Great Britain forced the British North American Colonies to seek new markets, they turned, as we have seen, to the United States. Those who looked to the United States to relieve the prevailing financial depression might be divided into two classes, the advocates of reciprocity and the advocates of annexation. In the former class were to be found the firmest adherents of the British connection, men unfaltering in their allegiance to the British Crown, who recognized the prevailing discontent as commercial, not political. Lord Elgin likewise realized the gravity of the situation which he too, moreover, rightly attributed to commercial discontent, not political dissatisfaction.

Depend upon it, our commercial embarrassments are our real difficulty. Political discontent, properly so-called, there is none. I really believe no country in the world is more free from it. We have, indeed, national antipathies hearty and earnest enough. We suffer, too, from the inconveniences of having to work a system which is not yet thoroughly in gear. Reckless and unprincipled men take advantages of these circumstances to work into a fever every transient heat that affects the public mind.[2]

He expressed his confidence that he could carry Canada " unscathed through all these evils of transition" if he could only guarantee to Canadians the same natural prosperity as the Americans possessed. If, however, free navigation and reciprocity with the United States were not secured for them without delay, he feared that " the worst " would come and at no distant day." [3]

---

[1] C. D. Allin and G. M. Jones, *Annexation, Preferential Trade and Reciprocity*, p. 36.

[2] Theodore Walrond, *Letters and Journals of Lord Elgin*, pp. 70-71.

[3] *Ibid.*, p. 71.

To this first group, including in its ranks the Governor-General of Canada, Lord Elgin, belonged the honor of both rightly diagnosing the ills which afflicted the colonies, and of indicating the true remedy to be applied. They urged upon the British Parliament the necessity of securing reciprocity for the colonies with the United States.

The second class, to which belonged the advocates of annexation to the United States, cannot be ignored. If what Lord Elgin said with regard to the cause of the general feeling of dissatisfaction throughout the British North American Provinces was substantially true, there was still sufficient cause for anxiety on the part of those who feared that the loyalty of the colonists could not sustain the material loss which was apparently involved in the British connection; for did not the colonists see their neighbors to the south enjoying an ever-increasing prosperity, a prosperity in marked contrast to their own condition? The advocates of annexation had not lightly come to their decision; indeed, there were many who quite reluctantly concluded that the British North American Colonies must become a part of the Republic. To them the price which the maintenance of British relations involved was too great. To them Great Britain spelled financial bankruptcy, the United States on the contrary, financial success. Indeed Lord Elgin himself feared that many more of the colonists would embrace the belief that annexation was the only possible alternative, if a reciprocity treaty were not speedily secured.

In a consideration of the causes underlying the disaffection which undoubtedly existed in certain sections of Canada, and resulted in the annexation movement, the effect of the passage of the Rebellion Losses Bill of 1849 must not be overlooked. The Baldwin-LaFontaine administration, which represented the moderate Liberals of both Canada East and Canada West, supported the Rebellion Losses Bill, a meas-

ure to indemnify the sufferers in the recent rebellion of
1837. Baldwin in his support of the measure pointed out
that it simply did for Canada East what had already been
done for Canada West, for a similar act had been passed by
the assembly of Upper Canada, October 22, 1840, in the
closing days of its existence — an act, moreover, rendered
operative by the Draper government in 1845.[1] He argued
that he was only asking for Canada East what the assembly
had already granted to Canada West, and therefore could
not justly refuse. At once there was violent opposition to
the bill. The cry was at once raised by the Conservatives
of Canada that the bill had been introduced by a French
Ministry which desired to compensate French traitors who
deserved punishment, not compensation. The government
later disproved this accusation by its appointment of a committee that showed its moderation and wisdom in the rejection of 429 out of the 2244 French claims on the ground
that those who had submitted them had been implicated in
the rebellion.[2] However unjustifiable the opposition to it,
the Rebellion Losses Bill threatened to bring about racial
war in Canada. This bill was undoubtedly devised with the
idea of satisfying the French Canadians. Long Elgin wrote
Earl Grey, Secretary of State for the Colonies, in 1852:
" I was aware of two facts, firstly, that M. LaFontaine
would be unable to retain the support of his countrymen if
he failed to introduce a measure of this description; and
secondly, that my refusal would be taken by him and his
friends as a proof that they had not my confidence." The
Tory forces were united in opposition. When the passage
of the bill was apparently imminent, they besought the
Governor-General to veto it. But Lord Elgin, acting in

[1] John Boyd, *Sir Georges Etienne Cartier, his Life and Times, A
Political History of Canada from 1814 until 1873*, pp. 97-98.

[2] Jean Charlemagne Bracq, *The Evolution of French Canada*, p. 111.

accordance with his conception of responsible government, which was to act on the advice of his ministers, signed the bill. Its opponents, infuriated by its passage, insulted the Governor-General. With the passage of the Rebellion Losses Bill, responsible government was won. Great was the service which Lord Elgin had rendered Canada. He had upheld the principles of responsible government, and in so doing had done much to conciliate French Canadians, who henceforth had implicit faith in his fairmindedness.

His attitude toward the question of French nationalism was ever a conciliatory one. " I for one," he had written in May, 1848, "am deeply convinced of the impolicy of all such attempts to denationalize the French. Generally speaking, they produce the opposite effect from that intended, causing the flame of national prejudice and animosity to burn more fiercely." [1] He recognized the stabilizing effect French Canada, essentially conservative, would exert in determining the course of Canadian political life. " Who will venture to say that the last hand which waves the British flag on American ground may not be that of a French Canadian?" Lord Elgin's faith in the loyalty of the French Canadians and their confidence in him, and personal attachment to him, did much to prevent the spread of annexation sentiment in Canada East.

Nor in a consideration of the causes promoting the annexations movement in Canada must the defeat of the Conservatives by the Reformers in 1848 be ignored. Having long regarded themselves as the loyal element in the colony, the Conservatives resented keenly the fact that Lord Elgin in accordance with his conception of responsible government should have asked the Reformers to form a government.[2]

---

[1] Theodore Walrond, *Letters and Journal of Lord Elgin*, p. 54, Elgin–Grey Correspondence: Elgin to Grey, May 4, 1848.

[2] *Cf.* Reginald G. Trotter, *Canadian Confederation, Its Origins and Achievement—A Study in Nation Building,* chap. ii, p. 13.

In the bitterness of their defeat they raised the cry of French domination, and attempted to arouse both racial and religious hatred. Naturally, therefore, they would bitterly oppose the Rebellion Losses Bill, and the aftermath of that agitation greatly discredited the Conservative party. " The extreme section of the party, embittered by the series of humiliations they had received from the local and British governments, and discouraged as to the future of the country, foreswore their allegiance to the Crown and entered upon an active campaign for annexation to the neighboring Republic." [1]

The Reform party was also divided into two sections, the Radical or Clear Grit section, and the conservative element. The Clear Grit section of the Reformers like the extreme Conservatives were inclined to favor American institutions. The moderate Reformers, more influential in the government, sought to check the spread of republican doctrines, but were greatly hampered in their efforts there, due to the widespread economic depression in the British North American provinces. Lord Elgin claimed that as a direct result of Great Britain's substitution of free trade for protection, property in many places had depreciated fifty per cent and three-fourths of the business men of Canada were ruined. The local government itself, on the verge of bankruptcy, could render no assistance.[2]

Out of the economic distress, and social discontent born of party strife and racial hatred, emerged in April, 1849, a new organization, the British North American League. Montreal was the headquarters of the League, but other branches were organized in Canada East and Canada West. The leader of the organization was George Moffatt of Mon-

[1] *Ontario Historical Society, Papers and Records*, vol. xiii, art. x, C. D. Allin, " The British North American League," 1849.

[2] *Ibid.*, vol. xiii, art. x.

treal, an influential Conservative. In a public address the social, political, and economic evils from which Canada was suffering were described, and a convention summoned to consider remedies. Although the address stated that no impairment of the imperial connection was contemplated, the purpose of the gathering was left vague in order to attract the malcontents. So many annexationists joined the Montreal Association that the loyalists became alarmed. The election of delegates to the League Convention at Kingston was therefore bitterly contested, and since only one of the five delegates elected by the Montreal Association belonged to the annexationists, many of the annexationists withdrew. There were two views as to the origin and character of the League, the Conservative, voiced by John A. Macdonald, and the Liberal, expressed by his political opponent, Alexander Mackenzie. Since the League was recruited almost entirely from the Tory Party with a few annexationists, and a few disgruntled Reformers, the Conservative view was favorable and the Liberal unfavorable. Macdonald ascribed to the League the honor of determining Canadian history in its advocacy of confederation as the true solution of the situation. Mackenzie regarded the League as " a queer Mixture of Tories and annexationists [and in addition] all the disappointed items." He, therefore, likened it to David's famous army at the cave of Adullam: " every one that was in distress and every one that was discontented gathered themselves to the meeting of the League." He contended that the League, condemned and ridiculed by the Liberal newspapers, collapsed because its members advocated extreme Toryism, extreme disloyalty, and threatened the French. The League, however, made three definite contributions to Canadian political development, for it created the Liberal Conservative party, advocated an independent fiscal policy, and proposed a federal union of the British American Provinces. The League, an unofficial body, found it difficult to open up negotiations with the governments of Nova Scotia and New Brunswick.[1] The reason for the refusal of the Maritime provinces to consider proposals from the League for a legislative or federal union was expressed in a letter of Howe's, the Reform leader of Nova Scotia, to Moffatt, May 8, 1849, in which he stated that such proposals if made by the government of Canada would be treated with respect, but if made by a party in opposition would not for a moment be entertained."[2] Opposed by Joseph Howe, the League found it impossible to form an organization in Nova Scotia. Although a New Brunswick Association similar to the British American League of Canada was organized, nothing was done to further the cause of confederation, except to give it a certain publicity. Although the League was never formally disbanded, its members took no part as an association in the election of 1850, but the majority of them returned to their political party, the Conservative.

Since Montreal suffered most severely from the new trade measures, it was natural that the disaffection toward Great Britain should there find expression in the significant Manifesto of October, 1849, to the people of Canada. This document was a calm, dispassionate discussion of actual conditions in Canada, contrasted with conditions in the United States. The remedy urged was peaceful separation from the mother country, followed by annexation to the United States.

In view of the many evils which afflicted the country, the framers of the manifesto claimed that the people of British America must forget all differences of party, origin, and creed, in a united and determined effort to find the remedy

[1] *Ibid.*, vol. xiii, art. x.

[2] A. Chisholm, *Speeches and Letters of Joseph Howe*, vol. ii, p. 25.

that must be applied. The prevalent and deep-seated distress everywhere noted throughout Canada was attributed to Great Britain's withdrawal of her former preferential tariff to her colonies in consequence of her adoption of free trade. Thus in spite of her vast natural resources Canada was unable to secure a loan, although offering security greater than either Great Britain or the United States considered necessary to procure similar loans. Although " super-abundant water power and cheap labor ", a combination usually insuring the development of manufactures, were both found in Canada East, foreign capitalists hesitated to invest money in a country where, in their opinion, the institutions did not possess the permanency which alone could inspire confidence in its security. As an instance of the contrast between Canada and the adjoining states the fact was cited that while Canada had only three lines of railway scarcely fifty miles in length with the stock of the three lines depreciated from 50 to 80 per cent, the United States had " a network of thriving railways ". The system of Provincial government necessarily involved the reference of certain matters to Great Britain, which was often indifferent to provincial needs; it was declared both expensive and unsatisfactory.

In the event of war, moreover, between Great Britain and the United States, Canada must — due to her geographical position — be the chief sufferer, however indifferent she might be to a quarrel which might in no sense concern her. Since party animosities of long standing in Canada showed no sign of diminishment, new issues which would eradicate these differences should be welcomed by the Canadian people. The framers of the manifesto claimed that statesmen in Great Britain, certain clear-sighted observers of conditions in Canada living in the United States, and people from all classes in British North America were firmly convinced that a Canadian political revolution was imminent. Such a conviction undoubtedly tended to discourage desirable settlers who quite naturally desired a country whose government possessed stability. Contented with a brief statement of the evils, the annexationists enumerated the six remedies which they said were ordinarily suggested:

1. " The revival of protection in the markets of the United Kingdom."

This remedy which would afford only partial relief could not be considered, since the suffering of the poor in Great Britain, which would necessarily result from the revival of protection, would mean sooner or later a second reversal of Great Britain's trade policy, one which, moreover, would only complete the ruin of British-America.

2. " The protection of home manufactures."

Without access to the United States markets this remedy was declared inadequate.

3. " A federal union of the British-American Provinces."

Free trade throughout British-America and a decrease in governmental expenditure, the two chief benefits claimed by the advocates of the measure, the annexationists declared would be no remedy, since all the benefits of free trade might be secured under existing conditions, while the lessening of expense was declared problematical.

4. " The independence of the British North American Colonies as a Federal Republic."

Independence was declared too costly a boon, involving as it would military expenditure on a large scale in order to secure its maintenance against the United States, without at the same time removing the evils which retarded material prosperity.

5. " Reciprocal free trade with the United States, as respects the products of the farm, the forest and the mine."

The fifth remedy was declared merely an instalment of advantages which might be otherwise secured, and likewise was declared inadequate.

6. The sixth remedy " consists of a friendly and peaceful separation from British connection, and a union upon equitable terms with the great North American confederacy of sovereign states."

Since this remedy involved a political revolution, the framers of the manifesto admitted it merited serious consideration.   Towards Great Britain the annexationists declared they entertained the most friendly feeling; moreover, they believed that Great Britain by her continuance of military protection on the condition that the people of British America defray all expenses really signified a desire to sever the connection.   The various advantages of a union with the adjoining Republic were enumerated.   American capital would be released for investment in Canada, thereby equalizing the value of real estate on both sides of the boundary line.   The foreigner would no longer hesitate to invest his money in a land of such vast natural resources, now that the fear of instability in the form of government was removed.   Public credit would, therefore, be restored.   Not only would American capital be used to introduce manufactures which had hitherto flourished solely in the United States, but the markets of the United States would also be open free of duty.   American capitalists would build railroads in the Canadas and Maritime Provinces over which their produce might be carried to the United States.   No longer would the agricultural products of Canada fail to secure the same prices as similar products in the United States, and further the cost of living would be reduced in consequence of the lowering of the prices on such articles as tea, coffee and sugar.   The value of Canadian timber would be greatly enhanced, for no longer would a heavy duty be levied upon it. The shipbuilding industry would flourish, for the shipping trade of the United States was bound to increase. The form of government under the United States system, the annexationists declared, would be much more economical than the Provincial government under Great Britain. No longer would the menace of war, an ever-present contingency under present conditions, exist. Opportunities for public service and distinction open to the citizens of the United States might, henceforth, be theirs; for no longer would the Canadians be citizens of a country dependent upon Great Britain but citizens enjoying all the advantages open only to those who belong to an independent country.

The closing portion of the manifesto dealt with the benefits which would accrue to both Great Britain and the United States in consequence of annexation. Chief among these advantages was the lessening of the chances of collision between them with all the inevitable clashing of interest due to the close proximity of British-America to the United States.[1]   The Manifesto thus concluded:

We address you without prejudice or partiality—in the spirit of sincerity and truth—in the interest solely of our common country, and our single aim is its safety and welfare. If to your judgment and reason our object and aim be at this time deemed laudable and right, we ask an oblivion of past dissensions; and from all, without distinction of origin, party or creed, that earnest and cordial cooperation in such lawful, prudent and judicious means as may best conduct us to our common destiny.[2]

To this document were affixed the names of many promi-

---

[1] C. D. Allin and G. M. Jones, *Annexation, Preferential Trade and Reciprocity*, chap. vii, pp. 106-115.

[2] *Ibid.*, p. 114.

nent Canadians, including J. J. C. Abbott, a future prime
minister of Canada, John Rose, later finance minister under
Sir John A. Macdonald, and D. L. Macpherson, later Lieutenant-Governor of Ontario. The leading commercial men
of Montreal were well represented by the Molsons, Tor-
rances and Workmans, men prominent in the banking circles
of Montreal and all connected with the establishment of
Molsons' Bank in Canada.[1] The two naturally opposed
parties, the ultra-conservative and the Rouge, were well
represented, as can be readily perceived, if the list is
scanned.[2]

A survey of the newspapers of this period seems to prove
that the numerical strength of the annexationists in Canada,
even at the period of greatest financial depression, was not
great, and that, in proportion as business conditions im-
proved, it gradually diminished. The press was directly
under the control of the political leaders who themselves
were the editors [3]—as Principal Grant of Queens University,
Canada, said, " at that time in the history of the world it
was almost impossible to be an editor without being a politician also." [4]

The Toronto *Globe,* the official organ of the Liberal party
of Canada West, under the leadership of George Brown,
was untiring in its denunciation of the annexationists. A

[1] *Montreal History and Gazetter,* 1892.

[2] J. L. Morison, *British Supremacy and Canadian Self-Government,*
pp. 212-213. To *le parti Rouge* belonged the radicals of Canada East,
followers of Papineau, the French-Canadian leader of the rebellion of
1837. Upon Papineau's return from exile he was elected to the Canadian
Assembly as a supporter of LaFontaine, the French Liberal leader.
Papineau soon found himself at variance with the Liberal party, and
became known as the leader of the independents, the radicals of Canada
East.

[3] *Cf. History of Canadian Journalism,* edited by a Committee of the
Press Association 1908.

[4] *Ibid.,* p. 2.

loyal Scot, he exerted an almost incalculable influence in
Canada West — an influence, moreover, ever in favor of
Great Britain. No public man in Canada has ever exercised
such power through the medium of the newspaper. Thus
did Sir Richard Cartwright truly say: "There were probably many thousand voters in Ontario especially among the
Scotch settlers who hardly read anything except their *Globe*
and their Bible, and whose whole political creed was practically dictated to them by the former." [1] This newspaper,
the ever-resolute and consistent opponent of annexation, was
naturally inclined to underestimate the strength of the movement. "As a popular movement the whole thing has been
an entire failure; it has not found a resting place in any
section of the country, nor with any political party." [2]
Undoubtedly with the *Globe,* the wish was father to the
thought.

The Toronto *Examiner,* [3] the newspaper of the radical
section or " Clear Grits " of Canada, founded by Francis
Hincks, Prime Minister of Canada in 1854, assumed a
vacillating attitude toward the question of annexation. This
radical section of the Liberal party adopted an extremely
critical attitude toward the Baldwin administration, which
it regarded as the reactionary wing of the party. Hence
many of its comments with regard to its policies might be
taken to indicate a predisposition toward the republican form
of government. Although the *Examiner* did not openly
support annexation, it indicated its belief that in the natural
course of events, the bond which united the British North
American Provinces to Great Britain would be severed.
This newspaper further declared its opinion that the inter-

[1] Sir Richard Cartwright, *Reminiscences,* pp. 9-10.

[2] The *Globe,* March 5, 1850.

[3] *A History of Canadian Journalism,* edited by a Committee of the
Press, p. 167; Merged into *Globe* 1857.

vening step, namely, the independence of the provinces, must be consummated before the idea of annexation with the neighboring republic could even be considered.

The *British Colonist,* a Conservative newspaper established by Hugh Scobie in 1838, the chief competitor of the *Globe,* likewise adopted a vacillating policy which indicated a certain changefulness in public opinion. In its issue of July 3, 1849, the annexation sentiment found expression. "Our opinion, declared repeatedly within the last three years, has been that commercial wants and intercourse would bring it [annexation] to pass in a short period independently of collateral circumstances of a purely political nature." But ten days later, July 13, this newspaper denied that it had committed its columns to an advocacy of annexation, and declared that it had merely reviewed the facts in connection with the course of the movement. On July 27, 1849, it discussed the external influences determining the case, namely the influence of a colonial office, the attitude of the manufacturers of England, and lastly the encouragement which might be received from the United States. Later, perhaps influenced by the definite pronouncement against annexation by the British American League[1] to which many of the Conservatives of Canada West belonged, the *British Colonist,* September 11, 1849, reaffirmed its loyalty, and returned to its allegiance in its declaration that it was "opposed to any agitation in favor of separation from Great Britain."

The Toronto *Patriot,* the newspaper of the High Church Tories,[2] unfaltering in its attachment to Great Britain, warned its readers against encouraging the annexationists,[3]

---

[1] *Cf. Ontario Historical Society—Papers and Records,* vol. 13, art. x, Allin, C. D., "The British American League 1849."

[2] *A History of Canadian Journalism,* edited by a Committee of the Press, p. 168. Ogle R. Gowan, a prominent member of the Orange Order was one of the editors of the *Patriot.*

[3] The *Patriot,* October 12, 1849.

and the views of this newspaper were endorsed by the majority of the Tories of Canada West. Even the *Globe* naturally anxious to make political capital, and bitter in its denunciation of those who supported annexation, admitted that " a large and respectable portion of the Canadian Conservatives are thoroughly attached to Great Britain, and will not knowingly be led into annexation agitation." [1]

Until the advent of the *Canadian Independent* in September, 1849, the annexationists had no official organ. Even those newspapers of Canada West sympathetically inclined toward separation had refused to support annexation. Hence the annexationists had long felt the need of an official newspaper to spread their propaganda in Canada West. The policy of this newspaper, as announced by itself, was " to promote by peaceable means separation from the mother country." The *Patriot,* the Conservative newspaper of the High Church Party and the *Globe,* the leading Liberal newspaper, both signified their disapproval of the policy of the *Canadian Independent* by their refusal to publish its prospectus.

A survey of the newspapers of Canada East reveals that the annexationists of that province received much greater support from the press than did their fellow annexationists to the westward. The *Herald,* the *Courier,* and the *Witness,* three papers of the English-speaking people of Montreal, openly advocated annexation. The Montreal *Herald,* under the leadership of the editor, E. Goff Penny, clerk to the secretaries of the Montreal Annexation Association, R. McKay and A. A. Dorion, became the most active annexationist newspaper in Canada East.[2] Since a state of political tran-

---

[1] The *Globe,* June 20, 1849.

[2] *Cf. The Canadian Historical Review,* vol. v, September, 1924, Arthur G. Penny (grandson of E. Goff Penny), " The Annexation Movement 1849-50, p. 237.

sition always necessarily involves much suffering, this newspaper advocated speedy incorporation with the United
States.[1] The *Courier,* a Conservative newspaper, claimed
that the mal-administration of the government was responsible for the spread of annexation sentiment in Canada.
" When men find things irretrievably bad, they must needs
think of desperate remedies. Annexation is that remedy." [2]
The *Witness,* fond of giving a semi-religious tone to its
editorials, characteristically saw the hand of God leading the
people of Canada toward annexation.

The Montreal *Transcript and Commercial Advertiser,* a
Conservative newspaper, opposed to annexation, declared :

Taking the newspapers as our guide-book, we are forced to the
conclusion that, in this city, the friends of annexation are to be
found in the ultra-Conservative party and the most democratic
and republican of the French. One by one, the Conservative
journals have come over to that doctrine, and many influential
Conservatives, who not long ago would have rejected the address
with scorn, are now its shameless and unflinching advocates.
And it cannot be doubted but that a great part of their supporters
go with them in this strange and sad revulsion of feeling.[3]

Furthermore this newspaper in its discussion of the underlying causes which had led to the issuance of the Manifesto
admitted the sincerity of certain signers who regarded annexation as the remedy for the evils from which the country
suffered.[4] This admission of the disinterested patriotism
which had prompted a number to sign, was followed by a
declaration that annexation would not relieve the evils, but
rather increase them. The next class of signers referred to
were the merchants who had suffered severely from the

---

[1] The *Herald*, October 3, 1849.

[2] The *Courier*, October 3, 1849.

[3] The Montreal *Transcript and Commercial Advertiser*, October 4, 1849.

[4] *Ibid.*, October 11, 1849.

withdrawal of protection and were unwilling to wait to see what time would do. "Among them are some quondam free-traders who are in an amazing hurry to falsify their own theories. Doubtless they felt uneasy at the economic outlook; but with the many evidences of a revival of trade among them and knowing full well as business men the liability of all countries to periods of commercial depression, they act impatiently in seeking to drive the country into immediate annexation."[1] The third class referred to, described as the most zealous, though not the most numerous, were the holders of real estate in the city who in their desire for higher rents looked upon annexation as a mere Montreal property movement.[2] The annexationists were accused of " accentuating the evils of the country, and in assigning to the whole province a condition of wretchedness which is mainly existent in Montreal. To all such clamours, we need only reply that prosperity will return in time without the abandonment of British allegiance."[3] The *Transcript* declared the question of annexation had not yet become a national one, and until it did, had small chance of success.[4] The annexationists who formed a respectable but small party were not in a position, this newspaper declared, to dictate the policy of the country.[5]

The Montreal *Pilot,* a Liberal newspaper founded by Francis Hincks, likewise a resolute opponent of annexation, declared: "The warp is high rampant Toryism; the weft, a few scattered British, Irish, French, and American Liberals, whose presence there is somewhat of a mystery."[6]

[1] *Ibid.*, October 13, 1849.
[2] *Ibid.*
[3] *Ibid.*, October 11, 1849.
[4] *Ibid.*
[5] *Ibid.*
[6] The *Pilot*, October 11, 1849.

By far the largest portion of the names affixed to the annexation address were, it declared, members of the League. In the same issue this newspaper declared that it " would not lend its columns to the dismemberment of the empire." The warning issued by the *Pilot* to all Reformers to avoid all entangling alliances, reads like a modern United States newspaper opposed to the entrance of its country into the League of Nations.

Upon the publication of the manifesto, the *Gazette,* a Conservative newspaper, followed a devious course, similar to the vacillation shown by the *Colonist* and the *Examiner,* newspapers of Canada West. It declared that it was " unable to go as fast as the signers of the manifesto." [1] Its readers were urged to give due consideration to the terms of admission to the Union. " Wisely and slow " was the advice of the *Gazette;* nevertheless, it concluded thus : " The feeling is without a doubt spreading that the final result of all our moves in Canada, unless checked by Great Britain will be into the arms of the United States. We believe so ourselves." Twelve days later the *Gazette* announced its preference for Canadian independence, not annexation; " because we are convinced that it is worth a trial, and that it is attainable, while we believe that Great Britain will never consent to a bare, unqualified demand to hand us over to the United States." [2]

The French Canadian newspapers divided in accordance with party lines. *L'Avenir,* the official organ of the Rouge party, the newspaper of Papineau, approved the manifesto thus : " C'est un appel fait à toutes les classes, et à toutes les parties, d'oublier les anciennes causes de division, pour se reunir dans le bout d'obtenir ce dont le pays a le plus puissant besoin, le prospérité avec l'annexion." [3] In an

[1] The *Gazette*, October 11, 1849.

[2] The *Gazette*, October 23, 1849.

[3] *L'Avenir*, October 13, 1849.

earlier issue this paper had asserted its conviction that annexation with the United States would not mean a surrender of French nationality: " The United States, far from
extinguishing in our hearts the sacred fire of nationality,
would fan it into a blaze. For they knew well that in confiding the safety of the St. Lawrence to the French of
Canada, it would be as well guarded as was New Orleans
by the French of Louisiana." [1]

The ministerial press, including *La Minerve* in Montreal,
and *Le Journal de Quebec,* were outspoken in their criticism
of the annexationists; while *L'Ami de la Religion et de la
Patrie* urged the French Roman Catholics to be faithful to
the British Crown. The Roman Catholic priests in Canada
East have ever exerted their powerful influence in favor of
the British connection. As a direct result of the conciliatory
policy of Great Britain toward the Roman Catholic Church
in Canada from 1763 until the present, this Church has ever
sought to keep her adherents loyal to the British Crown.

The report of Lord Durham contained a fine tribute to
the loyalty of the priests in Lower Canada. Since the
French Canadians were exclusively Roman Catholic, Great
Britain at the conquest had left their church in possession
of its endowment. The right that the priests possessed to
tithe the land was, however, restricted to those lands owned
by Roman Catholics. In spite of the fact that they lost their
tithes as soon as the land passed into the hands of Protes-
tants, Lord Durham declared that the Catholic priesthood
of the province had " to a remarkable degree conciliated the
good-will of persons of all creeds." Their practice of the
Christian virtues had been, he claimed, productive of much
good in the provinces. Possessing incomes considered large
in accordance with the ideas of the country, and enjoying
also the advantages of education, they exerted a powerful

[1] Quoted from the *Globe*, April 4, 1849.

influence, for they lived on terms of kindly intimacy with the humblest *habitants* of the rural districts. As an administrator of the province through troubled times, Lord Durham believed that the Catholic clergy were entitled to an expression of his esteem, for in " the absence of any permanent institution of civil government" the Catholic church had proved itself a powerful organization in its loyal support of the British government.[1]

Care should be taken not to over-estimate the strength of the annexation movement in Canada, a movement which moreover had its origin largely in commercial discontent. Sir John Abbot,[2] in a speech in the Senate, March 15, 1889, explained the annexation manifesto as an " outburst of petulance " on the part of a small section in Canada East. With the exception of a few Americans living in Montreal, he claimed, the signers of that manifesto had " no more serious idea of seeking annexation with the United States than a petulant child who strikes his nurse has of deliberately murdering her." Exasperated by the passage of the Rebellion Losses Bill in spite of their opposition, they had signed the paper. " Before the year was over," he claimed, " it was like the shower of last season."

Sir Alexander Galt, a Canadian statesman of the first rank, and Canada's ablest finance minister, explained his support of annexation thus : "My prejudices were altogether against the annexation movement," he writes to Alexander Gillespie, Governor of the Land Company, in October, 1849, " but my very situation here has probably given me as good an opportunity of judging of the effect of the measure as any one in the province possesses, and I am thoroughly con-

[1] *The Report of the Earl of Durham*, Methuen and Company, second edition, p. 97.

[2] J. J. C. (now Sir John) Abbott in 1889 regretted that he had signed in 1849 the Montreal Annexation Manifesto.

vinced it is the only cure for our manifold ills. . . . All the plans for ameliorating our condition now before the country are based upon reciprocity with the United States, and are therefore only adopting one of the advantages which would flow from annexation." [1]

Neither political party in Canada had a right to claim a monopoly of loyalty to the British connection. Three great political leaders, Robert Baldwin, the leader of the Constitutional Reformers, George Brown, the Progressive Reformer, and John A. Macdonald, the Conservative chieftain, were all loyal to Great Britain. Due in a measure no doubt to their influence the numerical strength of the annexation party, if the district of Montreal is excluded from consideration, remained relatively insignificant. The vast majority of the people were loyal to Great Britain.

The radicals in Canada undoubtedly had imbibed many of the ideas of the Manchester School of Liberals. The leaders of the Manchester School, including Cobden and Bright, have been called " Little Englanders ". Their lack of faith in the binding force of the bond which united the British North American Provinces to the mother country was in marked contrast to the earlier Liberal Colonial Reformers, namely, Lord Durham and Charles Buller, whose faith did much to make possible a British Empire. The Manchester School looked forward to the time when the colonies would sever the bond, as inevitable. The Radicals in Canada derived considerable encouragement from the speech of Lord John Russell, Prime Minister of Great Britain, in the House of Commons, in which after an able defence of Lord Elgin's policy in connection with the Rebellion Losses Bill he considered the probability of the future loss of the colonies:

[1] O. D. Skelton, *The Life and Times of Sir Alexander Tilloch Galt*, p. 153.

I anticipate indeed with others, that some of the colonies may so grow in population and wealth that they may say—" Our strength is sufficient to enable us to be independent of England. The link is now become onerous to us—the time is come when we think we can in amity and alliance with England, maintain our independence." I do not think that the time is yet approaching. But let us make them as far as possible fit to govern themselves—let us give them, as far as we can, the capacity of ruling their own affairs—let them increase in wealth and population; and, whatever may happen, we of this great empire shall have the consolation of saying that we have contributed to the happiness of the world.[1]

Is it any wonder that the radicals in Canada received this public utterance of the Premier of Great Britain as an endorsement of their own position? This concluding part of a speech, which Lord Elgin otherwise commended, he referred to as the sting in the tail. In his despatch to the Colonial Secretary, Earl Grey, he pointed out that such remarks, from one so high in authority, were liable to do incalculable harm in the colonies. He discussed at length his opinion that Lord John Russell and his political followers had too rashly assumed that the colonial relations were incompatible with maturity and development. Then he contrasted the two systems of government in North America and claimed that the colonists had " no reason to envy any state in the Union," since they had greater control of their destiny than a state which must submit to a " tariff imposed by twenty other states, and pay the expenses of war undertaken for objects which they profess to abhor." Yet he admitted that every State in the Union had a certain advantage over every province, for it was " invested with all the dignity of manhood, and introduced into a system which, despite the combativeness of certain ardent spirits from the

---

[1] *Hansard Parliamentary Debates*, 3rd ser., 1850, vol. 108, p. 567.

South, every American believes and maintains to be im-
mortal." Under the British constitutional system, elastic
as it was, he saw no reason why the links which bound the
colonies to the British Crown should not be made at least
as lasting as those which united the American States. In
order to achieve this result, however, the British government
must cease telling the colonies that the colonial relation was
merely provisional, and "must allow them to believe that,
without severing the bonds which unite them to Great Britain, they may attain the degree of perfection, and of social
and political development, to which organized communities
of free men have a right to aspire."

Then followed his description of the effect of Lord John's
speech on Baldwin, the leader of the constitutional Reformers, a man of singularly placid demeanor, who, apparently
greatly moved, had said in the Council Chamber in regard
to the latter part of Lord John's speech, "if the anticipa-
tions therein expressed prove to be well founded, my interest in public affairs is gone forever. But is it not hard
upon us while we are laboring, through good and evil report,
to thwart the designs of those who would dismember the
empire, our adversaries should be informed that the difference between them and the Prime Minister of England is
only one of time?"

In his reply to Baldwin, Lord Elgin attempted to reassure
him by stating that he believed "no man living was more
opposed to the dismemberment of the empire than Lord
John Russell" and that in the sentence referred to, the
Prime Minister had merely given expression to a "purely
speculative" and in his judgment "most fallacious" opinion. Lord Elgin admitted that he left the Council Chamber
disheartened, for his "audience was disposed to regard a
prediction of this nature, proceeding from a Prime Minister,
less as a speculative abstraction than as one of that class of

prophecies which work their own fulfilment ". Admitting
that he might be inclined to exaggerate the evil effect of this
speech, he expressed his conviction that there could not be
" any peace, contentment, progress, or credit " in Canada
while the idea prevailed that England regarded the colonies
as " a millstone about its neck " to be cast off as soon as it
could be conveniently managed. In order to attract capitalists a stable form of government must be assured. The
question from the British point of view was also a momentous one. " What is it indeed but this: Is the Queen of
England to be the Sovereign of an Empire, growing, ex-
panding, strengthening itself from age to age, striking its
roots deep into fresh earth and drawing new supplies of
vitality from virgin soils? Or is she to be, for all essential
purposes of might and power, Monarch of Great Britain
and Ireland merely — her place and that of her line in the
world's history determined by the productiveness of 12,000
square miles of a coal formation, which is being rapidly
exhausted, and the duration of the social and political
organization over which she presides dependent on the annual expatriation, with a view to its eventual alienization, of
the surplus swarm of her born subjects?" Now that " the
idea of maintaining a Colonial Empire for the purpose of
exercising dominion or dispensing patronage had been for
some time abandoned, and that of regarding it as a hot-bed
for forcing commerce and manufactures more recently re-
nounced ", he believed, " a greater amount of free action
and self-government might be conceded to British colonies
without any breach of Imperial Unity, or the violation of
any principle of Imperial Policy, than had under any scheme
yet devised fallen to the lot of the component parts of any
federal or imperial system." [1] Faith, when faith was needed

[1] Theodore Walrond, *Letters and Journals of Lord Elgin*, Letter to
Earl Grey, Toronto, March 23, 1850, pp. 115-120.

to insure the perpetuation of the bond, had been vouchsafed to the Governor-General of Canada.

Lord Elgin and the vast majority of the people of the British North American Provinces, who looked upon the annexationists as traitors, welcomed the portion of Lord John Russell's speech in which he said that "the Crown could give nothing but a decided negative" to the proposal that "the province of Canada should be annexed to the United States." The opponents of annexation were further heartened by the despatch of Earl Grey, January 9, 1850, to Lord Elgin, in which he said "Her Majesty confidently relies on the loyalty of the great majority of her Canadian subjects, and she is therefore determined to exert all the authority which belongs to her, for the purpose of maintaining the connection of Canada with this country, being persuaded that the permanence of that connection is highly advantageous to both." Lord Elgin received further instructions to resist to the utmost any attempt to bring about a separation, and to bring all implicated in such an undertaking to a court of justice. Since the above-mentioned despatch was the official answer of the British Government to the annexation manifesto of 1849, no longer could the annexationists of Canada deceive themselves with the hope that the British Government was prepared to grant their request for a dissolution of the bond.

Meanwhile the advocates of reciprocity with the United States, ever since the Canadian House of Assembly had on May 12, 1846, agreed on an address to the Queen requesting her to begin negotiations, had been untiring in their efforts.[1] Pakenham, the British Minister at Washington, was instructed to bring the matter to the attention of the United States Government whenever a favorable opportunity presented itself. As the Walker Tariff Bill signed by

[1] *Canadian Archives, Series G*, 125.

President Polk, July 30, 1846, was then under discussion he delayed the opening of negotiations until its passage. The same year he presented Robert J. Walker, the Secretary of the Treasury, with a memorandum in which was expressed the desire of Her Majesty's government for reciprocity between British North America and the United States.[1]

Successive efforts were made by the Canadians. In 1848, Lord Elgin sent Hamilton Merritt[2] of St. Catharines, an influential advocate of free trade, to convince Congress of the desirability of reciprocity, and on January 6, 1851, despatched Francis Hincks, Inspector-General of Canada, on a similar mission. In a communication which Hincks addressed to R. M. McLane, Chairman of the House Committee on Commerce, he even threatened retaliation.[3] Until very recently he said the provinces of Nova Scotia, New Brunswick, Prince Edward, and Newfoundland had been among the best customers of the United States for breadstuff, but that within the past year Canada had arranged with three of these provinces for a free exchange of their natural products, an arrangement which he claimed would divert from the city of New York to those provinces a very large amount of Canadian trade. He further stated that " Canada would reenact the differential duties in favor of British manufactures, and by closing the Canadian canals to American shipping, she would inflict most serious injury to the trade of Chicago, Cleveland and other lake ports." [4] Both the efforts of Merritt and Hincks to secure a treaty were unavailing.

[1] *Johns Hopkins University Studies*, 1922, Charles C. Tansill, " The Canadian Reciprocity Treaty of 1854," pp. 17-18.

[2] *Ibid.*, p. 17; O. D. Skelton, *The Life and Times of Sir Alexander Tilloch Galt*, p. 286.

[3] *Johns Hopkins University Studies*, 1922, " The Canadian Reciprocity Treaty of 1854," p. 36.

[4] *Ibid.*, pp. 17-18.

Between 1847 and 1851, British North America made successive overtures to the United States regarding both the fisheries and reciprocity,[1] but from 1852 to 1854 the question of the fisheries was even more intimately associated with that of commercial reciprocity, for the Americans were conscious of the value of the fisheries of the Maritime Provinces.[2]   At the meeting held in Toronto, 1851, the province of Canada agreed to cooperate with Nova Scotia in the protection of the fisheries by providing two sailing vessels to cruise in the Gulf of St. Lawrence and along the coast of Labrador.   Nova Scotia was to continue to employ two vessels in the protection of the fisheries and the New Brunswick Government was urged by her delegates to this convention to provide at least one vessel to be employed in the Bay of Fundy.[3]   The Nova-Scotians viewed from a distance with distrust the reciprocity treaty, and on September 2, 1852, held a public meeting in the hall of the Province Building " in consequence of learning Great Britain contemplated surrendering to the United States the privilege of fishing on the coasts of the Colonies ".   Here the citizens prepared a memorial to the Queen and also urged the Lieutenant-Governor to use his influence to delay action until the interests of Nova Scotia which they believed were about to be sacrificed could be presented.[4]   Realizing that there was a certain opposition to the extension of fishing privileges to Americans, the United States sent Israel D. Andrews, for-

[1] *Collections, Nova Scotia Historical Society*, 1910, vol. xiv, Wallace Graham, Judge of the Supreme Court of Nova Scotia, " The Fisheries of British North America and the United States Fishermen.

[2] *Johns Hopkins University Studies*, 1922, " The Canadian Reciprocity Treaty of 1854," p. 42.

[3] *Collections, Nova Scotia Historical Society*, 1910, vol. xiv, Wallace Graham, " The Fisheries of British North America and the United States Fishermen," p. 17.

[4] *Ibid.*, p. 19.

merly United States Consul at St. Johns, New Brunswick, as a special agent to Nova Scotia to influence public opinion. Opposition in the Maritime Provinces to the proposed reciprocity treaty was so strong that in his despatch of May 4, 1854, from St. Johns, he stated that "after several interviews with the Governor and the leading men of the Council, it was not deemed advisable to have a public discussion at this time, as it might increase the opposition of the North Eastern Coasts."[1] As "a professional organizer",[2] Andrews rendered valuable service. The Canadian advocates of reciprocity naturally had expected support from the Southern members of Congress, since there was a low tariff sentiment in the South. At first they were disappointed in their expectation, for many Southerners considered reciprocity as the preliminary step to annexation, and since the Southerners were opposed to the admission of any more free-soil states to the Union, they naturally opposed reciprocity. Their influence made itself felt, for two successive reciprocity bills, one in 1847, and the other in 1849, passed the House of Representatives, only to be defeated in the upper chamber; but there was a gradual change of opinion. The Southerner came to look upon reciprocity as the alternative offered in place of annexation. Hence the desire to prevent annexation which had at first militated against the bill, in 1854 operated in its favor.

Lord Elgin, by means of his knowledge of human nature, proved himself a very able advocate of reciprocity. To him reciprocity, likewise, appeared as an alternative to annexation. Hence with all the persistence of a Scot, he labored to secure it. This diplomacy is described in the words of his secretary, Laurence Oliphant, who accompanied his chief

[1] *Johns Hopkins University Studies,* 1922, Charles C. Tansill, " The Canadian Reciprocity Treaty of 1854," pp. 66, 73-74.

[2] O. D. Skelton, *The Life and Times of Sir Alexander Tilloch Galt,* p. 289.

on his mission to Washington. " He is the most thorough diplomat possible,—never loses sight for a moment of his object, and while he is chaffing Yankees, and slapping them on the back, he is systematically pursuing that object "; [1] and "Thus was concluded in exactly a fortnight a treaty to negotiate which had taxed the inventive genius of the Foreign Office, and all the conventional methods of diplomacy, for the previous seven years." [2] In the language of Oliphant, this treaty was " floated through on champagne ".

The Reciprocity Treaty of 1854 dealt with such matters as the fisheries, the navigation of the St. Lawrence, and tariff legislation.

In consideration of mutual free trade in many natural products, including fish and products of fish, and of the liberty to fish on the American coasts as far south as the 36th parallel, it was agreed that, in addition to the liberty secured by the treaty of 1818, " the inhabitants of the United States shall have in common with the subjects of Her Britannic Majesty, liberty to take fish of every kind except shellfish, on the sea coasts and shores and in the bays, harbors and creeks of Canada, New Brunswick, Nova Scotia, Prince Edward Island and of the several islands thereunto adjacent, without being restricted to any distance from the shores, with permission to land upon the coasts and shores . . . and also upon the Magdalen islands, for the purpose of drying their nets and curing their fish, provided that in so doing they do not interfere with the rights of private property or with British fishermen in the peaceable use of any part of the said coast in their occupancy for the same purpose.[3]

The fishermen of the United States were alone benefited by the above provision, for seldom did the British North Amer-

[1] Margaret Oliphant, *Life of Laurence Oliphant*, vol. i, chap. i, p. 120.

[2] Laurence Oliphant, *Episodes in a Life of Adventure*, p. 56.

[3] *Collections, Nova Scotia Historical Society*, 1910, vol. xiv, Wallace Graham, " The Fisheries of British North America and the United States Fishermen," pp. 20-21.

ican fishermen desert their own fishing grounds and fish in American waters. In return for the right given Americans to navigate the river St. Lawrence and the Canadian Canals, the Canadians were given the right to navigate Lake Michigan with their vessels. The United States government also agreed to urge upon the State governments that they permit the Canadians to use their State canals on terms of equality with the American.[1] This latter privilege, however, was never accorded to Canadians.

In 1855 the treaty was carried into effect by acts passed by Congress, and by the Legislatures of the United Kingdom, Canada, Prince Edward Island, New Brunswick, Nova Scotia, and Newfoundland. In spite of its ratification by their legislatures, the Reciprocity Treaty of 1854 was never popular in the Maritime provinces, and especially was this true of Nova Scotia, whose people did not think they had been sufficiently consulted.[2] There followed, however, an era of prosperity for both countries which would appear to be largely the result of the Reciprocity Treaty. The Americans had " a balance of trade in their favor " amounting to twenty millions according to United States returns, and ninety millions according to provincial returns.[3]

The people of the western states were now given a choice between two natural trade routes, the Great Lakes and the St. Lawrence, and the Erie Canal and the Hudson. The Canadian Government sought to induce the Americans to use the Canadian route by the offer of a refund of 90 per cent to those vessels which had paid tolls for the use of the Welland Canal upon their entrance to the St. Lawrence.

[1] O. D. Skelton, *The Life and Times of Sir Alexander Tilloch Galt*, p. 292.

[2] A. H. U. Colquhoun, *Chronicles of Canada*, vol. xxviii, " The Fathers of Confederation," p. 14.

[3] O. D. Skelton, *The Life and Times of Sir A. T. Galt*, p. 295.

The American Government claimed that this was unfair discrimination in favor of the Canadian route, and was in direct violation of the treaty.

At the time of its passage the Canadian tariff was moderate, but within five years there was a rapid growth of protectionist sentiment. The United States complained that Canada, the sole offender among the British North American possessions, by the adoption of a protective tariff on manufactured goods had violated the treaty. In his defence of the imposition of higher rates on manufactured goods, Galt, finance minister of Canada, claimed that they were absolutely necessary in order to meet the heavy expenditure of the provinces, and were levied to aid Canada, not to injure the United States; moreover there could be no violation of the treaty, since in it there had been no mention of manufactured goods, and the United States had insisted upon a strict interpretation. With regard to the charge that discrimination was involved in the change from the specific to the *ad valorem* basis of levy duties, he claimed that

the change made in 1859 was merely a reversion to the basis which existed when the treaty first went into force, and contended that it merely put Montreal on a level with New York instead of being discriminated against as formerly. The provision for refunding canal tolls, further, gave an advantage to the Canadian route, indeed, but left United States and Canadian vessels on an equality, and it was equality as to vessels that the treaty prescribed. Moreover, the United States had not carried out nor tried to carry out, the treaty provision of urging the separate states to open their canals to Canadian vessels; until they did and until they abolished the tolls, they had no standing in court.[1]

The few newspaper comments in British North America on the election of Buchanan as president in 1856, seemed to

[1] *Ibid.*, pp. 297, 298, Despatch of Galt, March, 1862, to Privy Council.

indicate that the people of British North America generally regarded his election as favorable to the further extension of trade between the two countries, since the Democrats had declared themselves opposed to a protective tariff.   There was, however, the prevalent feeling in British America that the Southern Democrats who had been instrumental in securing its passage had approved the Reciprocity Treaty for a political, not a commercial reason, and therefore might sacrifice their traditional trade policy of low tariff for the same reason.[1]   Both the Liberal and Conservative press in the fifties favored a policy of reciprocity with the United States. No Canadian administration, either Liberal or Conservative, was willing to admit the principle of direct protection.   To the charge of the *Globe*[2] that the Canadian Government controlled by the Conservatives in 1858 had adopted the policy of protection favored by the manufacturers, and opposed by the farmers, the *Leader*,[3] a Conservative newspaper of Canada West, replied that the higher Canadian tariff was necessary to meet the increased governmental expenditure on public works, and was in no sense an imitation of the preferential tariff of the United States.   In referring to the appointment of Mr. Hatch by the United States government to investigate the alleged violations of the Reciprocity Treaty, the *Leader* contended that before no impartial tribunal could Canada be found guilty.   No narrow interpretation of the treaty such as the Americans had shown in the imposition of consular fees which amounted to a tax, had been permitted by the Canadian government.[4]

The Reciprocity Treaty of 1854 was ratified at a time when the free-traders of both countries were in the ascen-

[1] The *Pilot*, December 3, 1856.

[2] The *Globe*, November 12, 1858.

[3] The *Leader*, November 19, 1858.

[4] *Ibid.*

dant. Soon there followed a reaction in both countries in favor of protection. The absence of the Southern Senators from Congress on the secession of the Southern States largely accounted for the change of official sentiment in the United States. As the *Globe,* July 22, 1861, truly remarked: " The Reciprocity Treaty was carried and has since been maintained by the influence of Southern statesmen, who believed that it would be a means of preventing the annexation of Canada to the Republic, a thing which they dreaded, and foolishly enough, thought likely to happen."

Protectionist sentiment was increasing in both countries. In Canada, it was said, the tariff of 1859, and the tariff of 1858, " of which it was an enlargement and expansion, were the first ever framed in this country for the avowed purpose of developing home manufactures, and in obedience to a popular demand." [1] The Canadian Government was very far indeed from accepting the protectionist principles advocated in a protectionist convention in Toronto, held in the spring of 1858 when it was apparent that some changes in the tariff were necessary. The Canadian Ministry resolutely refused to admit the principle of direct protection, and the principal opposition to the changes introduced in the tariff had its origin within the ranks of the protectionists. The refusal of Galt to recognize direct protection, and his adoption of a revenue tariff arranged with the various interests of the country in mind was a keen disappointment to the protectionists. To the Sheffield Chamber of Commerce, which believed that Canada should adopt the free-trade policy of Great Britain, the colony appeared to have

---

[1] Compiled by John Maclean, *The Tariff Hand-book showing the Canadian Customs Tariff, with the various changes made during the last thirty years, also the British and American Tariffs in Full and the more important portions of the Tariffs of France, Germany, Holland, Belgium, Italy and Switzerland, all taken from the best authorities,* p. 52.

entered on a protectionist trade policy, while to the Canadian protectionist, the course was ruinous free trade.

An " Association for the Organization of Canadian Industry " had been organized in Toronto in 1858. This association included in its membership many of the influential manufacturers of Canada. They made certain formal demands on the Canadian Government for increased duties on manufactured goods. Galt, who was then finance minister of Canada, realized the need of increased revenue and therefore complied with the wishes of the manufacturers. The explanation of the tariff of 1859 may be found in Galt's own words:

The fiscal policy of Canada has invariably been governed by considerations of the amount of revenue required. It is no doubt true that a large and influential party exists, who advocate a protective policy; but this policy has not been adopted by either the Government or Legislature, although the necessity of increased taxation for the purpose of revenue has, to a certain extent, compelled action in partial unison with their views, and has caused more attention to be given to the proper adjustment of the duties, so as neither unduly to stimulate nor depress the few branches of manufacture which exist in Canada. The policy of the present Government in readjusting the tariff has been, in the first place, to obtain sufficient revenue for the public wants; and, secondly, to do so in such a manner as would most fairly distribute the additional burdens upon the different classes of the community; and it will undoubtedly be a subject of gratification to the Government if they find that the duties absolutely required to meet their engagements should incidentally benefit and encourage the production, in the country, of many of those articles which we now import. The Government have no expectation that the moderate duties imposed by Canada can produce any considerable development of manufacturing industry; the utmost that is likely to arise is the establishment of works requiring comparatively unskilled labor, or of those competing with American makers, for the production of goods which

can be equally well made in Canada, and which a duty of 20%
will no doubt stimulate.   That these results should flow from
the necessity of increased taxation, is no subject of regret to the
Canadian Government, nor can it be alleged as any departure,
on their part, from the recognized sound principles of trade, as
it will shortly be shown that the Government were compelled
to obtain increased revenue; and it is believed that no other
course could be relied on for this result than that adopted.[1]

In answer to the complaint of the British Government
against the increased duties levied on manufactured goods,
Galt declared the fiscal independence of Canada in unmis-
takable and unforgettable language:

Self-government would be utterly annihilated if the views of
the Imperial Government were to be preferred to those of the
people of Canada.   It is, therefore, the duty of the present government distinctly to affirm the right of the Canadian legislature
to adjust the taxation of the people in the way they deem best—
even if it should unfortunately happen to meet the disapproval
of the Imperial Ministry.   Her Majesty cannot be advised to
disallow such acts, unless her advisers are prepared to assume
the administration of the affairs of the colony irrespective of
the views of its inhabitants.[2]

Since this pronouncement by Galt, the constitutional right of
Canada to settle her fiscal policy has not been questioned.

From the adoption of free trade by the United Kingdom
in 1846, until the present, the fiscal policy of the United
States, and not that of Great Britain, has exercised a greater
influence in Canada.   To the protests of the United States
at the increased rate of duties, Galt had retorted, " it is not
for the high tariff pot to call the lower tariff kettle black ".[3]

[1] The Quebec *Gazette*, October 4, 1850.

[2] O. D. Skelton, *The Life and Times of Sir Alexander Tilloch Galt*,
p. 330, quoted from source.

[3] *Ibid.*, p. 297.

CHAPTER II

The Negro in British North America

Slavery in the Early Days—British North American Legislation on Slavery—Anti-Slavery Sentiment—Depreciation in the Value of Slave Property in the British Provinces—Effect of the Pro-Slavery Legislation of the United States—Press of British America United in its Condemnation of Fugitive Slave Law 1850—Northward Trek of Negroes—Destitution—Organization of the Anti-Slavery Society in Canada 1851—Negro Settlements in British North America—Political Events in the United States—Effect on the Extension of Slavery—Sympathy for the Refugee—John Brown in Canada—Harper's Ferry Insurrection—Southern Resentment against Canada—The Negro Safe in Canada.

The question naturally presents itself as to how far the presence of the colored race in the British North American Provinces determined the attitude which these provinces adopted toward the American Civil War. Negro settlements at the outbreak of the war were to be found not only in the Canadas, but also in the Maritime provinces. The negro will, therefore, be considered not merely as an economic issue, but as a moral issue, affecting the relations of the two countries.

The presence of the negro in Canada was not something new, for in Lower Canada as far back as 1689, slavery had been recognized by France, and sixty years later slavery was also to be found in Nova Scotia.[1] Before the separation of Upper and Lower Canada in 1791 slavery had spread westward into Upper Canada and a few hundred negroes and some Pawnee Indians were to be found in bondage throughout the scattered settlements of the southwestern portion of

[1] *Collections of the Nova Scotia Historical Society*, vol. x, T. Watson Smith, " Slave in Canada," chap. i.

Upper Canada.[1] At the termination of the Revolutionary War the rumor that two thousand slaves had escaped to British territory caused considerable consternation to their masters, especially when it became known that the British Commander-in-Chief, Sir Guy Carleton, had issued a " proclamation guaranteeing their liberty to all slaves who when taking refuge within the British lines had formally claimed the protection offered by British commanders." [2] The demand of Washington for their surrender was refused, for such a restoration would have been a violation of good faith on the part of the British authorities. These fugitives were reassured by the grant of certificates of freedom from the British government, and were given grants of land, and rations such as were distributed to the United Empire Loyalists. In 1791 John Clarkson, an anti-slavery leader, was sent to Nova Scotia by the Sierra Leone Company to arrange for the transportation back to Africa of all freedmen desirous of returning there. One thousand one hundred and eighty negroes from Nova Scotia and New Brunswick are said to have availed themselves of this opportunity.[3] At the termination of the American War of Independence the total number of United Empire Loyalists, including men, women and children, some accompanied by their slaves, has been estimated as between eighty and one hundred thousand. About two-thirds of the exiles had settled in Nova Scotia and New Brunswick, and the remainder in the valley of the St. Lawrence.[4] The slaves who accompanied their

[1] Wilbur H. Siebert, *The Underground Railroad from Slavery to Freedom*, chap. vii, p. 190.

[2] *Collections of the Nova Scotia Historical Society*, vol. x, p. 21.

[3] *Ibid.*, vol. x, p. 23; vol. vii, "Story of Deportation of Negroes from Nova Scotia to Sierra Leone" (read by ex-Governor Archibald 12th March, 1885).

[4] *Canadian Magazine*, vol. x, art. vi, "The Makers of the Dominion of Canada," by Bourinot, Sir John G.

masters to the Maritime provinces were classified as servants.

In Canada East the negroes have never been numerically strong. This fact may partly account for the failure of the legislature of that province to pass any legislation on the subject of slavery. Petitions were presented to the House of Assembly to safeguard the rights of the slave owners. One motion to consider the question of slavery was referred to a committee of five consisting of Papineau,[1] Grant, Craigie, Cuthbert, and Dumas. Cuthbert introduced on behalf of the committee, April 30, 1800, a bill which provided for the gradual liberation of the slaves, and the prevention of any further introduction of slavery. This bill was referred to the Committee of the Whole, but was never heard of again. The Courts of Canada East, however, refused to uphold the rights of the slave owner. The Court of King's Bench at Montreal discharged a slave of a Mr. Fraser who had been committed by three justices of the peace to the house of correction in accordance with his master's wishes. The legislature of Canada East also refused to aid in the restoration of the fugitive slave to his master. When the Secretary of State of the United States requested the delivery of a slave, Sir James Kempt referred the matter to the Executive Council, which reported that, " the law of Canada does not admit a slave to be a subject of property."[2] Slavery, however, was never formally abolished in Canada East, until the passage of the Act of 1833 by the Imperial parliament which fixed the date August 1, 1834, as the date for the emancipation of all slaves in the British Colonies.

In Canada West where there were more slaves the case

[1] Joseph Papineau, the father of Louis J. Papineau the rebel, was one of the outstanding men of his day, a commanding influence in public meetings.

[2] *Journal of Negro History*, vol. v, W. R. Riddell, " Slavery in Canada "; *Canadian Archives, State K.*, p. 406.

was somewhat different, for the Upper Canada legislature had passed an act September 28, 1793, which formally provided for gradual emancipation.[1]   Hence technically at least Canada West was in advance of Canada East in anti-slavery legislation.

According to Judge Marshall, who was appointed chief justice of the Court of Common Pleas for Cape Breton in 1832, an escaped slave was brought before Chief-Justice Bowers, who " legally and justly decided that this province was not debased with that cruel and abominable slave system which John Wesley appropriately characterized as the sum of all villainies." [2]   Judge Thomas C. Haliburton, on the contrary, denied that there had ever been a judicial decision rendered in Nova Scotia on the subject of slavery.[3]   In New Brunswick no judicial decision condemning slavery was ever rendered; nevertheless the conviction gradually grew in the Maritime provinces that the slave owners there could not expect much recognition from the law courts, and as a natural consequence the value of slaves greatly depreciated.[4]   An indication of the general uncertainty with regard to slavery was to be found in a bill of sale made out in King's County 1807 in which appeared the words " if a negro can be considered property in Nova Scotia." [5]   The last effort made by the slave owners to protect themselves resulted in a bill for " securing them their property or indemnifying them for its loss." It passed its second reading, January 11, 1808, but never became law.[6]   Partly, no

---

[1] *Canadian Archives, Q 2792*, p. 335.

[2] *Nova Scotia Historical Collections*, vol. x, T. Watson Smith, " The Slave in Canada," p. 111.

[3] Judge Thomas C. Haliburton, *History of Nova Scotia*, vol. ii, p. 280 (published 1829).

[4] *Nova Scotia Historical Collections*, vol. x, pp. 113-114.

[5] *Ibid.*, p. 115.

[6] *Ibid.*, p. 117.

doubt, as the result of this uncertainty, the number of slaves remaining in the Maritime provinces was reduced at the beginning of the nineteenth century, although a few remained in the southwestern portion of Nova Scotia.[1] In the first census of New Brunswick one thousand four hundred and three colored people are listed, the majority of them no doubt at one time slaves.[2] As far back as 1781 the legislature of Prince Edward Island passed an act which contained a recognition of slavery. The act of 1825 did not abolish slavery but repealed the previous legislation of 1781. Although legally possible in Prince Edward Island until the Imperial Act of 1833, slavery gradually ceased to exist in that province as in the other British provinces, and the last recorded sale of a slave was in 1802.[3]

If the actions of the law-makers and judges in British America indicated an opposition to pro-slavery legislation, quite a contrary tendency was discernible in the United States where the pro-slavery legislation gradually led the negro to regard the British North American Provinces as the Promised Land. As one fugitive expressed the feeling of his race: " He led me across the water to Canada, the land that we negroes call rock and our land of promise." [4] The number of negroes who went north to British America, however, remained relatively insignificant.

As far back as 1787, the federal constitution had safeguarded property rights in slaves, in the clause which said " no person held to service or labour in one state, under the laws thereof, escaping into another, shall, in consequence of any law or regulation therein, be discharged from such ser-

[1] *Ibid.*

[2] *Ibid.*, p. 118, foot-note—1st General Census in New Brunswick, 1824.

[3] *Cf. Journal of Negro History*, July, 1921, W. R. Riddell, " The Baptism of Slaves in Prince Edward Island.

[4] J. G. Kohl, *Travels in Canada and through the States*, vol. i, p. 104.

vice or labour, but shall be delivered up on claim of the party to whom such service or labour may be due." [1]   In the Northwest ordinance of 1787 was inserted a fugitive slave clause, which stated " that any person escaping into the same from whom labor or service is lawfully claimed in any one of the original states, such fugitive may be lawfully reclaimed and conveyed to the person claiming his or her labor or service aforesaid." [2]   It was in 1793 that the first federal law which provided for the return of the fugitive slave was passed.   This law had two clauses which related to fugitives from justice, and two to fugitives from labor. This bill passed the Senate unanimously, and the House by a vote of forty-eight to seven.[3]   As the Southerners did not regard the act as effective, it was amended from time to time until the passage of the Fugitive Slave Act of 1850.[4] This act of 1850 was a powerful instrument to create anti-slavery sentiment in the North, for the question of owner-ship was to be determined by the simple affidavit of the slave owner without permitting the negro to testify in his own behalf; in addition, heavy penalties were to be imposed upon all who harbored the refugees, and the federal commissioners were to receive ten dollars for every slave returned to his master, and only five for each negro discharged.

The Fugitive Slave law of 1850 was universally con-demned by the press of British America.   The injustice of the rigorous provisions which provided every facility to the slave-holder for the recovery of his property, but denied to

[1] *The Constitution of the United States*, art. iv, sec. ii, clause 3.

[2] *Journal of Congress*, vol. xii, pp. 84, 92.

[3] *Annual Report of the American Historical Association*, 1893, James A. Woodburn, " The Historical Significance of the Missouri Com-promise," p. 252.

[4] *Ontario Historical Society*, vol. xvii, Fred Landon, " Canada's Part in Freeing the Slave," p. 74.

the negro protection against false arrest, was generally recognized. The defeat of the amendment offered by Mr. Dayton in the Senate, which would have provided for the negro trial by jury, was likewise condemned. In its condemnation of the bill, characterized as " harsh and vindictive in spirit and necessarily unjust in its operation," the Quebec *Gazette* admitted that it was also influenced by the dread of the arrival on British soil of an increasing number of fugitives, many of them, moreover, of "depraved moral habits." [1] This newspaper boldly declared that fifty unions should have been sacrificed before the North submitted to the passage of such a bill. It was regarded as a degrading compromise which the North had made with the South, and which in its enforcement might involve suffering to many fugitives who for a score of years had enjoyed their liberty, residing in the Northern States, acquiring property and bringing up their families confident that they were in a land of freedom. To these slaves now, the only alternative to a return to bondage was an escape to British soil, preferably Canada West on account of the milder climate. The economic reasons sometimes urged in its behalf were declared an insufficient justification. " The cotton spinners of the North were afraid that the cotton growers of the South would renounce their alliance, and spin their cotton for themselves, and the North gave up its soil to the man-hunter as a hunting ground and provided beaters and game keepers to assist in the chase." [2] The indignation of the Northern anti-slavery people at the passage of such a bill, which found expression notably in New England, likewise did not pass unrecognized by the people of British America. Lengthy discussions of the question of the extension of slavery in the neighboring republic found

[1] The Quebec *Gazette*, October 4, 1850.
[2] *Ibid.*, October 11, 1850.

expression in the columns of the Montreal *Gazette*[1] and also in the *British Colonist* of Toronto.[2] The comment of the former newspaper on Webster's statement in regard to the constitutionality of the act was characteristic of the attitude generally adopted by the press of British America: " This measure may be constitutional and expedient in the sense of Mr. Webster; but neither of these will excuse its moral wrong."[3]

By this signing of the Fugitive Slave Bill, September 18, 1850, President Fillmore started a northward trek of both free and slave negroes, for the free colored person, as well as the escaped slave, no longer felt secure in the northern states. The free negroes who remained in the United States preferred to reside in the states bordering on Canada, to which they could flee if their freedom were endangered. The northwest migration continued until the opening of the Civil War. Various estimates of the number of negroes who entered Canada during the decade of the fifties may be found; for instance, one authority[4] claimed that fifteen to twenty thousand entered, and that the negro population increased from forty thousand to nearly sixty thousand, but the census reports of Canada[5] recorded a much smaller number. The census gives the following statistics: In 1851 out of a total population of 952,004, Canada West had 8,000 colored, mainly settled in the counties of Haldimand,

---

[1] The Montreal *Gazette*, October 4, 1850, October 14, 1850, November 4, 1850.

[2] The *British Colonist*, October 4, 1850, October 15, 1850.

[3] The Montreal *Gazette*, November 4, 1850.

[4] *Journal of Negro History*, vol. iv, Fred Landon, " The Negro Migration to Canada after 1850."

[5] Wilbur H. Siebert, *The Underground Railroad from Slavery to Freedom*, pp. 220-221. Siebert characterized the census reports of Canada as wilfully false.

Kent and Northumberland;[1] in 1861 out of a total population of 1,396,091, Canada West had 11,223 colored, an increase of 3,223 colored within the ten years, mainly settled in the Southwestern portion in the counties of Essex and Kent.[2] Canada East, out of a total population of 890,261 in 1851 had 18 colored people,[3] and in 1861 the colored population had increased to 190.[4] New Brunswick in 1851 out of a total population of 193,800, had 1,058 colored,[5] and in 1861 out of a total population of 252,047 had 1,581 colored.[6] Nova Scotia, out of a total population of 276,854 in 1851 had 4,908 colored,[7] and in 1861, 5,927 colored,[8] an increase of 1,109 colored within the decade prior to the Civil War. Although the two reports show a wide variance, there is sufficient evidence to substantiate the statement that the influx of negroes presented a serious problem for the British North American population to solve. Undoubtedly the emigration of the colored people from the United States would have been greater if the attitude of many Northerners had not shown a determination to resist the enforcement of the Fugitive Slave Bill of 1850. Henceforth the presence of numerous refugees in Canada forced the people of the British North American Provinces to look upon the question of slavery from an economic, as well as from a moral viewpoint.

Since many of the refugees upon their arrival in Canada

[1] *Census of 1851*, Canada West.

[2] *Census of 1861, Canada West.*

[3] *Census of Canada East, 1851.*

[4] *Census of Canada East, 1861.*

[5] *Journal of the House of Assembly of the Province of N. B.—1862,* Compilers Record, p. 4.

[6] *Journal of the House of Assembly of the Province of N. B.—1862.*

[7] *N. S. Journal, 1852,* Appendix 94, 1854.

[8] *Census of Nova Scotia, 1861.*

were utterly destitute, the Canadians realized the imperative
need of organized relief work for them. In February, 1851,
the Anti-Slavery Society of Canada was organized. All
previous attempts to organize such a society in Canada had
failed. A detailed report of the organization meeting, at
which the Mayor of Toronto presided and the Principal of
Knox College opened with prayer, appeared in the *Globe,*
March 1, 1851. The meeting endorsed four resolutions.
The first declared that "slavery is an outrage on the laws
of humanity" and that "its continued practice demands the
best exertion for its extinction." The second resolution
stated that the United States slave laws were "at open
variance with the best interests of man as endowed by our
great Creator with the privilege of life, liberty and the pur-
suit of happiness." The third resolution voiced the sympathy of the gathering with the abolitionists of the United
States, the fourth contained the proposition for the organization of the Anti-Slavery Society in Canada whose "object
shall be to aid in the extinction of slavery all over the world
by means exclusively lawful and peaceable, moral and religious, such as the diffusing of useful information and
argument by tracts, newspapers, lectures and correspondence, and by manifesting sympathy with the houseless and
homeless victims of slavery flying to our shores." The
headquarters of the Anti-Slavery Society was in Toronto,
but various branches were organized throughout Canada by
agents of the Society.

In carrying on the work of the organization the clergy-
men of Canada were well represented, for Dr. Willis, Principal of Knox College, a Presbyterian theological institution, was the first president, and the Reverend Mr. William
McClure, a Methodist clergyman, was the Secretary. To
further the task a large committee of prominent Canadians,
including in its ranks George Brown, editor of the *Globe,*

and Oliver Mowat, later a premier of Ontario, was appointed. Prominent among the champions of freedom, George Brown voiced his sense of responsibility in the words, " We, too, are Americans. On us, as well as on them, lies the duty of preserving the honor of the continent. On us, as on them, rests the noble trust of shielding free institutions." [1] Although he complained of the indifference of certain churches in Canada, Dr. Willis was instrumental in securing assistance from the Presbyterians, who in a Synod meeting passed a resolution declaring that slavery was inhuman, unjust and dishonoring to the common Creator as it is replete with wrong to the subjects of such oppression. The second resolution reinforced the first by calling upon the church to denounce legislation which violated the commands of God.

The Anti-Slavery Society in Canada continued its work throughout the fifties, and the sixties, until the need for an organized relief body for the negroes in Canada no longer existed. At the close of the Civil War the Society felt that it was no longer necessary to continue, in view of the fact that many of the negroes had returned to the United States where they could find climatic conditions which suited their manner of living. During its period of activity considerable money had been spent in relief work, for at the annual meeting of the Society in 1857 the treasurer reported that more than two thousand two hundred dollars had been spent in relief work, and more than four hundred negroes had received financial assistance. [2]

The money expended, however, represented but a small portion of the relief work done. To the southwestern por-

[1] *The Makers of Canada Series*, vol. xix, John Lewis, George Brown, p. 114.

[2] *Journal of Negro History*, vol. iv, Fred Landon, " The Anti-Slavery Society in Canada."

tion of Canada West, easily accessible by way of Detroit, in the decade of the fifties, flocked many fugitive slaves. Here, too, an effort was made by Canadian sympathizers to welcome the fugitives, often destitute, supply their needs and settle them upon the land. Necessarily, with the settlement of an increasing number of negroes in Canada, the question of slavery assumed a new significance in the eyes of the Canadian people, for was not their own national life intimately affected? Since the negroes never came in such numbers to either Canada East or the Maritime Provinces, the people of those provinces never came into such intimate contact with the colored race.[1] Naturally a few refugees came northward through New England and settled in either Canada East or the Lower Provinces, but these settlements in comparison with those of Canada West were relatively insignificant.

The largest of the negro refugee colonies in Canada West was the Buxton settlement, consisting of nearly nine thousand acres to the south of Chatham. A company generally known as the Elgin Association was incorporated in 1850 " for the settlement and moral improvement of the colored population of Canada, for the purpose of securing crown or clergy reserve lands in the township of Raleigh and settling the same with colored families resident in Canada of approved moral character." [2] The land was surveyed and divided into small farms of fifty acres. The negroes were encouraged to buy these farms at the low price of two dollars and fifty cents per acre in ten annual payments. Certain regulations were enforced; for instance, the negro must build a house in accordance with certain specifications,

[1] Wilbur H. Siebert, *The Underground Railroad from Slavery to Freedom*, p. 191.

[2] *Cf. Journal of Negro History*, vol. iii, Fred Landon, " The Buxton Settlement in Canada."

namely 18 feet by 24 feet and 12 feet high, 30 feet from
the road with a garden in front. The negro did not receive
a deed to his land until he had complied with all the requirements. Although in many respects considered the most important of the negro colonies, Buxton was only one of many.
In the Dresden settlement, usually considered second in importance, a manual labor school, known as the Dawn School,
was established. The Colchester Settlement, twelve miles
from Amherstburg, was established by some benevolent
Quakers for the fugitive slaves.[1] The negroes were most
numerous in the southwestern portion of Canada West.

Not all the inhabitants of Canada West were prepared to
welcome the influx of an alien race, uneducated and un-
accustomed to freedom. The negroes were in many respects
as irresponsible as little children, but unfortunately, not as
guileless. The fact that indignation meetings were held in
Toronto, Chatham, and other towns would seem to indicate
that the negro was not as universally welcomed as the abo-
litionist would wish us to believe. At such a gathering held
in Chatham, the county town of the district in which the
negroes were most numerous, the plans of the Elgin Association or Buxton Company settlement were unqualifiedly
condemned. " A resolution was passed in condemnation of
the sale of public lands to foreigners, the more so when
such persons belong to a different branch of the human
family and are black." A Vigilance Committee was also
appointed to watch the negro settlements. Necessary funds
were voted to carry on an active campaign against the
negroes, the majority of whom were regarded by those who
attended this meeting as worthless idlers who simply depreciated the value of property wherever they settled.[2] The

[1] *First Annual Report of the Anti-Slavery Society of Canada*, pp. 16-17.
[2] *Journal of Negro History*, vol. iii, Fred Landon, " The Buxton Settlement in Canada."

white race shunned the districts in which the colored race settled. Even at public sales, the auctioneer was instructed not to accept a bid from a colored person. In the course of a debate in the Legislative Council, June, 1858, Colonel Prince, representative from the county of Essex, is reported to have made the statement: " In the County of Essex the greatest curse that befell them was the swarm of blacks that infested the country. They were perfectly inundated with them." [1]

The negroes frequently became aggressively offensive, claiming the right, for example, to send their children to the schools which white children attended, even when the community had provided separate schools for the colored children. In the Detroit *Free Press,* January 20, 1860, is to be found an account of a negro disturbance at Chatham.

They now threaten that if any distinction of color is suffered to exist in any department of the public affairs, they will burn the town. The blacks parade the streets in squads, abusing and insulting the whites, frequently resorting to violence. Nor is their violence confined to the males. Females when met upon the sidewalks are roughly pushed into the gutters to give place for the black ruffians, and the authorities of the town discreetly keep out of the streets at night for fear of personal violence.

Thus the actual presence of the negroes in Canada aroused a certain antagonism to the race in districts where the negroes did not prove themselves law-abiding members of the community. Racial prejudice was, therefore, accentuated.

The few newspaper comments [2] on the election of Buchanan as President in 1856, showed that the people of Brit-

[1] The *New York Herald,* January 5, 1860.

[2] The Quebec *Mercury,* November 11, 1856, December 5, 1856; the *Acadian Recorder,* November 8, 1856, November 15, 1856; the *Leader,* November 7, 1856; the *Globe,* March 9, 1857.

ish America were primarily concerned with the effect that his election would have upon the slavery question. Without exception the press of Canada West, Canada East, and the Maritime Provinces, whenever sufficient interest was felt in the election to mention it, regarded the success of Buchanan as a victory for the Southern slave owner. Nowhere was surprise expressed, for had not the North ever yielded to the South The election of Buchanan, therefore, was generally considered but one more concession to the South, added to a long series. The reason usually assigned for this policy was that in spite of their championship of the slaves, the Northerners were after all only half-hearted in their efforts, placing the Union first, and the cause of freedom second. What further proof of the above contention was needed when the majority of the free men of five or six of the Northern states had voted for Buchanan and Fillmore,[1] two candidates closely identified with the slave interest?

The Dred Scot decision which aroused so much comment in American newspapers failed to evoke a corresponding interest in the press of British North America. A satirical editorial did appear in the Quebec *Mercury* of March 21, 1857, under the heading, "Negroes are not Men." Here the whole argument that a person of African blood cannot be a citizen is reviewed. The Supreme Court of the United States

sets aside all the legislation of the United States on the subject for the last fifty years and overrules all the decisions of the Supreme Court in which the questions were involved from the commencement of the government. All the acquisitions of territory from the origin of government are thus made subservient to the extension of slavery.

[1] *Cf.* G. Ticknor Curtis, *Life of James Buchanan*, vol. ii, p. 177, electoral vote of the five free states: Pennsylvania, New Jersey, Indiana, Illinois, California.

The judicial decision of the Supreme Court disfranchised those negroes who had voted in accordance with the constitution of certain Northern States.

Strange though it may seem to Americans, the Congressional election of 1858 in the United States apparently aroused more interest in British North America than the presidential election of 1856—an increased interest which may in a large measure be accounted for by the outrages committed by the pro-slavery party in Kansas within the interval of time which had elapsed. The probable consequences of the Republican victory of '58 were carefully analyzed by the *Globe* of November 5th and 16th, 1858. The Democratic victory in Illinois in which Douglas, the repealer of the Missouri Compromise, defeated Lincoln, referred to as " the Free Soil Republican candidate," seemed to indicate that Douglas the " little giant " was the strongest Democratic candidate for the presidency in 1860.[1] Many of the Democrats who had deserted Buchanan in 1858 might rally under Douglas in 1860, since he had gained considerable popularity among the moderate men of the North by his condemnation of the " Lecompton Outrage " in opposition to the known wishes of Buchanan and the Southern party. Since the sole possibility of success for the Democratic party was in a union of the moderate men of the North with a united South, Douglas was considered the most likely candidate of that party.[2] In its issue of November 16, 1858, the diversified interests represented in the new Republican party were discussed. There were those who had joined the Republican party to prevent the extension

[1] Edward C. Smith, *A Dictionary of American Politics,* p. 157; *cf.* James Albert Woodburn, *Political Parties and Party Problems in the United States,* chaps. v, vi. The Free Soil Party organized in 1848 had been merged in the new Republican party of 1856.

[2] The *Globe,* November 5, 1858.

of slavery but would hesitate to carry the struggle further against slavery; those of the old Whig party in Maryland, Virginia, Kentucky and Missouri desirous of sharing the Republican spoils; and those who belonged to the anti-slavery associations—the old Liberty men of 1840 or 1844 who had forced upon Whigs and Democrats the slavery issue; and lastly the Free Soilers, many of whom had joined the Republican party when their party was merged with the Republican in 1856. Holding the balance of power in the Republican party, the anti-slavery men could not be ignored in the selection of a presidential candidate.

Thus the press of British America in all its comments upon the elections in the United States showed itself primarily interested in the outcome because of the probable effect on slavery. In spite of a certain amount of racial prejudice against the negro due in part at least to his conduct, both the press and Anti-Slavery Society in Canada were influential in arousing considerable sympathy for the refugees. This fact no doubt influenced John Brown in his selection of Chatham, Canada West, for his secret convention, May 8 and 10, 1858. Here John Brown outlined his plan for freeing the slaves and a constitution was adopted for his followers; later copies of this constitution presented in the courts of Virginia furnished incriminating evidence against Brown. More than a year elapsed before he attempted to carry out his plans, as outlined at the Chatham convention. Declaring its belief that the Harper's Ferry insurrection, characterized as " an act of madness," [1] would intensify public feeling on the eve of a presidential election, the *Globe* nevertheless commended the motives that prompted Brown to risk " liberty and life for the advancement of an alien and despised race." [2] Not only would the Southerners,

[1] *Ibid.*, October 20, 1859.
[2] *Ibid.*

naturally aroused, refuse to be identified in any way with those whom they regarded as responsible for the outrage, but also the conservative party in the North, alarmed at the prospect of Civil War, might be tempted to join them. This newspaper in its issue of November 2, 1859, stated its conviction that the effect of the execution of Brown would be to perpetuate his memory as "a brave man who perilled property, family, life itself for an alien race." Three weeks later the *Globe* prophesied Civil War in the near future if the tension between the two sections of the United States continued. "No force which the South could bring to bear would keep the slaves down were the North anxious that they should be free. Dissolution of the Union would not help the case. The effect would be rather the reverse. The South have not shown wisdom or statesmanship in arousing the spirit of the North by their frantic attempts to extend the peculiar institution." [1] Furthermore this paper believed that the execution of Brown would do much toward arousing the spirit of the North. On December 12th, 1859, the *Globe* continued to say with reference to the cotton states that "if a Republican President is elected next year, nothing short of a dissolution of the union will satisfy them." [2]

The incriminating evidence against Brown at his trial revealed that the plot had been definitely planned at the secret convention held at Chatham, Ontario. Governor Wise of Virginia was very much incensed against the Canadians. Speaking to the Legislature of Virginia, he said: "This was no result of ordinary crimes. It was an extraordinary and actual invasion, especially upon slave-holders and upon their property in negro slaves. . . . A provisional government was attempted in a British Province, by our countrymen,

---

[1] The *Globe*, November 22, 1859.

[2] *Ibid.*, December 12, 1859.

united to us in the faith of confederacy, combined with Canadians to invade the slave-holding states . . . for the purpose of stirring up universal insurrection of slaves throughout the whole South." Referring to the spirit of the North, he continued: " It has organized in Canada and traversed and corresponded thence to New Orleans and from Boston to Iowa. It has established spies everywhere, and has secret agents in the heart of every slave state, and has secret associations and underground railways in every free state." [1] On December 22, 1859, Governor Wise addressed a gathering of medical students of Philadelphia, who had deserted their college and gathered in Richmond, thus: " With God's help we will drive all the disunionists together back into Canada. Let the compact of fanaticism and intolerance be confined to British Soil." [2]

The feeling of resentment against Canadians for their so-called aid was not justified by the evidence presented at the trial. No doubt the fact that Brown held his convention in Chatham, in that section of Canada where the negroes were more numerous than in any other, was due to his hope of receiving active support from the negroes in Canada. His expectation was not realized. The negro, safe himself, had no intention of risking his new-found happiness for the sake of the slave in the South.

It is true then, to a certain extent at least, that the presence of negroes in British North America must have helped to determine the attitude of these provinces toward the American conflict. As has been elsewhere noted, slavery received in the early days a certain recognition in all the provinces. So strong, however, was the anti-slavery sentiment throughout British North America that the provincial

[1] *Cf.* the Toronto weekly *Globe*, December 6, 1859; *Journal of the Senate of Virginia*, 1859, pp. 9-25.

[2] The *Globe*, December 28, 1859.

law courts prior to 1834 failed to support the legal demands of the slave owners for the protection of their property; consequently, the value of slaves depreciated. Upon the passage of the Fugitive Slave Law in 1850 the question of the negroes assumed a new significance both from an economic and moral standpoint, for henceforth British America was the sole haven of the refugees. Although the negroes were to be found in all the provinces, their number remained relatively insignificant except in the southwestern portion of Canada West. To this section many of them crossed the border from the frontier towns of Niagara and Detroit, and lived together in settlements. Here too the people of Canada West came into an intimate personal contact with the negro that was not found elsewhere throughout the British provinces.

CHAPTER III

PUBLIC OPINION IN CANADA WEST

Power of the Press — Liberal Press — Conservative Press — Opposed
Coercion—Press of the Northern States—Transformation in Canadian
Feeling — Anderson Case — Inaugural Address — Mason and Slidell —
Preparation for War—Canadian Militia Bill—Conscription in United
States—The Proclamation of Emancipation—The Alabama—Chesapeake
—Peterhoff—St. Albans Raid—Party Division—Canadian Loyalty.

The press of a country at one time guides and directs
public opinion, at another merely acts as the reflector and
register. It is not indeed by the study of a single newspaper, however influential that newspaper may be, that
public opinion can be accurately gauged, for no newspaper
is the spokesman of the entire people, but often the organ
of a certain organization, usually a political organization
within the country. Since this simple fact, self-evident to
all thoughtful people, has been frequently overlooked, the
rash and unconsidered statements, the work of politicians,
and not of statesmen, have threatened grave international
complications. One paper has spoken—the entire people are
held responsible. This is exactly what happened in the days
of the sixties. Once again, the Canadian press recognized
that the relationship between the British North American
Provinces and the United States, which since the War of
1812, with the possible exception of the years from 1837
to 1842, had been a matter of minor significance, had become of vital significance, for was not the peace of the English-speaking world again threatened? In the event of war
between the United States and Great Britain, Canada must

necessarily have been the battlefield.   Hence to Canada, as
the chief sufferer in the event of war, even more than to the
neighboring Republic, the preservation of amicable relations
was a matter of supreme importance.

What then was the attitude of the press of Canada West?
Did its newspapers consistently follow lines of political
partisanship?   These are a few of the questions which
naturally arise in the mind.   Was any one newspaper consistently the friend of the North, was any one paper consistently the friend of the South?   Must the newspaper
friendly to the North be anti-slavery, must that friendly to
the South be pro-slavery?   The American Civil War, of
course, was not in its initial stage a war for the liberation
of the slave, but a war for the preservation of the union;
as has been stated, the question involved was one of gram-
mar, namely whether the United States is or the United
States are.   Once again the Federalist party was arrayed
against the States Rights' party.   The great Lincoln, according to his careful and explicit statement, did not regard
himself primarily as the Emancipator of the slave, but as
the Protector and Savior of the Union:

My paramount object in this struggle is to save the Union, and
is not either to save or to destroy slavery.   If I could save the
Union without freeing any slave, I would do it; and if I could
save it by freeing all the slaves, I would do it; and if I could do
it by freeing some of the slaves and leaving others alone, I would
also do that.[1]

It is no wonder, therefore, in view of the declaration
made by Lincoln that the newspapers of Canada — even
those most friendly to the slave—sometimes failed to recognize the cause of freedom as dependent upon the success of

[1] Nicolay and Hay's *Abraham Lincoln, A History*, vol. ii, abridged
edition, p. 227.

the Northern army. Yet it was natural that the anti-slavery press in Canada West should generally regard itself as the ally of the North. For instance, the great Liberal organ, the *Globe,* a Toronto newspaper, under the leadership of George Brown and his brother Gordon Brown, unwaveringly followed an anti-slavery policy. In the opening days of the American Civil War, this newspaper was outspoken in its support of the North, and equally outspoken in its denunciation of the South. Yet this expression of opinion does not seem to have been prompted by any love of the North, but merely by its hatred of slavery. The emancipation of the slave, and not the preservation of the Union, was the subject of its solicitude, just the reverse order of importance as expressed by Lincoln. To the Liberal in Canada West, the moral issue which involved the freedom of the colored race was a matter of paramount importance. The negro ever found a firm friend and ally in the *Globe,* but this did not require any independence of judgment on the part of that paper in the opening days of the war, for the Liberals of Canada West regarded themselves as the natural allies of the North.

It did, however, require considerable moral courage as time went on, for the Northern States were soon regarded with disfavor by many Canadians, Liberals as well as Conservatives. The service to the Northern cause rendered by the *Globe* was in no sense inconsiderable, and the fact was undoubtedly due in a large measure to the influence of George Brown, the great Liberal leader. It is impossible to determine the number of Canadians whom Brown influenced to enlist in the Northern army. Various estimates have been made. According to one report 48,000 Canadians enlisted, and of these 18,000 were killed.[1] Sir John

---

[1] *Canadian Historical Review,* vol. ii, March, 1921, Wilfred Bovey, "Confederate Agents in Canada during the Civil War," p. 57.

A. Macdonald, first premier of the Dominion of Canada, is reported to have said that " there were 40,000 Canadian enlistments in the American army in the course of the Civil War." [1] If this estimate is correct, and Sir John A. Macdonald surely possessed sufficient data, then it seems probable that Brown through the columns of the *Globe* aroused considerable Northern sympathy. He more than any other public man in Canada West, served consistently the Northern cause, and this fact should be generally recognized. " The spirit that animated the youth of the North in this moral struggle was powerful in the minds of these young Canadians. There was present in Canada not a little of the feeling of responsibility for the honor of the continent that George Brown voiced, and both by peaceful means and by the sword the people of the British American Provinces had their part in striking off the shackles from the slave in the South." [2]

Just as the *Globe,* the official organ of the Liberal party, was largely instrumental in determining opinions expressed in Liberal newspapers, equally significant was the influence exerted by the *Leader,* the official organ of the Conservative party.[3] The *Leader,* which had been established in 1852 as a Conservative journal, was vigorously managed by Charles Lindsey throughout the period of the sixties. Its

[1] Collected by Arnold Haultain, a selection from Goldwin Smith's *Correspondence,* comprising letters chiefly to and from his English friends written between the years 1846 and 1910, p. 414; *The Makers of Canada,* vol. xviii, " Sir John A. Macdonald " by George R. Parkin.

[2] Goldwin Smith's *Letters,* p. 377.

[3] The newspapers of the sixties did not publish their circulation. Although the Public Archives of Canada, the Public Library of Toronto and the Office of the *Globe* were consulted, it has been impossible to secure this information. The eightieth anniversary number of the *Globe* published in March, 1924, reviewed the history of the paper since its foundation, but did not contain anything along the line of its early circulation.

influence had been greatly strengthened when in 1856 it took over the *Colonist,* a Conservative newspaper which formerly had been the chief competitor of the *Globe.*[1] Throughout the early sixties, the *Leader* had on its editorial staff George Sheppard from Richmond, Virginia.[2] The pro-Southern articles which appeared in this newspaper led the *New York Times* of January 1, 1862, to insinuate that the editor of the *Leader* was in the pay of the Southern Confederacy. This the *Leader* of January 6, 1862, denied. It was, however, only natural that this official newspaper of the Conservative party should be pro-Southern, for to the Conservative party naturally belonged the descendants of the United Empire Loyalists, whose intense pride in their tradition of loyalty to Great Britain was coupled with a feeling of antagonism toward the growing Republic to the south. Bitter memories of previous wars still survived. According to these critics, the cup of American iniquity was indeed full. Had not the recent rebellion of 1837, the work of a few over-zealous Reformers whose grievances the Family Compact[3] had refused to redress, been needlessly prolonged by republican assistance? The *Leader,* therefore, could hardly be expected to take a sympathetic attitude toward the Republic torn by internal strife. What seemed to concern the *Leader* was the question of how it would affect British interests. Unless both the North and South adopted a more conciliatory attitude toward each other, it declared, war would be inevitable with all the resultant injury to the foreign commerce of the United States. Since

[1] *A History of Canadian Journalism,* edited by a committee of the press, pp. 35, 169, 176, 177, 181.

[2] *The Canadian Historical Review,* March, 1922, vol. iii, Fred Landon, "The Trent Affair of 1861," p. 53.

[3] The office-holding clique in Canada West composed of descendants of United Empire Loyalists. *Cf.* J. L. Morison, *British Supremacy and Canadian Self-Government, 1839-1854,* pp. 18, 60, 101, 129-130, 133.

England was dependent upon the South for her cotton supply, at least a large part of it, she would naturally recognize the Southern Confederacy — in other words, the economic issue at stake would naturally outweigh the moral issue.[1]

Early in January, 1861, there appeared an article on what was to be considered the opening act of the Civil War— namely the firing of the rebels of South Carolina on the *Star of the West*.[2] Later in the month the prevailing situation in the neighboring Republic was discussed under an editorial:

This fact should always be borne in mind. Though the North may talk lightly of " bringing the South to her senses " by force of arms, a more awful responsibility could not be incurred by man. It is bad enough to commence a war with a foreign Nation, but the horrors of such hostilities sink into insignificance when compared with those of civil strife. Much better would it be that the South should be allowed to go on her own foolish way undisturbed, until by the laws of nature which will assuredly visit her with severest punishment, she discovers her errors, and returns to that union in which alone she can hope for freedom and prosperity.[3]

Here then is the suggested solution: let her go in peace, for verily when she finds out her mistake, will she return to the fold. Surely here is the doctrine of non-resistance, opposition to the use of force against the South, an attitude widely prevalent in the Northern states themselves in the early months of 1861.[4]

[1] The *Leader*, January 19, 1861; *cf.* also the *Patriot* (Conservative), January 23, 1861, reprint from the *Leader*.

[2] The *Globe*, January 11, 1861.

[3] *Ibid.*, January 25, 1861.

[4] *Cf. Smith College Studies in History*, vol. iii, no. 4, July, 1918, Lawrence Tyndale Lowrey, " Northern Opinion of Approaching Secession," October, 1859–November, 1860.

The *Patriot,* a Conservative newspaper in Toronto, like-wise denounced those who would advocate a policy of coercion in connection with the Southern States. Ever friendly as its columns were to the South, it feared that the important issues, which confronted the Southern leaders in their organization of a confederacy, were often overshadowed in their minds by the secession movement.[1] Taking its policy from the *Leader,* a long article from which it reprinted, the *Patriot* declared " that the time for compromise was past and that any attempt to hold the South as a conquered state would necessarily change the whole character of the federal government.[2]

In its issue of September 12, 1861, the *Globe* claimed that among the Conservatives, designated by it as " the Ministerialist and Corruptionist party of Canada," was to be found the pro-slavery party of Canada, and although many of the Conservative papers hesitated to come out openly in support of slavery, they nevertheless revealed their Southern sympathy. One Ministerial newspaper, the *Ottawa Gazette,* indeed had frankly defended American slavery.[3] To substantiate its charge against the Conservatives of Canada West, the *Globe,* September 16, 1861, quoted the *Mount Forest Express,* a Conservative newspaper: " Canadian journalism has now become largely recreant to the principle of human freedom. We are bound to say that the reproach attaches principally to Conservative journals, but this again with honorable exceptions, among which the Guelph *Herald* bears illustrious distinction."

Generally regarding the *Globe* as a friend, and the *Leader* as an enemy, the Northern press of the United States recognized the vast influence wielded in Canada West by the

[1] *Cf.* the *Patriot,* January 2, 1861.

[2] *Ibid.,* January 9, 1861.

[3] The *Globe,* September 12, 1861.

leading newspapers, representing officially as they did Liberal and Conservative opinion.[1] Thus the Utica *Morning Herald* of April 11, 1861, denounced the *Leader* as " a violent conservative, anti-reform, anti-democratic, anti-American journal," and in a later issue [2] that month commented upon a long article which had appeared in the *Globe* in which there was a recognition of the justice of the Northern cause, coupled with an expressed desire for its triumph.

The attitude adopted by the Northern press toward Canaian affairs was largely responsible for the transformation of Canadian opinion which undoubtedly took place. This transformation is clearly discernible in the columns [3] of the *Globe,* the natural ally of the North. An American correspondent of this newspaper placed the responsibility for the change upon the *New York Herald* as the chief offender: " That the change of feeling which has, I am sorry to see, taken place in the minds of many Canadians during the last three months in reference to the cause of the North is mainly attributable to the bombastic and defiant tone of the *New York Herald*, I do not for a moment question," but the editor in the same issue refused to consider the *New York Herald* as the sole offender, for there were others:

We are aware that the *Herald* is chiefly to blame for this, and that it probably did it to help the South, but the *Herald* was not alone in its work. Such papers as the Albany *Evening Journal,* the New York *Times* and the Buffalo *Commercial Advertiser* joined it. The New York *Tribune* was free from this charge, and the *World* and the New York *Commercial* had done everything in their power to cultivate friendly relations with Eng-

[1] *Cf.* the New York *Tribune,* December 17, 1861, the Utica *Morning Herald and Daily Gazette,* March 26, 1861, April 23, 1861, April 30, 1861.

[2] The Utica *Morning Herald and Daily Gazette,* April 23, 1861.

[3] *Cf.* the *Globe,* January 29, 1861, June 3, 1861, July 29, 1861, August 7, 1861.

land . . . a great deal of sympathy with the North has now disappeared, and there is amidst our population a very general sentiment of pleasure that the pride of the North has been humbled. We deprecate the existence of this feeling; we look upon the recent disaster [the Northern defeat at Bull Run] as a great injury to Canadian interests as well as the cause of humanity, but we cannot wonder that the people should smile at the present absurd position of a people whose leading journals were boasting only a week ago that they would wrest these provinces in defiance of the whole power of England.[1]

A week later, on August 7, 1861, the *Globe* again pointed out that the spirit of antagonism aroused toward the North was but the natural outcome following the tone adopted by the Northern press:

The insolent bravado of the Northern press toward Great Britain and the insulting tone assumed toward these provinces have unquestionably produced a marked change in the feelings of our people; when the war commenced there was only one feeling of hearty sympathy with the North, but now it is very different. People have lost sight of the character of the struggle, in the exasperation excited by the injustice and abuse showered upon them by the party with which they sympathized. It is not in human nature long to maintain cordial sympathy toward those who are pouring insult continuously upon you.

The *Globe* did not fail to note that the hostile attitude adopted by the *New York Herald* toward the British North American Provinces and Great Britain was not endorsed by the best thinking people of the North, but merely voiced the anti-British element in the United States, a noisy minority if the entire population were considered.

True, we are told that the people of the North do not participate in the feeling to which their press have given utterances—

[1] *Ibid.*, July 29, 1861.

and that the silly bravado, of which we have heard so much lately, is as distasteful to the great mass of reflecting Americans as it is to us. We believe this—and notwithstanding the unsatisfactory language of Mr. Lincoln's government as to the " peculiar institution," we do believe that the cause of liberty will be promoted by the success of the North. We cannot doubt that the supremacy of the slaveholder in the government of the Republic has exercised a most pernicious influence on the character and policy of the American people: we cannot doubt that if our Northern neighbors were freed from the demoralizing thraldom of the slaveocracy, they would give a more genuine testimony for freedom than they have heretofore done; and therefore we have heartily longed for and do yet heartily desire the complete establishment of Northern sentiment in the Government of the United States.

The support which the *Globe* extended to the Northern cause, therefore, was due not to any natural affection for the champion, but solely to a recognition of the moral issue involved in the conflict.

The charge that the *Herald* deliberately sought to arouse this feeling of antagonism in Canada can surely be substantiated by even a cursory survey of the newspaper. For instance, on July 14, 1861, an editorial appeared in the *Herald* which claimed that when " the programme of John Bull " had been made known, the Canadian press, which had previously sympathized with the Northern states, altered its policy in conformity.

Let us hear no more of Canadian liberty [it said]. The provinces are still tied to their Mother's apron strings, and whatever way she may jump or kick up her heels, they imitate her example. But as they have not yet attained to the stature or the good sense of manhood, we must excuse their childish course. When they are annexed to the republic, which is only a question of time— a question which may receive its solution before the termination of the present year—we will show them the way to act an independent part, and to assert the dignity and freedom of the Anglo-Saxon race.

In its comments on this editorial the *Globe* retaliated, accusing the *New York Herald* of using this garment of anti-British propaganda to conceal its hidden disloyalty to the Northern cause:

The New York *Herald* was long a supporter of the rebellion; one day a mob attacked the office; next day it took a somersault and became a rabid supporter of the war. . . . And because it is a friend of the Southern republic, it is endeavoring to force a war with England knowing well that within a week after the commencement of hostilities every Southern port would be open and every Northern port closely blockaded.[1]

On June 3, 1861, the *Globe* denied the charge of anti-Americanism laid by the Detroit *Tribune,* and claimed that ever since the secession movement had begun, the North had received its support, a support due solely to its recognition of the justice of the Northern cause. It however denied that the policy of the United States government had ever tended to " forward the true alliance which alone " could " prove permanent and useful." There was also a recognition of the fact that material interests bound Canada closely to the Northern states. Increased intimacy with the Americans had, moreover, increased Canadian respect for their Northern neighbors, and had produced in Canada a sincere desire for the preservation of the Union. This newspaper denied that the American rulers and American press had ever contributed to this good-will, for they had ever found " the promise of war with England an effectual election cry." Professing its inability to understand the hostile attitude of the United States, the *Globe* continued:

[1] *Cf.* the *New York Tribune,* October 21, 1861.

There appears to have been a vague idea on the other side of the lakes that the Nations of the world ought to combine together, England leading, to go mad with despair at the mere prospect of the Republicans shooting one another. Suppose we mourn in sack-cloth and ashes; sit by our hearth-stone and weep our eyes out; would that satisfy America? Or shall we one and all commit suicide as a tribute to the worth, the greatness and the goodness of the Republic? That with nothing less shall we be able to render the degree of homage which American citizens esteem to be their due, as we have most abundant evidence.

Thus it may be noted that the *Globe,* the natural ally of the North, was not guiltless of arousing a counter-irritation in the Republic, for there, too, the Canadian press was quoted as was the Northern press in Canada.

Considerable irritation continued throughout the British American Provinces as a result of the operation of the Fugitive Slave law—irritation not only against the neighboring Republic, but also against the mother country. One instance in 1861, namely the Anderson case, might be cited: Anderson, a slave who had escaped to Canada from Missouri, had slain a planter, Digges, who had attempted to arrest him. The State of Missouri under the Ashburton Treaty had demanded the surrender of Anderson to justice. Just how much justice could a slave expect who in his escape to freedom had killed a white man? To what a fate must he be surrendered! The Canadian government left to the Canadian courts the question of the interpretation of the law. Must a man who in self-defense had slain another be surrendered upon the demand of the courts of the slave-owning states? The matter was, however, apparently taken from the jurisdiction of the Canadian court, when upon the application of an attorney, Edwin James, to the Queen's Bench of England, on behalf of the fugitive slave, a writ of habeas corpus was granted by the Chief Justice of England, Lord Cockburn. Considerable irritation was aroused. The Canadians felt keenly the humiliating position in which they were placed by the transfer of this case from a Canadian court to an English court. Jealous of their rights, the Canadians asked themselves the question, is not this an infringement of our rights and liberties as a free people? Under responsible government should not the law courts of Canada have supreme jurisdiction in such a case? This was the question which agitated many Canadians. The *Globe,* while zealous on behalf of the slave, was even more zealous in safeguarding the independence of the Canadian law courts. Was the liberty of this man to be purchased at the price of Canadian liberty? The British Chief Justice, although aware of the hostile feeling that would be evoked, nevertheless had granted the request. The indignation of a large portion of the people of Canada West found utterance in the editorial of the *Globe,* January 30, 1861.

Certainly it is far from convenient, and very far from pleasant, to us as a self-governed people, to have the whole of our Judges snuffed out by one stroke of the pen of a Judge sitting 3000 miles off!—to have an English Bailiff crossing the Atlantic and by the warrant of an English Judge, who never put his foot in Canada, taking a prisoner out of our custody and carrying him off for trial to Great Britain! We would admit with great reluctance that this abstractly is either right or constitutional.[1]

Deeply humiliating, this newspaper considered, was the situation, which had arisen in Canada due to the failure of the Canadian government to assume its proper responsibility, which involved a refusal of the demand of the slaveholder as not within the treaty. Instead of performing its duty, the Canadian government had transferred it to the law courts, and " a foreign court " had been " compelled to

[1] The *Globe,* January 30, 1861.

step in and preserve the man from the imbecility of a Canadian Executive and Canadian Judge." [1] Strange indeed to Americans will appear this designation of an English court as " foreign " by Canadians; but such, however, was the Canadian conception of the rights which they enjoyed under responsible government that any interference on the part of a court of Great Britain with the Canadian judicial system would have aroused deep and widespread resentment in British America.

The *Leader* took issue with the *Globe*. Here the position was taken that under the existing international treaty, namely, the Ashburton Treaty, Anderson should be surrendered. The English press that had urged the fulfilment of international obligations, even if it were to involve the surrender of Anderson, was quoted with approval in the *Leader*, January 23, 1861. No matter how much sympathy his case must necessarily arouse, there was no other course open. The arguments advanced by those who claimed that "Anderson ought not to be given up, law or no law," were said to speak " better for the hearts than the heads." The *Spectator,* a Conservative newspaper of Canada West, agreed with the *Leader* that Anderson was a murderer, and that under the existing international treaty, he should be surrendered.

The tense situation in Canada West, the feeling of resentment, was relieved by the action of the Judges of the Court of Common Pleas, who discharged Anderson on the ground of informality in the warrant on which he was committed to the Brantford jail. Did the Canadian judges evade the issue at stake? This at least may be said in their favor, that they had prevented the transfer of the case from a Canadian to an English court. The Canadian people, through their judges, had spoken.

[1] *Ibid.*

Upon this question the Conservative newspapers of Canada West had been in complete agreement with the *New York Herald,* which the *Globe* in its issue of February 16, 1861, had characterized as " the pro-slavery Satanic press of New York." Furthermore must it not have been a source of gratification to this Satanic press, and also to the Missouri slaveholders, to find arrayed on its side the official newspaper organ of the Canadian government? The inference may be drawn that the Liberal party in this case at least favored the slave, and incidentally the North, while the Conservative party favored the slave-owner, and incidentally the South. The *Herald* undoubtedly did all in its power to stir up a bitter anti-British feeling with the underlying purpose perhaps of driving the forces of Great Britain into an alliance with the South.[1] If this were the design of the *Herald,* its apparent agreement with the Conservative press of Canada West did not signify any vital sympathy, for there was a wide gulf between the anti-British New York paper and the loyal Conservative press of Canada West. Thus in its anti-British policy, the *Herald* was directly opposed to the Canadian press, Conservative as well as Liberal. Moreover, the outstanding figure in the Conservative party, the Attorney-General of Canada West, John A. Macdonald, ever aggressively British, was not the kind of man whom the *Herald* could use as a tool to further its designs against Great Britain.

The Liberals in Canada West, who through their outspoken sympathy for the slave had identified themselves with the North, were generally dissatisfied with the Inaugural Address of President Lincoln. They had looked for a definite pronouncement on the subject of slavery, and there was none. The statement by Lincoln that secession was illegal

---

[1] As elsewhere noted on p. 73, the *New York Herald* was believed to be secretly friendly to the South. *Cf.* the *New York Tribune,* October 21, 1861.

did not concern the Liberal to whom the moral issue involved, and not the legal, was of paramount importance. There was a feeling of uncertainty as to the course of action which might be expected from the government at Washington which was indeed a keen disappointment to the anti-slavery men, of whom there were many in Canada West. The *Globe* in its issue of April 16, 1861, was more discriminating in its appraisal of actual conditions in the Republic: in its recognition of the determination of the North to withstand Southern demands—a determination so strong that in the event of aggression on the part of the South the President might look for support to a united North.

The people will spring to arms with an alacrity worthy of their cause. The Border States may then find reason for postponing secession, and the South for retracing its steps. The North has as noble a cause to fight for as any for which blood has ever been shed. Every motive which impels men to do well and bravely is theirs. If they stand as nobly by their cause as their cause is noble, they cannot fail of success.

The Leader, March 5, 1861, in its comment on the Inaugural Address of President Lincoln, commended the moderation of tone, the implied recognition of the gravity of the situation in its abstinence from all threats of coercion. It likewise differed from the *Globe* in its estimate of prevailing conditions in the republic. To the *Leader,* strongly monarchical in its sympathies, the American controversy was directly attributable to the evils inherent in a republican form of government.[1] In its editorial of March 14, 1861, it clearly indicated its inner convictions that republicanism was a failure. Was any further evidence required?

[1] The Canadian leaders frequently contrasted the monarchical and republican form of government, always to the advantage of the former under which they considered their government possessed greater stability than was to be found in the United States. Republicanism, not federalism, was criticized.

One fact is certain, that under but slight pressure it has literally collapsed.   At this moment the Executive does not know whether to advance or recede.   To this add the conflicting opinions which meet you at every turn.   Some assert that the true policy is to pour troops into the South, retake the fortresses, collect the revenue at the entrance of the ports, in short to commence the horrors of Civil War.   On the other hand, moderate men declare that the first shot fired will drive the slave Border States into immediate alliance with the extreme South.

The Conservative viewpoint, as voiced in this newspaper, was that the weakness inherent in the United States Government was the lack of a strong centralized form which would have made secession impossible under ordinary circumstances.   No attempt, moreover, had been made, this newspaper declared, to treat specifically the Southern grievances, which had included the fear of a servile insurrection on the inauguration of Mr. Lincoln, and the tariff which had taxed the South in order to support Northern manufacturers.   These grievances might, however, have been adjusted if the President had not been elected by a party the members of which had " engaged in the contest with the hope of reward and profit."   This was called the " vicious principle " in the American constitution to which was attributed much of the unrest which had resulted in the Civil War.   The *Leader* further indicated its sheer inability to recognize slavery as the root source of disunion in the Republic.   " Slavery cannot be the real cause of difference, otherwise the South and North could in twenty-four hours compose their dissensions, for the leading Northern politicians all declare their anxiety in no way to injure the South.   But men have reasoned themselves into the necessity of taking some desperate step, and their pent-up anger cannot have vent unless in attacking the very Union."   Yet the *Leader* failed to indicate how the question of slavery might be adjusted without injury to the South.

Toward the close of the opening year of the American Civil War the Mason and Slidell incident found the press of Canada West united in its indignation at the insult which had been offered to the British flag in the removal of these men from a British vessel. As is well known, Captain Wilkes, the commander of the American warship, the San Jacinto, had stopped a British mail steamer, the Trent, on the high seas, and compelled the surrender of Mason and Slidell, two diplomatic representatives of the Southern Confederacy. If the British commander had resisted, a much more serious situation between the United States and Great Britain would have arisen, and hence his prudence was commended. The action of Captain Wilkes was declared an outrage on the British flag, and an infraction of international law, for which there could be no possible justification. If such conduct were permitted, no nation could be neutral in any war, for if neutral ships could be searched, so could neutral territory. The Southerners in Canada would be no longer safe, if the action of Wilkes were legal, for the Northerners might capture them, and carry them off to either Fort Lafayette or Fort Warren. The seizure of Mason and Slidell was declared not only wrong, but also absurd and stupid, for in seizing them the American officers had done more to accomplish their errand of arousing feeling against the North than anything they could possibly have done themselves. Although the *Globe* expressed its conviction that the British government would deal temperately in the matter, it nevertheless also recognized that the capture of the Southern diplomats would strengthen " the hands of the not uninfluential parties in Great Britain " who were striving to induce the government to interfere in the American quarrel. If the war were waged vigorously and the union saved, the United States had, this newspaper declared, nothing to fear from Europe. The suggestion

was also made that it would " add infinitely to the strength
and dignity of the American government," if the captives
were at once freed, without waiting for Great Britain to
remonstrate. It would also show that the North had " confidence in the goodness of its cause," and did " not fear the
tongues of traitors well-poised though they might be." [1]

The article which appeared in the *Leader* the following
day, November 19, 1861, was much more inflammatory.
In comparison with the article the opinion as expressed by
the *Globe* the previous day appeared a very moderate and
conciliatory one. Here the virulence of attack was plainly
discernible: " Wilkes, however, understands the temper of
his Northern countrymen. He knows the capture of leading
" rebels " however accomplished, would be applauded, and
that any insult to the British flag would commend him to
the graces of the sweet democracy who reign and rule in the
republic." In its comments on a telegraphic despatch to the
effect that the president and his cabinet were elated, this
newspaper declared that it was a puerile exultation which
revealed how fragile was their hope of ultimate success.
If Great Britain objected and demanded satisfaction, the
despatch announced, the United States government would
disavow the act, make an apology, and promote Wilkes.
This the *Leader* announced as "Northern respect for international obligations," and the "Northern mode of recipro-
cating the scrupulous fidelity with which the government
and people of England and her colonies have adhered to
their profession of neutrality." Then it reviewed and condemned the position of the *Evening Post* of New York
whose attitude had previously won its commendation. The
Evening Post had admitted that it might be necessary to
apologize for the capture, but had denied the logical sequence

[1] *Cf.* the *Globe*, November 18, 1861.

of its own position, namely, the surrender of Mason and Slidell. The *Leader* asked, " Of what avail, then, will be the suggested apology?" for " the thief who repents makes restitution." The release of the Southerners was the only evidence that the United States government could offer to Great Britain of the sincerity of its regret. The article which appeared the following day further declared that this outrage should reconcile the British to the disruption of the Union. In the words of the *Leader:*

We have no interest, political, social, or commercial, in the preservation intact, of a Union whose rulers and people are alike indifferent to the obligations of law and comity; and we may be not unreasonably satisfied with a disruption which by humbling the North, and removing a prime source of its prosperity, may ultimately teach it the pleasure and profitableness of an adherence to right, and a cultivation of the courtesy which is due to neutral and friendly powers.

The *Ottawa Tribune* might be regarded as the spokesman for the Roman Catholics of Canada West. More Roman Catholics were to be found in Ottawa than in any other section of that province, a condition due no doubt to its proximity to Canada East, a province predominantly Roman Catholic. Declaring that British America enjoyed one of the most liberal governments, this paper declared that "Canadians of all classes and creeds will defend the soil from foreign aggression." [1] Like the Roman Catholics of Canada East, they preferred the monarchical to the republican form of government, believing that under the former system of government their religion was more secure, for " they had not forgotten how, when peace and prosperity flourished in the States, Irish nationality was a butt for the ridicule and sneers of native-born Americans, and how the abomi-

[1] The *Ottawa Tribune,* December 20, 1861.

nable doctrines of Know-Nothingism were cherished and received with popularity throughout the length and breadth of the nation." [1]

To many people in Canada there thus appeared only one natural outcome to the Mason and Slidell incident, namely war. The *Leader* intimated that the expressions both anti-British and anti-Canadian found in the columns of the *New York Herald* were simply a reflection " of the dominant antipathies of the people amongst whom it circulates." The *Globe* likewise recognized the seriousness of the situation:

The cry of war rings throughout the land. At the corner of every street, you hear the excited discussion as to the Mason and Slidell outrage, the next news from England, the erection of forts, and the probabilities of a fight with the Americans. The excitement no doubt had its origin in the insolent tone of the *New York Herald* and the other American journals—but the flame has been fanned by violent articles in the ministerial Press of Canada, got up systematically for partizan purpose.

Here the warning note was sounded. If the Ministerial Press of Canada sought further to inflame popular resentment, then must it needs bear a portion of the responsibility for the war. Intense excitement prevailed. The words of Palmerston, uttered when the news reached England of the outrage, " I don't know whether you will stand it, but I'll be damned if I do," were quoted with approval by many a Canadian. If Great Britain had declared war, Canada necessarily would, as we have observed, have been the chief sufferer, since Canada would have been the battlefield. But not alone in Canada West, but also in the other British Provinces, the people were animated by the spirit of determination—a determination to face the issue unflinchingly, to demand redress for the outrage, whatever might be the

[1] *Ibid.*, January 3, 1862.

consequences to the practically defenceless Provinces. If war came, the British North American Provinces were prepared to act as a unit in the defence of British soil. The surrender of Mason and Slidell averted war.

Confronted with the prospect of a war with the United States, Great Britain had recognized the loyal response of British North America. The bond which united these provinces in a love to the mother-land had been strengthened by a common danger. The situation in Canada as far as seen by the British press appeared in the London *Times* of December 11, 1861. Later this article was reprinted in the *Globe,* January 1, 1861. Canada, unprepared but undaunted, commanded an increased respect in Great Britain. There was also a recognition of the significance of Canadian loyalty, not from a materialistic, but from an imperialistic standpoint. The Canadian view of international laws was, the *Times* declared, similar to that of the French press: " The deck of an English ship is a part of the soil of England and ought to give exactly the same protection to strangers as the soil of England itself. The seizure of such a ship is a high-handed insult to our flag, and a challenge to maintain its rights. In answer to such a challenge the people of England will give no uncertain sound." [1] Such language used by the Canadians upon whom the first results of any war between Great Britain and the United States would fall had aroused the admiration and respect of the mother country.

Another sign of the general excitement in Canada was the mass meeting which had been called for December 31, 1861, at St. Lawrence Hall, Toronto, to consider the question of war, since war had appeared imminent. Although the danger of an Anglo-American conflict as a result of the Mason and Slidell incident had passed, the meeting consid-

[1] *Cf.* the *Globe,* January 1, 1862.

ered the question of preparedness in the event of any future emergency. A series of patriotic resolutions were passed in the midst of great enthusiasm. " Defence, not defiance " was the motto adopted. Since it was declared the duty of every Canadian to aid in the defence of his country in the event of war, a volunteer force for Canada " worthy of her position as one of the most important and loyal of the dependencies of the British Empire " was advocated.[1]

January, 1862, a Commission was appointed to consider the question of the military defence of Canada. To this Commission belonged four members of the government, Cartier, McNab, Galt and Macdonald; two members of the provincial forces, Colonel Campbell and Colonel Cameron; while Lord Lyons, the British minister at Washington, represented the British War Office. As a result of their deliberations a Militia Bill was framed. This bill became a government measure, and hence was freely discussed by the press, supported by the *Leader,* and opposed by the *Globe.* The militia was to be divided into two classes, the "Active Militia " and the " Sedentary Militia ". The former class was to be subdivided into three parts — " the Volunteer Force, the Regular Force and the Reserve Force—the latter class to consist of the Service Sedentary Force and the Retired Sedentary Force." In his role as Commander-in-Chief of the British forces in Canada, the Governor-General was empowered to accept all who might offer themselves for service as volunteers.[2] The Liberals claimed that the British Provinces were not able to bear the additional burden of taxation involved in the passage of this bill which according to the estimate of Galt, the finance minister, would be $1,000,000 yearly. Retrenchment was therefore necessary.[3]

[1] *Ibid.*

[2] *Cf.* the *Globe,* April 24, 1862.

[3] The *Globe,* May 5, 1862.

The arguments in favor of the Militia Bill, taken from Mr. Galt's speech, May 6, 1862, were presented by the Conservative press. " The government would ask for only $832,000.00 the first year," and to raise the required amount " he did not propose to have recourse to direct taxation." The need of providing a force large enough to place the province on a defensive footing was urged.[1] As a result of this bill, the Conservative Ministry suffered defeat. The bill was thrown out by a majority of seven. The vote of the members from Canada West was thirty to twenty-four in favor of the bill.[2] The defeat of the Militia Bill was partly due to the fact that the bill had become a party measure; moreover, the Trent affair had been satisfactorily adjusted, and the feeling of immediate danger was lacking. The Canadians allowed a modified Militia Bill to pass in 1862. It provided for 25,000 men under drill, and a reserve force of 25,000—a force which, with the cooperation of the Imperial troops, many Canadians deemed sufficient. The vote of $500,000 for Militia also showed that the Canadians saw the desirability of making provision for the increased efficiency of the Militia. The news of the defeat of the original Militia Bill, and the passage of a modified one was a keen disappointment to the Imperial Parliament.[3]

The Canadian newspapers, in August, 1862, claimed that the President's proclamation commanding a draft had been followed by an exodus from the Northern States into Canada of those who were desirous of avoiding it, and that the draft-evaders fled not only to the towns and villages on the frontier, but also to the inland towns of Canada. Many were the uncomplimentary comments on their appearance which appeared in the Canadian newspapers. Not to these

[1] The *Leader*, May 7, 1862.

[2] *Ibid.*, May 21, 1862.

[3] The *Globe*, June 18, 1862.

fugitives, but to another class, namely, the thousands of British subjects scattered throughout the United States, did the Canadians look for a permanent addition to her population as a result of the Civil War; moreover, it was believed that the Conscription Act finally passed by Congress, March 3, 1863, would hasten their departure to Canada.[1]

Then came the Proclamation of Emancipation for the slave — a measure long anticipated by many Canadians. Thus did the *Globe,* the steadfast friend of the slave, in its issue of September 23, 1862, acclaim the news:

President Lincoln has proclaimed the emancipation of all the slaves in States and parts of States found in rebellion on the 1st of January next, and declares that he will press upon Congress the adoption of the measures which we recommended last session, to recompense the loyal States for freeing their slaves. This is avowedly a war measure.   Mr. Lincoln proclaims emancipation because he cannot save the Union and end the war without doing so.   Nevertheless the act is right and will have important results.   A large portion of the Slave States will be in rebellion on the 1st January next; and long ere that, we trust, there will be an army of colored men on foot who will be able to fight for their own freedom.

The *Leader,* October 25, 1862, likewise recognized the Proclamation as a war measure but declared that it would fail " to effect any good in that or any other respect."   Again in the *Globe* of January 6, 1863, this proclamation, announced by President Lincoln " as an act of justice warranted by the Constitution under military necessity," was further discussed.   Since the Southern rebellion was without a precedent in United States history, new measures must be taken to meet this national emergency.   Then the impracticability

[1] References to the draft evaders are to be found in the *Leader,* August 7, 1862; the *Globe,* August 11, 1862; *ibid.,* August 12, 1862, contain extracts from the Canada West newspapers, the Chatham *Planet,* the London *Free Press.*

of compensating the slave-owners, a remedy which had been suggested, was mentioned. The need for compensation had likewise vanished in the face of the rebellion.

Throughout the Civil War the Northern States frequently complained that ships were being built in British waters for the Confederates. The damage done by the *Alabama,* a Confederate vessel built in British waters, especially inflamed the North against Great Britain. Once again there was grave danger of international complication. The matter was thus calmly discussed by the *Globe,* November 20, 1862: " If on inquiry it be found that England in allowing the ' Alabama ' to depart from one of her ports, has broken international law, then we hope to see the fault owned, and justice immediately done." In its discussion of international law this newspaper, after referring to the complaint of Great Britain during the Crimean War that ships for Russia had been built in American ports, cited the reply of President Pierce in which after stating that " Americans being neutrals, had a right to sell to the belligerent powers contraband of war, or to take munitions of war upon board their private ships," he admitted that they had no right " to fit out within the limits of the United States a vessel to commit hostilities against any State with which the United States is at peace, or to increase the force of any armed vessel intended for such hostilities against a friendly State," [1] but went on to say that the law had not been broken by Americans. The *Leader* [2] likewise attempted by quoting merely a portion of President Pierce's speech to prove that there was ample justification for the building of the Confederate ship in the precedent that had been established by the United States. The position maintained by the Conservative journal

---

[1] *United States' Presidents—Messages and Papers,* vol. v, 1849-1861, p. 332, Third Annual Message, Washington, December 31, 1855.

[2] The *Leader,* November 24, 1862.

was however untenable, for he had explicitly stated that a neutral had no right to allow a vessel to be fitted out in its ports for the benefit of one belligerent to the detriment of the other.   The *Leader* also quoted with approval Lord Russell's statement to Mr. Adam in which he pointed out " how difficult it would be to interfere with the private interests of British manufacturers for the alleged cause of complaint." [1] This view was simply the natural, traditional, pro-British attitude of the official Conservative press.

Throughout the year 1863 there was considerable discussion as to whether vessels built for the South in England should be permitted to leave.   The *Globe* consistently maintained that Great Britain should not permit ships " fitted out in England to burn and destroy on the high seas the vessels of a friendly power, but it is an injury to morality and civilization in which British mechanics and sailors are active participants." [2] The damage inflicted by Southern privateers, notably the *Chesapeake* and *Peterhoff,* built in English waters, was a constant source of friction.   On October 15, 1863, Earl Russell in a speech signified that the future policy of Great Britain would prevent any further annoyance of a similar nature.

Perhaps an even more serious cause of friction between the two countries than the Confederate vessels built in British waters was the presence of Confederate agents in Canada during the American Civil War.   In 1864 in Canada there was a secret military and political society organized by Jacob Thompson, of whom it may be said that from the day as member of President Buchanan's cabinet he opposed the sending of troops to Charleston until the Washington government offered a reward of $25,000 for his capture, the North had no more implacable enemy.   Holding a commis-

[1] *Ibid.,* November 24, 1862.
[2] *Ibid.,* April 13, 1863.

sion from the Southern Confederacy, he arrived in Canada, April, 1864. With Thompson in Toronto by July, 1864, there was also C. C. Clay, another authorized Confederate agent with similar authority. A series of plots were then planned, for whose furtherance considerable money was expended. Various plots, including the seizure of the American steamer, the *Michigan,* and the attempt to burn New York City—an attempt which merely resulted in a scare to New-Yorkers—were frustrated. Thompson expressed the difficulty under which the Confederate agents in Canada labored, as follows: " The bane and curse of carrying out anything in this country is the surveillance under which we act. Detectives or those ready to give information stand at every street corner. Two or three cannot interchange ideas without a reporter." [1]

The St. Albans raid, one instance of the irregular border warfare waged by Confederates from Canada during the American Civil War, caused considerable excitement in Canada West, as well as in Canada East. Lieutenant B. H. Young had been authorized by the Confederacy to organize a company for special service. The parting words of James A. Siddon, Secretary of War of the Southern Confederacy, were: " Lieutenant, you go upon a dangerous mission, and you and your command shall be fully protected." [2] The nature of this service, Young confided to C. C. Clay, who was residing temporarily at St. Catharines, Canada West, consisted in the burning of certain New England villages

[1] *Cf. Canadian Historical Review,* vol. ii, March, 1921, Wilfred Bovey, "Confederate Agents in Canada during the American Civil War," pp. 46-50.

[2] Compiled by L. N. Benjamin, *The St. Albans, Vt., Raid or Investigation into the charges against Lieut. Bennett H. Young and Command for their acts at St. Albans, Vt., on the 19th October, 1864, Being a complete and authentic report of all the proceedings on the demands of the U. S. for their extradition, under the Ashburton Treaty,* p. 172.

and robbing them of whatever he could convert to the use of the Confederate government. Clay approved this plan, which the Confederates regarded as justifiable retaliation for the wrong inflicted by Sheridan and his soldiers in the Shenandoah Valley. On October 19, 1864, a party of Confederate soldiers, comprising about twenty-five in number, mostly escaped prisoners, attacked the small village of St. Albans, Vermont, fourteen miles from the Canadian frontier. This Confederate company robbed three banks of $150,000 in cash, fired upon the citizens, killing one and wounding others. Then they seized horses, and rode swiftly toward the Canadian frontier.[1] The citizens of this small town were naturally terrified. A company of citizens was quickly organized to go in pursuit of the Confederates, who were on Canadian soil before they were overtaken by their pursuers. As the Confederates were arrested on Canadian territory, they were consigned to the Canadian authorities for safekeeping. At once extradition proceedings under the Ashburton Treaty were begun. The defence for the Confederates considered the strength of its position to consist in the possession of documents which established the authority of the raiders from the Southern Confederacy. The defence was successful, and the prisoners released.[2]

Throughout Canada much indignation was aroused, chiefly directed against the Confederates for their attempts to use Canada as a base of operations against the North. A small proportion of the people also resented the order given by General Dix to the officer near St. Albans to cross the frontier to capture the Confederates on Canadian soil. The *Globe* regarded the repeated outrages on the Canadian fron-

---

[1] *Cf. Canadian Historical Review*, vol. ii, March, 1921, p. 50.

[2] *Cf. ibid.*, p. 57; compiled by L. N. Benjamin, *The St. Albans, Vt., Raid or Investigation into the charges against Lieut. Bennett H. Young and Command for their acts at St. Albans, Vt., on the 19th October, 1864*, p. 57; James Ford Rhodes, vol. v, pp. 333-334.

tier as attempts on the part of the Confederates to involve Great Britain in a war with the North, in order to secure Southern success. " Plunder may be one object, but the sanction which these desperadoes must receive from Southerners of a better class proceeds, we fear, from a different motive. It is a noticeable fact, that while this outrage at St. Albans was in progress, two Confederate agents presented themselves in Quebec and were chagrined by the government declining to take cognizance of them. Had they been received by the Governor-General, the circumstance would have afforded an admirable pendant to the robbery of the banks and murder of the citizens of St. Albans." [1] The people of the province, both Liberals and Conservatives wherever their sympathies lay, were practically unanimous in their decision that Canada must not be used as a base for military operations directed by the Confederates against the North. As the Southern refugees continued to violate the laws of international comity, there was a steadily growing feeling throughout the province that by so doing they had forfeited not only all claim to sympathy, but even the protection heretofore assured them under the British flag.

Surely the fact that the Confederate agents in Canada did not accomplish more was due to the desire of the majority of Canadians to maintain the neutrality enjoined by the British Government. The Liberal press commended the strict neutrality maintained by the British government; and at the same time blamed the *Leader,* with its pro-Southern attitude, for its proposal that Great Britain should " interfere to secure the independence of the South—an interference which would almost certainly be followed by a bloody war between the two countries in which Canada would be the battle-ground." [2]

[1] The *Globe*, October 21, 1864.
[2] The *Globe*, November 27, 1862.

Commending, therefore, the strictly neutral attitude of the government of England under the leadership of Lord Palmerston and Lord John Russell, the *Globe* said the people of the North should have been satisfied, and their journalists should have refrained from abuse of England, which had only lessened the popularity of their cause in Europe. Thus the significance of the maintenance of this neutrality was recognized :

Neutrality is best for England, but for Canada is absolutely essential, and it is an outrage for a Canadian journal to endeavor to make the British Government believe that any Canadian out of the Asylum desires an interference in American affairs, which would involve the Province in a disastrous contest with its neighbors. The people of Canada are ready to defend themselves when attacked, and are prepared to sustain the honour of the mother country. But they are not prepared to support any Government in a wanton interference in matters with which it has no concern, and more especially they have no desire to fight on behalf of the Southern slave power. There are enough of evil influences at work which threaten to bring the two countries into collision, without the press and people of Canada adding their share to the witches' cauldron. They have a simple duty to perform Men will differ in opinion about North and South, but our evident policy is to observe a strict neutrality as a people towards both sections, and maintain as much cordiality with our neighbors as is possible, while so lively a controversy is being carried on upon matters which come to the hearts of everybody.[1]

The Canadian newspapers of the sixties followed very closely party lines, the Liberal newspapers of Canada West taking their cue from the *Globe,* and the Conservative newspapers from the *Leader.* Party discipline was more rigidly observed by newspaper men in the period of the sixties than

[1] *Ibid.*

in the twentieth century. Few editors showed any independence of judgment in their editorials; indeed, many of the editorials were largely reprints from one of the two leading newspapers.

Notable therefore for its opposition to the customary attitude among Liberal newspapers was the *Huron Signal,* which proudly proclaimed its independent policy, a policy at variance with its political party. One may well wonder whether the key to an understanding of the opinions voiced in the newspaper is not to be found in the fact that more negroes had settled in the Southwestern peninsula than in any other section of Canada West. From the outbreak of the American Civil War, the *Huron Signal* was just as consistent in its advocacy of a Southern policy, as the *Globe* was of a Northern. Frankly announcing its sympathy with the South, it declared that the war was not one for the abolition of slavery, but simply a contest for supremacy on the part of two divisions of one family in which the Southerners were valiantly fighting for their freedom.[1] Differing with the other Liberal newspapers and agreeing frequently with the Conservatives of Canada West, this newspaper resented on behalf of its Liberal contemporaries the charge sometimes found in the Conservative press that the friendly attitude toward the North of the Reformers betokened disloyalty to Great Britain.[2] Independent in the expression of its opinion, this paper was still loyal to the Liberal party.

Towards the question of annexation the Canadian press, both Conservative and Liberal, was united in its opposition. Here again the press was reflecting not only the sentiment of the vast majority of the people of Canada West, but also of the other British American provinces. This was not a party question, for Liberals and Conservatives were now

---

[1] The Huron *Signal*, November 6, 1861.

[2] *Ibid.*, January 15, 1863.

united in a common loyalty to Great Britain. The small minority, the dissatisfied element, which may be found in the most favored countries, had been effectually silenced by the threatened disunion of the Republic. To them no longer did the Republic offer alluring prospects of greater commercial prosperity. Since the question of annexation with the United States was outside the realm of party politics, the *Globe,* May 3, 1861, in an editorial may be regarded as the spokesman of the British North American Provinces:

But though we Canadians were very much astonished to hear that we were panting to be annexed to the United States, large numbers of the Americans were not surprised at all. How could they be? . . . Do they not look with contempt upon us poor Provincials, who—as they think—pay an enforced homage to Queen Victoria? . . . Well, it is no use arguing with them, it is no use telling them that we don't see the Republic through their spectacles.

The *Leader,* with its strongly monarchical leaning, clearly indicated in its columns its opinion that republicanism was a failure, due to the lack of a strongly centralized government found in that form of government. The monarchical and republican forms of government were thus contrasted, always to the advantage of the former. Thus the *Leader* repudiated anything that savored of republicanism. It even went so far as to insinuate for political purposes that the sympathizers with the Northern cause who were principally to be found in the Liberal ranks, were disloyal to the British connection with a secret yearning toward a union with the neighboring Republic. The Conservative newspaper was well aware that this insinuation was false, but equally well did it know that it could make political capital out of it. Waving the flag has brought a party victory to many a politician. In its issue of November 19, 1861, thus appears the following statement: " There are among us persons who laud as the perfection of wisdom the most despotic acts of a republican government, and who condemn every act of their own. . . . [They] are always assuming that every institution is good or bad in proportion as it approaches to extreme democracy or recedes from that infallible standard of perfection." This opinion of republicanism persisted in Canada throughout the sixties. The chaotic conditions in the Republic were attributed by "John A", as Macdonald was affectionately called, to the evils which he as the leader and spokesman of the Conservative party, quite naturally considered inherent in that form of government." [1] This sentiment persisted; John A. Macdonald remarked in April, 1863, with fine assurance, " our French brethren will fight side by side with us against the foreign foe." [2]

In the Conservative newspapers of Canada West were also to be found occasional references to the hardships which the Western States had to endure due to their connection with the Eastern States of the United States. [3] Since the manufacturing interests of the Eastern States had been built up at the expense of the West, the *Patriot* claimed that Western jealousy of the East was justifiable; moreover, the war itself had further increased Eastern prosperity, for the moneyed men of the East had induced Congress to pass outrageous tariff bills, such, for instance, as the Morrill Tariff, by which capital was retained in the East. [4] The championship of the interests of the Western States by the Conservative press of Canada West may be partially

[1] The *Globe*, April 10, 1863, reprint from Kingston *News* of speech of John A. Macdonald.

[2] *Ibid.*, April 10, 1863.

[3] *Cf.* the *Patriot*, January 29, 1862.

[4] *Cf.* article from Cleveland *Herald* quoted in the *Patriot*, January 19, 1861.

explained by the fact that the United Empire Loyalists disliked the Yankees.

As the American Civil War progressed, there was a growing inclination in Canada West, as well as in the other provinces, to study the problem of union in British North America. If war between Great Britain and the United States should come, a possibility which had presented itself on more than one occasion, the British provinces, separated as they were, could not hope to defend themselves. The rapid advance of American settlement in Minnesota had aroused the fear of the Canadians that the Red River territory, and even Vancouver Island and British Columbia, might be eventually absorbed in the United States.[1] Gradually the belief spread that a union of the British provinces was necessary, if absorption by the United States were to be prevented. As early as April 19, 1861, Macdonald in the House of Assembly urged confederation.[2] Realizing then that the provinces could be more easily defended if united, both John A. Macdonald and George Brown in their presentation of the arguments in favor of confederation were earnest in their advocacy of it as a precautionary measure.[3]

A survey of the newspapers of Canada West during the period of the American Civil War seems to prove that the people, generally, were divided in accordance with party lines, the Liberals sympathized with the North and the Conservatives with the South. Thus the situation is summarized in the *Globe* of February 20, 1862, with an approach to accuracy, if due allowance is made for a certain intolerance toward the opposite political party:

[1] Reginald G. Trotter, *Canadian Confederation*, p. 314.

[2] Joseph Pope, *Memoirs of Sir John A. Macdonald*, vol. i, chap. xi, p. 228.

[3] *Parliamentary Debates on the subject of the Confederation of the British North American Provinces*, chap. vii, p. 32 (Macdonald) and p. 107 (Brown).

But the keenness of discussion among Canadians is also sharpened by the fact that our fossils, our remnants of antiquity, our devotees of Church and State alliances, entertain the liveliest sentiments of regard for the slave-aristocracy of the South, while Liberals are inclined to sympathize with the free North. This division of sentiment is not universal, though it is so near it, as to be as accurate as such generalizations usually are. There are some Conservatives who think rebellion against constituted authority so dreadful a crime, that they cannot approve of insurrection even against Abe Lincoln's Government, and there are some Radicals so wedded to the right of revolution that they can see no harm in the action of the Southern people. But the Puritan by nature in Canada generally takes the side of the Puritan in the States, and the Cavalier by birth, education and ecclesiastical connections, takes that of the man enslaver. Hence has arisen considerable bitterness in the discussion of the Civil war, which, however, will speedily disappear as it proceeds to a close. There were few of any party in Canada who desired to bring their prejudices on either side into practical operation; the wise policy of neutrality adopted by the Mother Country has commended itself to the good sense of our people.

This was a natural division. To the Conservative party, as we have said, belonged the descendants of the United Empire Loyalists, deeply attached to the monarchical system of government, and prone to look with disfavor upon anything that savored of republicanism. To the Liberal parties belonged those who were just as deeply attached to the monarchical system, but imbued with a spirit of friendliness toward the neighboring republic and desirous of a closer reciprocity in commercial matters. Neither political party had a monopoly of loyalty toward the Mother Country. George Brown and John A. Macdonald were political chieftains whose loyal attachment to Great Britain was unquestioned. The oft-quoted asseveration of Macdonald, " a British subject I was born, a British subject I will die," might equally well have been uttered by Brown. Thus, in every instance when serious international complications between Great Britain and the United States threatened, the press of Canada West, regardless of political lines, was found united in its support of the Mother Country. The Liberal press, steadfast friend of freedom, was often sorely tried by the anti-British and anti-Canadian tirades of the *New York Herald*. A revulsion of feeling undoubtedly took place as the war progressed, a revulsion which the *Globe* claimed was to a large extent directly traceable to these abusive articles, and to the fact that at certain crises, war appeared imminent between Great Britain and the United States. If further evidence is needed to support the above statement, the fact might be cited that at the beginning of the American Civil War, when the children played " North and South ",[1] few were to be found on the Southern side, but as the war progressed, few could be found to take the side of the North. Here the children merely indicated in their play the change in public opinion.

[1] *Reminiscences of E. W. Thomson*, p. 307.

CHAPTER IV

Public Opinion in Canada East

The Question of Nationality—Characteristics of French Canadians—
Annexation—The Press—Neutrality—Anderson—Mason and Slidell—
War Preparations—Lack of Northern Sympathy—Defeat of Militia Bill
—Railroad Construction—The Intercolonial Railway—Arrival of British
Transport—Canadians in Northern Army—Confederate Plots—St. Albans
Raid—French Canadian Leaders—French Canadian Loyalty.

The main differences discernible between Canada West
and Canada East are due to nationality; there is a definite
line of demarkation between Canada West, an English-
speaking province, and Canada East, predominantly a French-
speaking province.[1] The attitude of the majority of the
people of Canada East toward the American Civil War was
largely determined by certain French national characteristics,
for as every one knows, the French of Canada East have
clung tenaciously, even to the twentieth century, to their
national customs and traditions. Lord Durham, upon his
arrival in Canada, soon recognized that a national feud existed within the French province. Actual conditions as he
found them there in 1839 are thus described: " I expected
to find a contest between a government and a people: I
found two nations warring in the bosom of a single state:
I found a struggle, not of principles, but of races; and I
perceived that it would be idle to attempt any amelioration
of laws or institutions, until we could first succeed in termi-
nating the deadly animosity that now separates the inhabi-

[1] *Census of Canada East 1861*; total population 1,110,664; French origin
847,320.

tants of Canada East into the hostile divisions of French and English." [1]

The French-Canadian majority was essentially conservative and monarchical. Both Lord Durham and Lord Elgin recognized the French Canadians as forming the conservative or stabilizing element against the inroads of radicalism and republicanism. Thus did Lord Durham state his recognition of French-Canadian conservatism: " They remain an old and stationary society, in a new and progressive world. In all essentials they are still French; but French in every respect dissimilar to those of France in the present day. They resemble rather the French of the provinces under the old régime." [2] Lord Elgin did all in his power, as has been elsewhere noted, to satisfy the national pride and aspirations of the French, and by so doing, he undoubtedly did much to retain a continuance of French Canadian loyalty to the British Crown. With the exception of a very small section of the French-Canadian people, mainly to be found in the ranks of the Rouge party, the people of Canada East were loyal to Great Britain in 1861. The origin of *le parti rouge* was described by *La Minerve,* the radical newspaper of Canada East, thus: " Le parti rouge s'est formé à Montreal sous les auspices de M. Papineau, en haine des institutions anglaises de notre constitution déclarée vicieuse, et surtout du gouvernement responsable regardé comme une duperie, avec des idées d'innovation en religion et en politique, accompagnées d'une haine profond pour le clergé, et avec l'intention bien formelle, et bien prononcée d'annexer le Canada aux États-Unis." [3] Not one of the founders of the Rouge party, including A. A. Dorion, Papin, D'Aoust, Laberge, and the

---

[1] *The Report of the Earl of Durham,* second edition, pp. 8-9.

[2] *Ibid.,* pp. 17-18.

[3] John C. Dent, *The Last Forty Years,* chap. ii, p. 190.

rest, was over twenty-two at that time.[1] It was, however, dominated by the personality of a much older man—Louis Joseph Papineau—the rebel of '37. The Rouges, admirers of the republican form of government, lacked the numerical strength which would have entitled them to serious consideration.

The loyalty of the people was due in part at least to the fact that under British government they had enjoyed certain religious privileges. Their religious leaders, the Roman Catholic bishops and priests, at all times counselled loyalty to the British Crown. "A large part of the Catholic clergy, a few of the seignorial families, and some of those who are influenced by ancient connections of party, support the government against revolutionary violence."[2] According to Francis Masères, a descendant of the Huguenots, naturally hostile, therefore, to the French Roman Catholics, only "eight or ten of the seigniors, perhaps twelve, are *noblesse,* according to the French ideas."[3] If not *noblesse* according to the French usage of the word, there were many refined gentlemen who had been granted large seignories in the early days of Canadian colonization. Their descendants with the conservatism natural to property holders, and the clergy of Canada East were united in their opposition to republicanism.

The French-Canadian majority was opposed to a union with the neighboring Republic. The opposition of the French Canadians was to a certain extent national, but to an even greater extent religious, for they had an undefined fear that their religion might be endangered if annexation to the United States were consummated. They could not

[1] O. D. Skelton, *The Life and Times of Sir Alexander Tilloch Galt,* p. 168.

[2] *The Report of the Earl of Durham,* second edition, p. 11.

[3] Jean Charlemagne Bracq, *The Evolution of French Canada,* pp. 10-11.

forget that the Revolutionary Congress had objected to the French laws, under which they enjoyed certain religious privileges. Moreover the commercial advantages that a union with the United States would have secured for them never affected to any extent the French-Canadian attitude toward annexation, since they have ever been primarily an agricultural, not a manufacturing or trading people.

In the sixties, even as today, Canada East enjoyed a certain isolation, due in part at least to the fact that the language spoken by the majority of the people was French. The people of Canada East in the days of the sixties still answered the description of them which is to be found in Lord Durham's Report. Simple, kindly, polite, hospitable in all their dealings with their fellow men, the French Canadians were unprogressive. They possessed the virtues, as well as the vices, of a somewhat static society. Holding little intercourse with the outside world, they were content. The slight intercourse they had had with the Yankee did not lead them to desire more. Yankee taunts that the French Canadians were slow and old-fashioned, and needed the infusion of Anglo-Saxon blood in order to progress, did not increase American popularity in Canada East. A story is told of an American traveling through Canada, who having " observed the antiquated ways of our French peasants," made the remark with bland self-assurance that if they (the Americans) got " the country into their hands, they would soon improve the old-fashioned French off the face of the earth."[1] This was exactly what the French-Canadians feared. As the views of the ultra-conservative *habitant* were inevitably opposed to those of the progressive and unsympathetic Yankee, they failed to find any common meeting ground. Since the French Canadians did not believe that

[1] J. G. Kohl, *Travels in Canada and through the States of New York and Pennsylvania*, vol. i, p. 134.

they could hope for the same tolerance for their established customs and traditions from their republican neighbors as Great Britain had shown, they believed that it was better to maintain the British connection than seek to better their condition by a union with their ambitious neighbor. Then the anti-Catholic feeling in New England made the French Canadians even more apprehensive that their religion might be assailed in the event of annexation. They feared that annexation to the United States would mean a disturbance of all that they cherished most; moreover, there was a strong Canadian sentiment which resented the encroachment of a foreign power.

Perhaps the loyalty which undoubtedly animated the majority of the French Canadians might be better defined as loyalty to Canada, than loyalty to Great Britain. If Canada were invaded, they were prepared to resist. John A. Macdonald declared that his prejudices against the French had been largely overcome, since he had realized the truthfulness of Colonel Taché's assertion: " My countrymen republican? They are monarchical in everything, in their religion, laws, institutions, principles and even their prejudices, and I venture to predict that the last shot fired on this continent in defence of the monarchical principle will be fired by a French Canadian." [1]

The French press of Canada East resented keenly any insinuation or reflection cast upon French-Canadian loyalty. The French-Canadian conception of the obligations imposed upon all Canadians by Great Britain's *Proclamation of Neutrality* likewise found expression in the press. " Nous n'avons pas parmi notre population d'individus qui ont vendu leurs services et leur plumes à la cause des États-Unis qui ont aidé à l'enrôlement des Canadiens pour l'armée du Nord,

[1] The Montreal *Gazette*, July 8, 1861.

malgré la plus stricte neutralité gardée par l'Angleterre, et commandée par elle à tous ses sujets. Nous n'avons personne qui regarde avec complaisance vers Washington et qui voudrait voir une partie du Canada annexée à la republique voisine." [1] Proudly proclaiming its adherence to the monarchical form of government, the French-Canadian press resented any implication that in the event of war between Great Britain and France, the French Canadians would embrace their opportunity to aid France instead of Great Britain. "Et, dans l'hypothèse où les sympathies des Canadiens-français seraient pour la France, advenant le cas d'une guerre avec l'Angleterre, elles n'auraient pas pour la mère patrie de conséquences funestes. Il n'en serait pas de même des tendances républicaines de certains meneurs haut-Canadiens dans le cas d'une guerre avec les États-Unis." [2]

The press of the English-speaking minority of Canada East in the sixties likewise asserted its loyal attachment to Great Britain, and also its firm belief that the press which represented the French Canadians could say as much for them. No newspaper which advocated any change in their relations with Great Britain, the Montreal *Gazette*, a Conservative newspaper, declared, could look for popularity in Canada.[3] While the English-speaking minority, a small but influential group in Canada East, was inclined to be antagonistic toward the French-Canadian majority, both, with a few exceptions, were attached to Great Britain.[4]

The press of Canada East as well as that of Canada West, rejoicing in the deliverance of Anderson, the fugitive slave, declared that nine-tenths of the people of Canada were op-

---

[1] Le *Journal de Quebec*, 3 Decembre, 1861.

[2] *Ibid.*

[3] The Montreal *Gazette*, July 25, 1861.

[4] The Montreal *Gazette*, July 25, 1861; the Quebec *Mercury*, March 7, 1861; the Quebec *Chronicle*, March 15, 1861.

posed to his surrender on the demand of Missouri slave-owners.[1] Since Anderson had been discharged on a mere technicality, as has been elsewhere indicated, the Montreal *Gazette* declared that in this decision there was no guarantee that the slave who fought his way to freedom would be safe in Canada West. This newspaper further expressed its conviction that both the Imperial and Canadian parliaments should pass declaratory acts interpreting the Ashburton Treaty in such a way that all extradition proceedings in similar cases would be prevented.

The press of Canada East as well as that of Canada West demanded the surrender of Mason and Slidell. Not only the English minority but also the French-Canadian majority was quite as ready as was the English majority in the west to resent the insult to the British flag involved in the removal of the Southern commissioners from a British ship. With a full realization of the seriousness of the situation, the French Canadians prepared to defend the soil of Canada against invasion. Even *Le Pays*, the French newspaper, which had formerly advocated annexation, now urged preparedness.

Though we consider war to be very improbable, and we believe in the good sense of England and the United States, it is nevertheless possible that folly may produce war. In that case, what ought the population of this country to do? To this question there can be but one answer; " March to the defence of our territory, provided we are furnished with arms, and our experienced militia be sustained by a sufficient regular army." There is no reason to fear that, in these respects, England will make default. Her unlimited resources will enable her to arm at once, and completely to arm all the militia of the country; and as to sending us troops, we do not think that the doctrines

[1] The Montreal *Gazette*, February 15, 1861; the Quebec *Mercury*, February 19, 1861.

of the *Times* recently so imprudently expressed upon the defence of the Colonies will be shared by the Government. The militia ought immediately to be armed and organized. Without arms there can be no soldiers.[1]

Referring to the defence of British America, the *Times* [2] contended that the value of the colony to the mother country did not justify the yearly expenditure required for the maintenance of this relationship, and hence the severance of the bond, whenever the colony so desired, should meet with no opposition in Great Britain. The press of Canada East deplored the probable effect in America of the tone adopted by the London newspaper toward the question of colonial defence. This attitude was declared not only ungenerous and unjust toward the colony, but extremely impolitic at this time, since it might encourage the Americans, believing Great Britain indifferent, to commit acts of aggression on Canadian soil.[3]

A set determination on the part of the French majority and the English minority to support to the utmost Great Britain's demands for satisfaction over the Trent affair was apparent. Everywhere the probability of war was discussed. " No one seems willing to be left out. The spirit of the people is fairly aroused, and ere the month of February we shall have nigh, if not quite, the 100,000 men enrolled whom the *Times* [4] has called for. Meanwhile Generals January and February will fight for us against an invading army. We have only to provide against a coup de main. We need not fear any regular military operations before spring." [5]

---

[1] The *Mercury*, December 26, 1861, translation from *Le Pays*.

[2] The *Times*, June 6, 1862.

[3] *Cf.* the *Mercury*, December 12, 1861.

[4] Article in *Times* calling for 100,000 Canadian militiamen quoted in full in Montreal *Gazette*, Dec. 23, 1861, under the heading " From Late British Papers," but date not given.

[5] The Montreal *Gazette*, December 18, 1861.

Canada was prepared to act.   Then, as has ever been the case in times of international crises, Canada was one in sympathy with the mother land.

To the people of Canada East, as to the people of Canada West, war had appeared imminent.   Thus the situation was described by the Montreal *Witness,* December 30, 1861 : " For the last fortnight Canada has been passing through a war in anticipation."   This Liberal newspaper which had warmly espoused the Northern cause welcomed the assurance of peace.   The Montreal *Herald,* another Liberal newspaper of Canada East, which the *Chronicle,*[1] a Conservative newspaper, accused of playing " double " to the *Globe* in its admiration of the Yankees, blamed the Washington government for the unfortunate situation that had arisen in Canada as a result of the Trent affair.   Furthermore this newspaper contended that Mason and Slidell should have been surrendered at once without allowing time for the presentation of British demands.[2]

To many in Canada East, the surrender of Mason and Slidell in compliance with British demands, appeared rather as a postponement of the conflict, than as an elimination of the possibility of war.   Hence the French press continued to preach the doctrine of preparedness in accordance with the time-honored, however unwarranted, belief that preparedness lessens the probability of attack.

Ainsi, il peut donc se faire que la difficulté présente entre les deux puissances se termine d'une manière pacifique, mais dès que la guerre sera terminée avec le Sud, les États du Nord, sous un prétexte quelconque déclareront la guerre à l'Angleterre pour entretenir la main de ses 600,000 soldats, et se dédommager des pertes qu'ils éprouveront probablement par la scission des États du Sud. . . . Il est donc prudent de se tenir sur nos gardes,

[1] The *Chronicle*, December 4, 1861.

[2] The *Herald*, December 31, 1861.

quand même l'affaire du Trent aurait une solution pacifique, et de continuer à nous aguerrir, à nous organiser en une armée nationale autant que possible, afin de pouvoir faire face aux premiers dangers, car, comme le dit un vieux proverbe, ce qui est différé n'est pas toujours perdu.[1]

Whatever may have been the sentiment of 1849, now in the face of conflict the *Gazette* asserted the loyalty of the English-speaking minority of Canada East. " Canadians are Britons—the great masses of the people are British, heart and soul, and the men or people who insult the mother country become at once the enemies and insulters of Canada. Britain's cause is our cause; and any one who reckons on gaining popular support for plottings to transfer our allegiance mistakes us sadly." [2]

An examination of the newspapers of Canada East in the sixties would lead one to believe that there was less Northern sympathy than in Canada West. Notable among the Liberal newspapers, which were more favorable to the North than their Conservative rivals, were the *Herald* and the *Witness,* two Montreal journals, the former under the editorship of Edward Goff Penny,[3] the latter edited by John Dougall. There was however no editor in Canada East that could rival in influence E. H. Parsons, editor and proprietor of the *Evening Telegraph and Commercial Advertiser* of Montreal, —a man who dreamed of a powerful Southern Confederacy, and ably championed the Southern cause.[4]

In its explanation of the lack of Northern sympathy to be found in Canada East, the *Gazette* declared, that it was partly due to the fact that the Northerners had never proved

[1] *Le Journal de Quebec,* 28 Décembre, 1861.

[2] The Montreal *Gazette,* July 25, 1861.

[3] *The Canadian Historical Review,* vol. v, Sept., 1924, p. 237.

[4] *A History of Canadian Journalism,* edited by a Committee of the Press, Toronto, 1908, chap. xxiii, p. 155.

their devotion to the cause of freedom by an offer to pay for the emancipation of the slaves. Their compliance with the fugitive slave bills which made the " Northerners contrary to their honest conviction slave catchers for the South ", had further alienated Canadian sympathy; furthermore, their abuse of Great Britain in spite of her neutrality, and the " absurd bluster about the conquest of Canada " had made the Canadians, although declared to be " the strongest aboli- tionists in the world ", rejoice at Southern successes. Be- lieving that an unworthy motive such as self-aggrandizement at the expense of the South, animated the people of the North in their struggle, and not the nobler one of human freedom, the people of Canada East thus justified their indifference. Not yet realizing the value of confederation, the Canadians thought the Southern States should be allowed, in accordance with the principle of self-determination, to establish a Southern Confederacy, especially in view of the fact that the Northern States, which would still remain a first-class power, could not urge the plea of weakness in support of their policy of coercion.[1]

In its issue of August 10, 1861, the *Gazette* contained an article entitled, " Irrational Attacks upon Great Britain." Great Britain's recognition of the belligerent rights of the Southern States was defended. Why was not France con- demned by the Northern press for a similar recognition? The reason assigned for this apparent inconsistency was the Northern desire for the acquisition of Canada. The feeling that the British people should give expression to their sym- pathy for the Free States in " overt acts " by aiding the strong North against the weak South instead of maintaining strict neutrality was proclaimed unreasonable.

Then, the fact that it was not the emancipation of the slave, but the preservation of the Union that had been an-

[1] The Montreal *Gazette,* July 25, 1861.

nounced as the ultimate object in view also accounted for the lack of general sympathy in Canada East as well as in Canada West. To the Canadians in Canada East, the slave question, the moral issue at stake, was of paramount, not secondary importance. Upon what ground, therefore, could the Northern States expect Canadian sympathy when the *World,* thus proclaimed the policy of the government? " We are not fighting to extinguish slavery. Slavery is recognized under the Constitution and the North would not interfere with the rights which the Southern States enjoy, by the Constitution in regard to their slaves. Only their own persistence in rebellion can damage slavery." [1] The freedom of all men in Canada was a source of Canadian self-congratulation. " Of all men on this continent, the people of Canada alone are truly freemen, a small community we yet make all men free and equal before the law, black and white and red, except that the red man is treated with greater tenderness than white or black." [2] A gradual transformation in the opinion of a considerable section of the people of Canada East had taken place. At the beginning of the conflict there had been a widespread regret that the Union was threatened. Gradually the conflict had assumed a new significance. The question became simply stated : " Can we give our sympathy to a civil war having for its object to force half a continent into a union against the consent of the governed? " [3]

Only a few months after the surrender of Mason and Slidell, May, 1862, the Militia Bill, the main provisions of which have been outlined in the previous chapter, was defeated by the votes of Canada East. French Canadian inertia and pacificism, now that the war excitement had abated, reasserted themselves and postponed action. The vote was

[1] The Montreal *Gazette,* August 24, 1861.

[2] *Ibid.*

[3] *Ibid.*

thus divided: thirty-two votes for the bill in Canada West, twenty-four against: twenty-one votes for the bill in Canada East; thirty-seven against. Fourteen supporters of Mr. Cartier, the French-Canadian leader, told him that they would not support the bill. The Militia Bill had unfortunately become a party measure. Then the fact that the immediate danger of war with the United States had been averted, made the people of Canada East, always slow to act, hesitant about the imposition of the increased taxes which the passage of such a measure would necessarily involve. The reason given by the French Canadians for the defeat of the Militia Bill was thus stated by *Le Pays,* August 7, 1862:

Has the Duke [of Newcastle], yes or no, been informed of what took place here, of the true reason which influenced our Legislature, of the enormous deficit in our finances, for the maladministration of our affairs? How can they ask that with a deficit of $5,000,000 brought about by the maladministration of our affairs, a maladministration which was sustained and encouraged during seven consecutive years by the deplorable predecessor of the present Governor, that we should think of placing on foot 50,000 active militiamen and 50,000 reserve men, in a country which is not opened up, and where half the men required by its real agricultural wants cannot be obtained? Is it not strange to see the Minister even of the Colonies, blame the Province for not having done what was absolutely impossible, for not finding the two millions which it had not, and then 100,000 men which it had not also?[1]

The French-Canadian press found ample justification for the defeat of the Militia Bill in the fact that the force which had been sent by Great Britain in consequence of the Trent affair was to be withdrawn. " Nothing could better justify in the eyes of impartial men, the opposition made to the

[1] Le *Pays,* August 7, 1862.

Militia Bill proposed by the ex-Ministry and which the good sense of the people immediately reduced to its proper value." [1]   Thus the French-Canadian attitude was defined:

Certainly Jean Baptiste had good reason to suspect the ultra zeal of those famished loyalists who desired to feed at his expense. He understood the question in time; and England now testifies to his good sense, to the rectitude of his judgment, as well as to the uprightness of his patriotism in recalling the surplus of her military forces; whilst those born blind appreciate our position so little as to continue to provoke the Federal Eagle to fall upon us, as if their rhodomontade were capable of provoking anything but its pity and contempt. They attempted to use the people's stout shoulders as a stepstone to power and then to master them as we would a horse with a bridle. Jean Baptiste is naturally patient; so much so, that they have begun to believe that like the ass of the mill he would bear every load. The Militia Bill filled the measure of his patience and marked the hour of his deliverance from his petty masters. [2]

The cry of disloyalty which was raised in England upon the arrival of the news of the defeat of the Militia Bill was attributed by the French Canadians to the fact that the reason for their vote against the measure was not understood. " But our legislature explained itself : it voted half a million for our defence! our volunteers put down their names, and swore, in shouldering the muskets which were placed in their hands to defend Canada, and assist the Metropolitan power to keep it under its protection." [3]

Lord Monck, Governor-General of Canada, in his speech at Montreal on the subject of " Imperial and Colonial Relations " claimed that the position taken by Le *Canadien* was

[1] The Montreal *Gazette*, August 12, 1861, quoted from Le *Canadien*.

[2] Le *Canadien*, quoted in the Montreal *Gazette*, August 12, 1862.

[3] Le *Courier de St. Hyacinthe*, quoted in the Montreal *Gazette*, August 12, 1862.

grossly ludicrous: " It speaks of the Militia Bill of Mr. Cartier's Government as tending to ruin the country by the weight of taxation. The fact is that the burden which that measure would have imposed would have been 1s 8d a head of the whole population." [1] Then Lord Monck quoted with approval the French newspapers *Le Journal de Quebec* and *La Minerve*, supporters of the Militia Bill. Lord Monck, however, realized that the Militia Bill owed its defeat not only to the fact that it meant increased taxation, but also to the fact that it had become a party measure. " There can be no doubt," Monck stated, " that the proposed militia arrangements were of a magnitude far beyond anything which had, up to that time, been proposed, and this circumstance caused many members, especially from Canada East, to vote against it; but I think there was also, on the part of a portion of the general supporters of government, an intention to intimate by their vote the withdrawal of their confidence from the administration." [2] Seldom has the Governor-General of Canada expressed his views on any question that has become involved in politics, for by so doing, he weakens his ability to work with the Ministers who under responsible government have the confidence of the Canadian people. In making a statement regarding the defeated Militia Bill, Lord Monck, however, did not wish to interfere politically, but simply to indicate, in his role as the Queen's representative, his opinion that its failure to pass was not due to any lack of loyalty to Great Britain. Since the surrender of Mason and Slidell had relieved the French Canadians of any immediate sense of danger, they were reluctant to assume an additional burden, a burden, moreover, which appeared to them as unnecessary.

During the last fifteen years railway activity had helped

[1] The Montreal *Gazette*, August 12, 1862.

[2] *Canadian Archives, Series G*, 231, Monck to Newcastle, 28 July, 1863.

to determine Canadian politics.   The foremost political leaders in Canada East, including Cartier, Taché, Hincks, and
Galt had advocated railway construction.   As far back as
1846, Cartier had announced: " Our policy is a policy of
railways." [1]   His first railway enterprise was in connection
with the Grand Trunk.   In 1854 when a few miles of this
railway had been completed Cartier clearly recognized its
significance, for he said in the House of Assembly: " I
have been entrusted with the bill which has given life to
the Grand Trunk, and I take more pleasure in that fact
than in any other of my life.   Even today this railway is
the main cause of our prosperity.   The Grand Trunk Railway Company is giving work to 1600 men, and has spent
since 1852, £2,500,000.[2]   Another able advocate of railroad construction was Francis Hincks, the Inspector General of Canada, who had in 1849 introduced the first
measure for government aid in the building of the Halifax
and Quebec railway.   The work on the Grand Trunk
begun in 1852 was interrupted in 1854 on account of the
Crimean War.   In the year 1860 the government opened
to traffic one hundred and eight miles from St. John to
Shediac on the strait of Northumberland.[3]   Not until the
sixties did the people of Canada East realize that, in the
event of the outbreak of hostilities with the United States,
railroad connection with the Maritime provinces would be
of incalculable value in the transportation of troops and supplies.   As early as 1829 the citizens of St. Andrews, New
Brunswick, had discussed the building of the Intercolonial,
a line connecting Halifax and St. John with Quebec and
Montreal.   Financial reasons prevented its construction at

[1] Alfred D. DeCelles, *The Makers of Canada*, vol. ix, *Sir Georges
Etienne Cartier*, p. 45.

[2] *Ibid.*, p. 48.

[3] *Cf.* Reginald G. Trotter, *Canadian Confederation*, chap. xii.

this time. With no seaport of her own open all the year, Canada East found herself in the sixties confronted with the possibility of having to secure re-inforcement in the event of war with the United States by way of the Maritime provinces, with all the delay that must ensue due to a lack of any railway connection. Galt had previously recognized both the commercial and military advantages of an Intercolonial Railway, for in a confidential letter dated November 17, 1858, to Sir Edward Lytton, Secretary of State for the Colonies, he had urged its construction. In this letter he stated that the position of Canada was peculiar, since in that country resided three millions of British-born subjects who through the winter months had no intercourse with Great Britain or the other British colonies except through the United States. Since the winter and early spring trade of Canada passed through United States territory, Canada was declared to be " at the mercy of the American Congress for the continuance of her trade between December and June ", for " the repeal of the American bonding law would at once arrest the whole commerce of the province," and " would entail ruin on every merchant and trader in Canada West." He further stated that the interest of Canada in the Intercolonial Railway was due to a desire to be freed from " a painful subordination to the United States "; moreover, he believed, that such a railway would strengthen the bond which united Canada to the mother land, and increase her intercourse with her sister colonies. Although he refused to guarantee that Canadians would use such a line as long as there were shorter and cheaper lines, he yet believed that in the event either of the adoption of a different trade policy or the outbreak of war, such a line would be valuable. " The provision of such an outlet " was declared to be " the security against its being needed." [1] Fully impressed with the value of such a railway,

---

[1] O. D. Skelton, *The Life and Times of Sir A. T. Galt*, pp. 245-246.

the three governments of Canada, New Brunswick and Nova Scotia sent a joint delegation to London in 1858.   There the delegates soon perceived that the members of the British cabinet with the exception of Sir Edward Lytton were not interested, and that he was unable to help them.[1]   In a despatch dated December 24, 1858, Sir Edward Lytton announced to Sir Edmund Head, then Governor-General of Canada, the refusal of the British government to subsidize a loan for the building of the Intercolonial railway on the ground that " the national expenditure must be regulated by the national resources, and however important may be the foregoing advantages, it has been found that objects of interest to Great Britain yet more urgent must yield to the necessity of not unduly increasing at the present moment the public burdens." [2]

The arrival of a British transport with troops for Canada at the time of the Trent crisis in 1861, emphasized anew the need of an Intercolonial Railway.   Seward permitted the soldiers to disembark at Portland, and proceed by way of United States territory to Canada.   The absurdity of such a situation from a military standpoint could not be overlooked by the advocates of railroad connection.   Here were troops sent out to Canada at a period of international crisis to aid the Canadians in the event of war between the United States and Great Britain, compelled to pass through United States territory in order to reach their destination.   The advocates of the Intercolonial Railroad urged its immediate construction.   The added strength which such a railroad would insure to the British Provinces would likewise, so the advocates of railroad connection urged, lessen the probability of attack.   American railroads approached the Canadian borders, and insured, if so desired, a rapid advance of Amer-

[1] Sir Charles Tupper, *Recollection of Sixty Years in Canada*, pp. 19-20.
[2] *Canadian Archives, Series G*, 156.

ican troops. It was not, however, until the days of Confederation that a definite agreement was reached to build the Intercolonial Railroad. Then the British government guaranteed a loan, but insisted for military reasons that the railroad, which would be of vital significance in time of war must not be built too near the border. When the question of the location of the Intercolonial railway was discussed in the Privy Council, Cartier, the Minister of Militia, objected to the selection of the shortest route from Rivière du Loup to St. John, and insisted that the longer route following the river shore through Rimouski, Bonaventure and Gaspé must be followed. The route suggested by Cartier was the one most useful for the defence of Canada, and the one, moreover, that brought the people of the lower St. Lawrence into contact with Montreal and Quebec.[1] The northern route, the one endorsed by Cartier, was the one finally followed in the construction of the Intercolonial Railway, which was not however, begun until 1867, with Mr. (afterwards Sir) Sandford Fleming as chief engineer.

The fact that many French Canadians enlisted in the Northern Army was due primarily neither to sympathy with the slave, nor to a desire for the preservation of the Union, but to the large bounties offered by the Northern States. The practice became so widespread that the Bishop of the Diocese of Three Rivers, the Bishop of Quebec, and the Bishop of St. Hyacinthe, the three leading Roman Catholic Bishops of Canada East issued letters addressed to the parish priests of the provinces to warn the members of their congregations against federal enlistment.[2] Thus the Roman Catholic Church of Canada East opposed the active participation of the youth of Canada East in the American struggle.

[1] Alfred DeCelles, *The Makers of Canada*, vol. ix, *Sir Georges Etienne Cartier*, p. 50.

[2] The Montreal *Gazette*, February 20, 1864.

The Roman Catholic priests were not entirely successful in their efforts t oprevent federal enilstments, for *L'Ordre* continued to bewail the infatuation of the French Canadians who despite the warnings of their pastors and friends joined the Northern army.[1]

In spite of the fact that there were many Southern sympathizers in Canada East, the press of that province was united in its condemnation of the St. Albans raid.[2] It was only natural that the people of Canada East should have been interested in the trial of the Confederate soldiers who participated in that raid, for the investigation took place in Montreal.[3] The French Canadians were willing that the Southerners should find a refuge in Canada, but unwilling to have their land used as a war base. They believed that it was the duty of Canadians to maintain a strictly neutral attitude, a policy of non-intervention.[4]

The presence of the negro in Canada East did not determine to any extent the attitude of the people of that province toward the American Civil War, for in that province the negroes had never been numerically strong. During the sixties the negroes who were in Canada East were to be found mainly in Montreal and the county of Ottawa.[5] The laboring class of French Canadians resented negro competition, and made a vain effort to arouse public opinion. The negroes were waiters, cooks, whitewashers, and barbers. Rarely, did they establish businesses of their own. Due to the fact that the negroes were not as numerous in Canada

[1] *Ibid.*, February 20, 1864, quoted from *L'Ordre*.

[2] The Quebec *Mercury*, November 23, 1864; the Montreal *Gazette*, October 20, 1864.

[3] Compiled by L. N. Benjamin, *The St. Albans, Vt., Raid or Investigation into the charges against Lieut. Bennett H. Young and Command for their acts at St. Albans, Vt., on the 19th October, 1864.*

[4] *Canadian Archives, Pamphlet 2639.*

[5] *Census of 1861, Canada East.*

East as in Canada West the question of slavery did not arouse the same interest.

The attitude of Canada East toward the American Civil War was partly determined by the belief that under the monarchical system of government greater liberty was allowed, than would be permitted under the republican government, for did not the French Canadians have more than the neighboring Yankee?

We have Royalty in its fullness, and, far from impeding liberty, it hourly enlarges its bounds; while in the meantime the Republican Government of Washington systematically imprisons all who dare to affirm the liberty of thought. But we are far, we hope so at least, from the day when, separated from the mother country, we shall be forced to choose between a Republic and a Monarchy. Let us say, notwithstanding, that the manners of us French Canadians, our laws, and even our instincts are monarchical.[1]

Under Great Britain, Canada East had a form of government which guaranteed the autonomy of the French Canadians. Then the French-Canadian priests regarded American Catholicism as too liberal, and wished to maintain the status quo of the Catholic Church in Canada.[2]

Like the vast majority of their constituents, the leaders of French Canada, La Fontaine and Cartier, were loyal to Great Britain. La Fontaine was the first French Canadian to realize the possibilities for the people that constitutional cooperation with the Reformers of Canada West afforded. He was the first great French leader to cooperate with the British Canadians, and Lord Elgin, as has been previously noted, showed his confidence in French integrity by his constitutional support of the Baldwin-La Fontaine administration. Cartier, likewise, showed his willingness to cooperate with

[1] *Le Journal de Quebec*, October 20, 1864, quoted in the Montreal *Gazette*, October 22, 1864.

[2] André Siegfried, *The Race Question in Canada*, pp. 123-124.

his British compatriots.   Jealously safeguarding French interests, he yet realized that the welfare of Canada was of paramount importance to the British Canadian, as well as the French Canadians.   The *habitants* of Canada East have continued to be the peculiar people of the Dominion, a stable force, however, whose allegiance to Great Britain has been proved by history.   Lord Elgin practically solved the French Canadian problem by the confidence which he reposed in La Fontaine, and thus stated his conviction of French Canadian loyalty:

Candour compels me to state that the Anglo-Saxon portion of our members of parliament contrasts most unfavorably with that of the Gallican.   The French have been rescued from the false position into which they have been driven, and in which they must perforce have remained, so long as they believed that it was the object of the British Government, as avowed by Lord Sydenham and others, to break them down, and to insure to the British race, not by trusting to the natural course of events, but by dint of management and statecraft, predominance in the province.[1]

The French Canadian journalists almost invariably preferred Great Britain to the United States.   They, like the vast majority of French Canadians, were essentially conservative and monarchical.   They did occasionally speak of the " jours qui doivent nécessairement venir, que nous le voulions ou que nous ne le voulions pas " [2]—a prophecy of independence. Their influence, however, was exerted on the side of Empire. In the sixties the French Canadians proved their readiness to act promptly whenever the soil of Canada was threatened. Notwithstanding the fact that they have not always seen

[1] *Elgin-Grey Correspondence:* Elgin to Grey, 2 August, 1851.

[2] Joseph Cauchon, *L'Union des provinces de l'Amerique Britannique du Nord,* p. 51.

eye to eye with the British Canadian, the truth of John A. Macdonald's tribute to French-Canadian loyalty must remain unchallenged.

We cannot always persuade our fellow Lower Canadians to our way of thinking, and the Lower Canadians sometimes cannot persuade us; but it is a glorious thing to think and believe that from the East to the West of Canada our French brethren will fight side by side with us against the foreign foe.[1]

[1] The *Globe,* April 10, 1863 (from the Kingston *News*).

CHAPTER V

Public Opinion in the Maritime Provinces

Early Settlers of the Maritime Provinces—the Presence of the Negro—
Howe, the Popular Leader — Pro-Northern Attitude of Nova Scotia
Legislature—The Travellers in Nova Scotia—Reinforcement from Great
Britain — The Trent Incident — Transportation of Troops — Colonial
Defence — Howe, the Spokesman and Conciliator — Transformation in
Public Opinion—Contentment under Responsible Government—Conscrip-
tion in the United States—Fiscal Independence—The Intercolonial—
Loyalty to Great Britain—Union—Political Leaders—The Press.

THE three-part division of the British North American
Provinces which we have followed leads now to a consideration of the attitude adopted by the Maritime Provinces toward the American Civil War. Once more we are confronted by English-speaking people a people, moreover, intensely proud of their tradition of loyalty to the British
Crown. Since the Treaty of Utrecht, 1713, Nova Scotia
had been a British Province. It was not, however, until
after the peace of Aix-la-Chapelle, 1748, that British colonists began to settle in Nova Scotia. In the following year,
1749, twenty-five hundred disbanded soldiers under the
leadership of Edward Cornwallis arrived and founded the
town of Halifax, to which place in 1750 the capital was removed from Annapolis. It is a matter of pride to Nova
Scotians that the first parliament ever called together in what
is now the Dominion of Canada met at Halifax, October 7,
1758. There twenty-two legislators summoned by Governor
Lawrence assembled in the court house to consider the problem of government. The town of Lunenburg about seventy
miles southwest of Halifax was founded in 1750 by two
thousand Protestant Germans whose number at the close of
the Seven Years' War was augmented by other Germans who

had served in the British army.[1]   In 1773, two hundred
Highlanders arrived at Pictou Harbor, the first of the Scotch
immigrants to settle Pictou and Colchester counties, and Cape
Breton.   At the close of the American Revolutionary War,
more than twenty-five thousand United Empire Loyalists
driven from the United States by the persecution, or, equally
potent, the apprehension of impending persecution, which
followed in the wake of that war, settled in the Maritime
Provinces.   Now the United Empire Loyalists, contrary,
perhaps, to popular opinion in the United States, were not
men regardless of the liberties of freemen, but were men
who contended that their rights might have been secured by
constitutional means, not by rebellion.   Upon their arrival
in Nova Scotia they, therefore, petitioned Governor Parr for
representation in the Assembly.[2]   The government of Nova
Scotia was then controlled by a small group of men known as
the Halifax oligarchy that elected the Council of Twelve
which was both legislature and executive.   Somewhat similar
in character to the Family Compact, this ruling clique was
even more powerful, having among its members the ablest
leaders of Nova Scotia, men, moreover, who believed that
the task of government should be entrusted to the trained
few, and not to the masses.   The petition of the Loyalists
was accordingly refused.   Nothing daunted by this rebuff,
they petitioned the home government for a share in the
political life of British America, henceforth to be their home,
and this time their request did not pass unheeded.   In order
to satisfy their desire for self-government, in 1784 the section of Nova Scotia in which the Loyalists had settled was
made into two new provinces, New Brunswick and Cape
Breton.   If the history of the Maritime Provinces is studied,

[1] Adam Shortt and A. G. Doughty, *Canada and its Provinces*, vol. xiii,
"Nova Scotia under English Rule, 1713-1775," by Archibald MacMechan.

[2] *Ibid.*, p. 232.

it will be found to be one; for until the year 1784, they were formally united under the general designation of Acadia.[1] In 1820 Cape Breton was re-annexed to Nova Scotia by a simple Order-in-Council against the wishes of the people.[2] Between 1800 and 1829, twenty thousand Scotch settled in Cape Breton. In the days of the sixties, as today the vast majority of the people of the Maritime provinces were English, Irish and Scotch.[3]

The man in public life who more than any other gave expression to popular opinion in the Maritime Provinces was Joseph Howe. To him the people of Nova Scotia owed a debt of gratitude, for he became the leader of the Reform party in its struggle for responsible government. The fact that responsible government was secured for the people of Nova Scotia without the shedding of blood was largely a tribute to the wisdom of Joseph Howe. The reform which he was able to bring about was a very gradual one. In 1840 he moved a series of resolutions which really consisted of a motion of want of confidence in the administration.

Resolved, that the House of Assembly, after mature and calm deliberation, weary of seeing the revenues of the country and the time of its representatives wasted, and the people of Nova Scotia misrepresented to the sovereign, the gracious boons of the sovereign marred in their transmission to the people, do now solemnly declare that the executive council, as at present constituted, does not enjoy the confidence of the Commons.[4]

In a series of letters to Lord John Russell, Howe urged the

[1] *Ibid.*, vol. xiii, Introduction, Andrew Macphail, p. 3.

[2] *Ibid.*, p. 230.

[3] *Journal of the House of Assembly of the Province of New Brunswick,* Compilers Record; *Nova Scotia Journal 1852,* Appendix 94; *Census of Nova Scotia 1861.*

[4] J. W. Longley, *The Makers of Canada,* vol. vii, "Life of Joseph Howe," p. 62.

fundamental principles of responsible government.[1]   In his
struggle for responsible government, he was instrumental in
bringing about the removal of two governors, namely, Sir
Colin Campbell and Lord Falkland, who were either in-
capable or undesirous of granting self-government to the
people.   In 1848, Howe obtained for the people of Nova
Scotia a governor, who carried on the government of the
province in accordance with the advice of his ministers who
were responsible to the House of Assembly.[2]

Prior to the sixties, what direct contact with the United
States had these provinces, which would help to determine
their attitude toward the American Civil War?   For one
thing, the presence of the negro in the Maritime Provinces
must have influenced public opinion.   From the beginning
of the settlement of Nova Scotia negroes were to be found
there, as is evidenced by a notice that appeared in the Boston
Evening Post of September, 1751, in which there appears
the statement " just arrived from Halifax and to be sold,
ten strong, hearty men, mostly tradesmen." [3]   Henry Clay
once complained that three thousand six hundred and one
slaves had been taken to the Maritime Provinces and demanded payment for them.   In 1827 Great Britain agreed
to pay the United States £250,000 or $1,204,960 for those
slaves, and at the same time freed the slaves for whom she
had paid.   This was a fitting prelude to the Act of 1833 to
carry out whose terms, Great Britain paid £20,000,000 to
free eight million slaves.   In Nova Scotia alone in 1851 were
to be found five thousand negroes, and in New Brunswick
over a thousand.   This number was augmented by over fif-

[1] A. Chisholm, *Speeches and Letters of Joseph Howe*, vol. ii.

[2] *Cf.* Adam Shortt and A. G. Doughty, *Canada and Its Provinces*, vol.
xiii, "Nova Scotia under English Rule, 1713-1775," by Archibald
MacMechan.

[3] *The Journal of Negro History*, vol. v, Riddell, W. R., "Slavery in
Canada," chap. vii.

teen hundred in the decade prior to the American Civil War.[1] In Canada East, as has been elsewhere indicated, the number of negroes was almost negligible except in Montreal, but this was not true in the Maritime Provinces. Here too there was a tendency for them to congregate in the towns, especially in Halifax. A traveler described the negroes whom he saw in that city. " Their habits and manners indicate an indolent disposition, but a merry group they appear to be. Whole families of them have assembled upon the market grounds, oily-faced wenches and chubby-cheeked Sambos, together with ' Uncle Sams ' and ' Aunt Chloes' of antiquated appearance." [2]

In addition to the above-mentioned contact between the United States and the Maritime Provinces due to the immigration of the negro to the latter, might well be considered the boundary dispute, which had been settled by the Webster-Ashburton Treaty of 1842 but had left bitter feeling rankling on both sides, for in 1838-1839 a quarrel between British lumber-jacks and Americans had led to what has been called the " Aroostook War." The legislatures of New Brunswick and Maine sent their militia into the territory, where war between the two countries, Great Britain and the United States, was averted, largely through the wisdom and moderation of Sir John Harvey and General Winfield Scott, the two generals in command, who arranged for a joint occupation of the disputed territory. Although this boundary dispute had been settled by the Webster-Ashburton Treaty of 1842, it had left bitterness on both sides, for the Maritime Provinces declared that the interests of the British North American provinces had been sacrificed to promote Anglo-American friendship, and Maine was no better satisfied than

[1] *Census of Nova Scotia 1851 and 1861; Census Journal of the House of Assembly of the Province of New Brunswick*, Compilers' Record 1851.

[2] Andrew Learmont Spedon, *Rambles Among the Blue Noses, During the Summer of 1862*, p. 134.

was New Brunswick. The United States government sought to conciliate Maine by a cash payment of one hundred and fifty thousand dollars.

Howe perhaps more than any other man in public life in British North America, had taken the trouble to familiarize himself with actual conditions in the United States. In 1855 he conceived the wild project of securing recruits for the Crimean War in the United States, and from a southern journey on this mission, and later visits, he became acquainted with the people, and formed warm friendships there. Upon his return to Nova Scotia in 1859, after a sojourn of six months in the United States, Howe, with friendliness in his heart toward the neighboring republic, in an address to the men of Colchester expressed his belief that daily the commercial relationship between the two countries was growing more intimate.[1]

Upon the outbreak of the Civil War, Howe found in the Maritime Provinces men who were foolish enough to regard the American conflict as their opportunity to force Maine to restore the land which they considered had been wrongfully wrested from them by the Webster-Ashburton Treaty of 1842. Equally mistaken did he consider those Americans who talked of the annexation of the provinces as a compensation in the event of the loss of the Southern States.

At the outbreak of the American Civil War, it was no secret that the Legislature of Nova Scotia, then controlled by the Liberals, sympathized with the North, for on April 13, 1861, the day on which Fort Sumter fell, Joseph Howe moved a resolution in which was expressed regret, and the earnest hope that peace would soon be restored in the United States.[2]

[1] A. Chisholm, *The Speeches and Public Letters of Joseph Howe,* vol. ii.

[2] *The Canadian Historical Review,* vol. i, 1920, Fred Landon, " Canadian Opinion of Southern Secession."

Yet in spite of all Howe's efforts, travelers [1] in Nova Scotia from the British Isles claimed that they found considerable Southern sympathy in the Maritime Provinces. One is, however, inclined to think that the extent of this sympathy was exaggerated, for the viewpoint of the travelers was necessarily a one-sided one, as they associated chiefly with the class in the British provinces, which viewed the situation in the United States from an intensely British attitude. Prone to admire the Southerner, and equally inclined to dislike the Yankee, they naturally associated with those who were likeminded, and found a ready welcome within the ranks of the descendants of the United Empire Loyalists. The people of Nova Scotia and New Brunswick who were commended for their loyalty to Great Britain were said to favor the establishment of an independent government in Dixie Land. [2] One traveler did not attribute this sympathetic attitude toward the Confederate cause to unselfish motives.

But the tendency of their biased feeling does not appear to be the real spontaneous emanation of sympathy with the South; it chiefly arises from a selfishness congenial to their own interests; for were the State Republic to be dissolved by the fire of Red Rebellion, and the Black Dynasty of Jeff Davis to arise phoenix-like from the ruins of the Union War, they flatter themselves with the idea that such would ultimately prove conducive to their prosperity as trading colonies. [3]

Materialistic motives, not altruistic, were said to actuate the people of New Brunswick and Nova Scotia.

The people of these Provinces believed that there was

[1] *Cf. Dawson Pamphlet,* " British North America; *cf.* James Ferguson, *Notes of a Tour in North America in 1861;* Andrew Learmont Spedon, *Rambles among the Blue Noses.*

[2] *Ibid.*

[3] Andrew Learmont Spedon, *Rambles Among the Blue Noses,* p. 206.

[4] *Ibid.,* p. 206.

ample justification for the despatch of British troops to Canada by the *Great Eastern* in view of the fact that the Queen's Proclamation of Neutrality had aroused the hostility of the Northern press.

Lord Palmerston would have been guilty of foolhardiness if he had not re-inforced the garrisons of Canada, at all events before the setting in of winter.   The number of troops sent out (about 3000) only brings the Canadian garrison up to the standard of 1854—since which period, the military force in that colony was largely reduced, owing chiefly to the requirements of the Crimean and Indian Campaigns.   It is very easy to charge the British Government with folly for sending these troops to Canada, at the present juncture; but suppose they were not sent, and that, owing to disturbances on the borders, growing out of the present difficulties, their presence was required at an in-clement period of the year when they could only be forwarded through the wilderness of New Brunswick,—would not Lord Palmerston be blamed by the very parties who are now so ready to find fault?   For our own part, we look upon reinforcements for Canada as a wise measure of precaution, warranted by the fact that an adjoining country is in a state of insurrection, and the salutary effect which the knowledge that the government has a disciplined force . . . is sure to exercise upon turbulent and evil disposed characters on the North-American frontier, who might be disposed to re-enact the scenes of 1838, on a much larger scale.   We do not imagine that the services of these troops will be required.   But suppose they should not, no great harm can be done.   The cost of their maintenance in Canada will probably not exceed what would have been paid for their support had they remained in England, where their services were not, and are not likely to be required.[1]

The capture of Mason and Slidell aroused the people of the Maritime Provinces, as it had aroused Canada East and Canada West.   Howe said that no British government could

[1] The Halifax *Morning Chronicle*, July 18, 1861.

have stood a week that did not demand reparation. He feared that the mob of New York which had applauded Wilkes would not permit any atonement by the government at Washington.[1] The Britishers of the Maritime Provinces recognized the seriousness of the situation. " The detention of a British vessel engaged in the public service and the arrest on board of her of Southern delegates to Europe is intelligence which awakens surprise and gives rise to serious surmises wherever the swiftly flying news arrives." [2] The question of international law at stake was discussed. The general opinion was that " no right of visitation and search can be exercised on board a public neutral vessel on the high seas." [3] They recalled the contention of the American people in the War of 1812 which was exactly this. When war was averted by the surrender of Mason and Slidell, the people of the Maritime Provinces rejoiced. " The British flag has been vindicated, yet not a shot has been fired by British cannon." [4] The people of the Maritime Provinces attributed the surrender of Mason and Slidell to the fact that Great Britain had supported her demands by a display of force. " There was no waiting for a second challenge, because there was no time. Already heavily laden transports were on their way: already British troops were hurrying West, and British frigates steaming to the Northern shores." [5] In view of what they characterized as unaccountable hatred of the Yankees for England, the Maritime Provinces believed the surrender of the Southern Commissioners merely meant a postponement of the day of conflict.

[1] *Canadian Archives, Joseph Howe Papers*, vol. viii, " Letters from Howe 1861-1865," " Letters to the Earl of Mulgrave, November 30, 1861.

[2] The *Morning Chronicle*, November 23, 1861.

[3] *Ibid.*

[4] *Ibid.*, January 4, 1862.

[5] *Ibid.*

[6] The *Acadian Recorder*, January 4, 1862.

In the *Morning Chronicle* of January 14, 1862, appeared a description of the forward movement of the British troops from Nova Scotia to Canada.

Winter will find its silent fastnesses, the precipitous reaches of the St. Lawrence, the leagues of snow-piled barrens, of mazy whitened forests, disturbed by the tread of armed battalions moving heavily through the sullen solitudes, and under gloomy pines and larches, like piles of angry thunder-cloud that drift across the desert " with fire reserved for other lands." The citadels of Canada and especially the defences on its Southern frontier will thus be strongly reinforced; and when spring opens up the St. Lawrence to the sea, other arms and other forces will depart from England for the Canadas. Canada is astir with preparations. Her patriotic sons have arisen by thousands for the protection of their homes. Her volunteers are ranked by many regiments; day by day new hundreds flock to drill, and the spring will find that province in possession of a formidable army of volunteer auxiliaries to the regular forces, and British North America will wear a front more warlike than it has worn for years.[1]

The people of the Maritime Provinces felt that the best guarantee of peace lay in military preparedness. The threatening tone of certain Northern newspapers, notably the *New York Herald,* was largely accountable for the feeling of an impending conflict which undoubtedly existed in the British Provinces. If the Southern States were lost to the Union, could not compensation be found in the annexation of the British North American Provinces?

The irritation aroused in the Maritime Provinces by the attitude of Great Britain toward colonial defence, elsewhere discussed, caused Howe considerable anxiety. In a letter to the Duke of Newcastle, Colonial Secretary, April 17, 1862, he pointed out the folly of wounding the sensibilities of a

[1] The *Morning Chronicle,* January 14, 1862.

loyal and gallant people. Howe considered that the matter
of colonial defence might be adjusted to the satisfaction of
both the colonies and the mother country. This was his
suggestion: " I wish your Lordship would send me to settle
this war question with the different provinces and to adjust
on some principle intelligible to us all, the strength of garrisons in time of peace and the proportions in which the
burdens of war, whenever it comes, ought to be borne.
These matters may be adjusted by negotiations, but they
never will be by speeches flung to and fro across the sea
which only create irritation." [1]

Throughout the period of the sixties, Howe ever exerted
his influence for the preservation of peace. For instance, in
a speech at Niagara, September 18, 1862, he pleaded with
the people of Canada to arm for defence, not for aggression.
Loyal to Great Britain, friendly to the United States, he
counseled prudence and forbearance. Referring to the
militia system of Nova Scotia, he said: " I asked the people
at home to study the use of arms for defence—not to invade
their neighbors; but if any one comes to invade their soil,
every man, every boy, every old man, and I believe every
woman will turn out to defend it." He counselled the people
of Canada, as he counselled the Nova-Scotians, to observe
the Queen's Proclamation. Since the neighboring Republic
had been forced to raise a large standing army, he seemed to
feel that prudence demanded a certain military preparedness
on the part of the British North American Provinces. [2] That
he was not wholly insensible to the danger of invasion is
revealed in his letter to C. B. Adderley, Colonial Under-
Secretary, December 24, 1862, for he said:

[1] *Joseph Howe Papers*, vol. viii, " Letters from Howe, 1861-1865—
Letters of Howe to the Duke of Newcastle," p. 279.

[2] A. Chisholm, *Speeches and Letters of Howe*, vol. ii, p. 380.

Should the Northern and Southern States settle down under separate forms of government tomorrow, it is clear that though our danger may be diminished, the odds will still be fearfully against us. We shall then have 20,000,000 of people, active, enterprising and sagacious, on our flank, with a navy only inferior to that of Great Britain and France, and an army, familiar with war, of at least two or three hundred thousand men.[1]

The danger of invasion, if danger there was, must necessarily be from the North, for were not the Southern States too distant to think of invading the British Provinces? Moreover, Howe added, " their labouring population, being slaves, can never be soldiers or sailors, and though the white men who own them are splendid material for defensive warfare, trust me, it will be a long time before they will march into Canada and leave their slaves behind them." [2] Then he reviewed the reasons for the maintenance of Anglo-American friendship on the North American continent.

The Northern States are our immediate neighbors, and next to the Mother Country, ought to be our fast friends and firm allies. We claim a common origin, our populations are almost homogeneous, bridges and ferries, stage, steamboat and railway lines connect our frontier towns or sea-board cities. Our commerce is enormous, and is annually increasing in value. Every third vessel that enters the port of Boston goes from Nova Scotia. Our people intermarry, and socially intermix, all along the frontier. For one man that I know in the Southern Confederacy, I know twenty in the Northern States. All these mutual ties and intimate relations are securities for the preservation of peace.[3]

Howe admitted that a transformation in public opinion had taken place in the Maritime Provinces as it had in the

[1] *Ibid.*, vol. ii, p. 389.
[2] *Ibid.*, vol. ii, p. 409.
[3] *Ibid.*

other British Provinces. The Northern press was held largely responsible for the change, for had not abuse of the mother country followed the Queen's Proclamation of Neutrality, and also the Trent incident? Undoubtedly, it is true that Southern sympathizers were to be found in the Maritime Provinces. Was this sympathy that which the weaker contestant in a struggle has never failed to inspire? Howe saw this changing sentiment, but continued to point out that in spite of this involuntary tribute, often paid to Southern courage by the Maritime Provinces in common with the other parts of British America, material interests bound the provinces to the North, more than to the South. At the conclusion of the war, he claimed that for every ton of goods sent to the Southerners, and for every young man sent to aid their cause, fifty tons of goods and fifty young men were contributed to the North.[1]

In his letter to Adderley, December 24, 1862, Howe paid a tribute to the colonial policy of 1839, inaugurated under Lord John Russell. To responsible government Howe attributed the contentment which was general throughout the British Provinces. Under responsible government British America had prospered. Great Britain could no longer be blamed for the misgovernment. If misgovernment was still to be found, the colonists had only themselves to blame. Thus the grant of self-government which removed the manifold causes of irritation under the old system, strengthened the bond which united the British North American Provinces to Great Britain. The blessings of republicanism could, therefore, arouse no response from a people who enjoyed the blessings of Constitutional monarchism. To many Britishers in the Northern Provinces, the American struggle with the threatened collapse of the Union seemed to typify the inherent weakness of republicanism. Therefore, although

[1] Halifax *Citizen*, July 29, 1865.

the Trent incident found the British provinces totally unprepared for war, there was general unanimity of opinion
that the just demands of Great Britain must be supported.
In the event of war between Great Britain and the United
States, the British colonists realized that they must be the
sufferers. The instant and vigorous response on the part of
the colonies was glorious—though later sacrifice proved
needless. The danger to the provinces was contrasted with
the security of the mother land: " Your homesteads were
safe, ours in peril. A British, not a colonial ship had been
boarded, but what then? The old flag that had floated above
our father's heads and droops over their graves had been
insulted, and our British blood was stirred without our ever
thinking of our pockets." [1]

The opinion throughout the Maritime Provinces that under
the impending Conscription Act of 1863 thousands of
British subjects would be forced to serve in the Northern
Army was widely disseminated. " Legally, British subjects
cannot be liable to conscription in the United States; but unfortunately, at the present time, law is not worth much in
that country, and the every-day experience of the past month
shows that the British subject who now ventures across the
border to take up his residence there, is very likely to find
himself shouldering a rifle, and practising the goose-step to
the tune of ' Yankee Doodle ' for his pains." [2] The accusation was sometimes heard in the Maritime Provinces, as elsewhere in British America, that attempts were made to kidnap
British subjects, and then force them to join the Northern
army.

The Maritime Provinces, throughout the period of the
American Civil War, suffered financial loss. During the
first year of the American struggle the closure of the

[1] *Joseph Howe's Papers, Letters from Howe, 1861-1865,* vol. viii, p. 451.
[2] The *Morning Chronicle,* August 23, 1862.

Southern ports diminished the exports of Nova Scotia by $840,500.00 and the revenue by $81,373.00. Howe explained that the increase in the tariff was necessary in order to supplement the diminished revenue, and to provide the additional sum necessary for the volunteer force of the province.[1]

The colonists of these provinces, Howe declared, believed that the two causes of complaint, namely, the high protective tariff and the defeat of the Militia Bill, urged against Canada in Great Britain, were unjust.

As respects the tariff of Canada let me observe that when self-government was conferred upon that province, the right to construct her own tariff was virtually conceded. By a Special Despatch sent to all the Provinces, when Lord Grey was Colonial Secretary, the right to impose what duties they pleased was specifically conceded, provided they were not discriminating, and were made to attach alike to importations from all countries. No restriction of the right to protect their own industry was stated. But in none of the Provinces have protective or discriminating duties ever been imposed.[2]

Like Galt, Howe expressed his conviction that under responsible government, fiscal independence was assured the British provinces.

The British troops marching on foot through the forests to their destination made the people realize that the completion of a railway between Halifax and Quebec should be a matter of military concern. The American railway lines insured a rapid advance of American troops to the Canadian frontier, but there was no British railway which would insure for Canada reinforcement in an emergency. To the people of Nova Scotia, the advocacy of the Intercolonial

---

[1] *Joseph Howe Papers*, vol. viii, " Letter to Mulgrave," March 24, 1862.
[2] *Ibid.*, vol. viii, p. 452, " Letter to Adderley," December 24, 1862.

Railway became inextricably involved in the maintenance of the British connection.

In case of hostilities with the United States, the facility which a railroad from Halifax through British territory would afford for the transport of troops and munitions of war would be of incalculable advantage. . . . Nor is it the least of advantages that would result from this facility that the knowledge of its existence would tend to avert hostilities that otherwise might grow out of a sense of comparative insecurity attendant on aggressive movements. No less than seventeen lines of American railroad lead through the United States to the borders of Canada, and give means of rapid and hostile approach. Not a single line of British railroad connects the Provinces together or affords communication from the Atlantic shore through national territory. None more than the inhabitants of Nova Scotia appreciate the advantage of peaceful relations with the United States. They, however, who are placed in close proximity are less credulous than others may be as to the impossibility of hostilities between the two powers. And yet it is apparent to all that the foreign relations of no Government are so subject as that of the United States to the influences of popular opinion or of party interests. The great work we advocate is as necessary to enable Her Majesty's North American Colonies to *promote their material progress in peace, as it is requisite for their common defense in war.* The undertaking we urge must be accomplished while the danger that prompts it is distant and contingent, otherwise it will come too late to avert the evils it is designed to counteract.[1]

The events of the American Civil War made the Maritime Provinces, as well as the other British North American provinces, realize anew the need of a closer union for defensive purposes. As early as 1854, the first parliamentary proposal for a union of all the British North American provinces was made in the Nova Scotia legislature, but nothing came of it.

[1] The *Morning Chronicle*, July 30, 1863.

There was, however, a strong sentiment in favor of a union
of the Maritime Provinces, for to many this merely meant a
reversion to the status of 1784; moreover, in these provinces
a strong community of interests had developed a local
patriotism.   This sentiment did not extend to Canada, a land
far distant due to lack of railway connection, and inhabited
by an alien race who spoke a different language.   In 1864,
Tupper, the Conservative leader of Nova Scotia, invited the
governments of the other eastern provinces to send delegates
to a conference to discuss a Maritime Union.   This conference which was attended by delegates of Canada as well as
of the Maritime Provinces, met September 1, 1864, at Char-
lottetown, but owing to the insistence of Prince Edward
Island that the capitol of the new Maritime government must
be located there, nothing was accomplished.   Then a month
later, October 10, 1864, a conference of delegates met at
Quebec to discuss the union of all the British North American provinces.   This conference formulated the provisions
of the later British North America Act.

The political leaders in the Maritime provinces as in the
other British provinces were intensely loyal to the British
Crown.   The Conservatives in Nova Scotia under the leadership of Dr. Charles Tupper (afterwards Sir Charles) won
a victory, April 28, 1863.   In January 1865, Macdonald, the
Conservative leader of Canada, was in anxious communication with Tupper, still in power in Nova Scotia, with regard
to the passport system which the United States had established along the frontier.   The fact that Blaine had failed
in his negotiations for peace seemed to afford relief, for the
Conservatives feared that peace between the two sections of
the United States would be followed by a war between the
United States and Great Britain.   Tupper never possessed
the hold on the popular imagination that Howe had, but his
influence was considerable among the Conservatives.

Intensely loyal himself to the British Crown, Howe thought that the mere mention of the dismemberment of the Empire should be followed by " social and political degradation." He was firmly convinced that the maintenance of the bond was to the mutual advantage of Great Britain and the British North American Provinces. The Manchester School of statesmen in England who talked of the creation of " new nationalities " aroused his indignation. The only alternative left to the British Provinces, if deserted by the mother land was, Howe declared, annexation to the United States.

If the British Government and people are tired of the connection with North America, or considered it hazardous or expensive, and were to say so, then the dishonor of breaking old ties would rest on them, and not upon us. But, in that case, any attempt to found a new nationality with thirty millions of people on the other side of the frontier of 1500 miles would be suicidal and absurd. With wounded pride, and heavy hearts, we should at once cast in our lots with that other branch of the family who drove our fathers into the wilderness for adhering to the old flag, and to the British institutions, but who would now receive their descendants with open arms. A few years of social, commercial and political association, would make us one people. But how would peace be bought for Britain by the abandonment of these noble possessions, by driving out four millions of people, and all their offspring to swell the ranks of the Republic—by adding 922,000 tons of shipping to the Mercantile Marine of her great commercial rival—by presenting her 69,000 Fishermen and sailors to aid in the equipment of her Navy, by handing over to her our seacoasts, fisheries and mines, and leaving the country without a harbour in which to repair a ship, or a ton of coal wherewith to supply a steamer? When all was gone, would not the arrogant spirit and aggressive diplomacy of the great Republic have still to be encountered? War would still be imminent, and, when it came, the outposts and depots of the Republic would have been advanced 700 miles nearer to

Europe. The battle would be fought in Ireland, instead of British America, with this additional element of mischief that every Irishman in the Provinces would be suddenly converted into a Fenian. The picture is not a pleasant one, but it is still more unpleasant to reflect that even Oxford Professors are to be found, who, lacking the higher style of statesmanship by which empires are kept together are not ashamed to seek notoriety by suggesting how easily they may be destroyed.[1]

Not only the greatest statesman, but also the greatest journalist that the Maritime provinces has yet produced, Howe wielded an almost incalculable influence. He himself was the editor of the *Nova Scotian* in Halifax, a paper which upheld the rights of the people to such an extent that " his newspaper office became known as the ' school of the prophets ' of reform and progress." [2] His friend and devoted follower, George E. Fenety, who had learnt the business under him and imbibed many of his principles, became the editor of the *Morning News* published in St. John, New Brunswick. His influence further extended to Prince Edward Island where another devoted follower, Edward Whelan, who had learnt the business in the Nova-Scotian office, edited the *Examiner*.[6] Thus the journalism of the three provinces was closely connected in personnel and in spirits. In addition to the papers mentioned above, the *Chronicle,* the *Free Press* and Halifax *Citizen* have been classified among the Howe papers.[4] The other great political leader, Tupper, did not identify himself as closely with journalism. He was however ably supported by the *Acadian*

[1] *Joseph Howe Papers*, vol. viii, " Letter to the Right Hon'ble Edward Cardwell," pp. 717-732.

[2] *A History of Canadian Journalism*, edited by a Committee of the Press, p. 138.

[3] *Ibid.*, p. 139.

[4] *Canadian Archives, Classified as Howe papers.*

Recorder, an influential Conservative newspaper of Nova
Scotia.   Undoubtedly the newspapers of the Maritime provinces throughout the sixties wielded considerable influence,
and expressed public opinion, for the people of these provinces were a reading people.   In their discussion and advocacy of a Maritime union, as an alternative to annexation
with the United States, the press, both Liberal and Conservative, like the political leaders of the provinces, revealed ever
a loyal attachment to Great Britain and a desire to maintain
the status quo.[1]

[1] Newspaper files consulted: the *Morning Chronicle*, the *Nova Scotian*,
the *Casket*, published weekly at Halifax and Antigonish, the *Islander*,
Acadian Recorder.

CHAPTER VI

The Government Attitude

Ammunition—Detention of Vessels—United States Agents in Canada—Illegal Arrest of British Subjects—Trent Affair—Military Activity—Landing of British Troops in New England—Naval Depots on the Lakes—Recruits in Canada—Sioux Refugees in Canada—Exportation of Live Stock and Anthracite Coal—Frontier Disturbance.

ONCE again in the period of the sixties the relationship of the government of Canada to that of the United States which for the two decades prior to the American Civil War had been of relatively minor significance, chiefly affected by the increasing trade between the two countries, assumed a new significance. To the sanity of leadership in the governments of these two countries may be attributed the fact that war was averted. Upon more than one occasion, as we have seen in studying press opinion, grave international crises arose. Whatever accusations might, with justice, have been brought against the individual British subject, not once did the Canadian Government deviate from the rules enjoined upon a neutral power. Confidential information of alleged Confederate plots, as soon as it was received by the Canadian government, was transmitted to the American government through the agency of Lord Lyons, the British minister. The Canadian government did not intend that the Confederates should abuse the hospitality and right of asylum, freely extended to Northerner and Southerner alike, and although a transformation in public opinion undoubtedly took place in Canada, the Canadian government maintained throughout the American struggle a consistent policy. An examination of the correspondence which passed between the two countries leaves one impressed with the idea that their governments, whatever might be the popular clamor, were one in their desire for the preservation of peace. Cordiality, courtesy, frankness and fair-mindedness characterized these communications. An idea of the Canadian Government's conception of neutrality can be obtained only through an examination of the attitude adopted by it in a variety of situations. A series of complications which called for government action will, therefore, be considered.[1]

The refusal of the Canadian Government to sell arms and ammunition to the Northern army was due to the Canadian conception of what the observance of strict neutrality implied. In the Canadian Archives records are to be found of the application for arms made to the Canadian government by the states of Illinois, Massachusetts, Ohio, and New York. Sir Edmund Head,[2] the Governor-General of Canada, promptly replied that he could supply arms only if a direct requisition were first secured by the United States from the British Minister at Washington. This information Sir Edward Head immediately transmitted to Lord Lyons for his consideration. Lord Lyons signified his approval of the decision in his written instructions to Her Majesty's Consul at New York, who, since the telegraphic communications of the government at Washington with the North were cut off, was asked in April, 1861, to transfer to Sir Edmund Head the telegram: " With reference to your Despatch of twenty-second, and to the application from the Government of Massachusetts, Lord Lyons is decidedly of opinion that nothing ought to be done without express orders from Her Majesty's Government." [3]

---

[1] These complications will be considered here only in so far as they are revealed in the government correspondence that passed between the two countries.

[2] Sir Edmund Head—Governor-General of Canada 1854-1861.

[3] *Canadian Archives, Series G., 229* " Letter of Lord Lyons to Sir Edmund Head," April 27, 1861.

In a despatch to Sir Edmund Head, Lord Lyons repeated the telegram form with additional remarks. Thus he continued to state his idea of the neutrality which he believed Great Britain wished to maintain:

Her Majesty's Government have not authorized me to obtrude advice or even to express an opinion upon the unhappy contest which is going on in this country. Much less have they given me authority to ask for material aid from her Majesty's Colonies for either party in the struggle. They are very far indeed from having manifested a desire to take part in the strife. They have on the contrary sought to avoid even the appearance of anything which might be construed to imply such a desire.[1] In his reply to Governor Morgan of New York, April 25, 1861, Sir Edmund Head had stated: " There are no arms in the Province which the Government has power either to sell or to lend."

Similar messages were sent to the other states which applied for arms. The state governments informed the Federal government at Washington of the decision of the Canadian government. The motive which prompted the refusal was not understood at Washington. In a letter to Lord Lyons, May 3, 1861, Seward chose to assume that the objection of the Canadian government to sell to the respective States did not necessarily imply an unwillingness to sell to the national government. Since the state troops were to be mustered into the national army, Seward urged that the arms might be sold direct to the national government. Lord Lyons forwarded to Sir Edmund Head a copy of Seward's note, together with a copy of his answer. In his reply, Lord Lyons expressed his opinion that " it would not be right to comply with any such application without express orders from Her Majesty's Government." [2]

[1] *Ibid.*

[2] *Series G, 229,* " Letter of Lord Lyons to Sir Edmund Head," May 3, 1861.

Official correspondence passed between the United States and Canada on the subject of the manufacture by the Southerners in Canada of ammunition known as " Greek Fire ", to be used in burning northern cities of the United States. The measures which were taken by Viscount Monck,[1] the Governor-General of Canada, to prevent the manufacture of " Greek Fire " were gratefully acknowledged as satisfactory by Secretary Seward.[2]

The government of the United States and that of Canada were at variance on the subject of Canada's responsibility for the detention in British waters of vessels suspected of being in the service of the South, and during the period of the American Civil War, considerable correspondence passed between the two governments on this subject. On the evening of April 27, 1861, Sir Edmund Head received a telegram from Governor Andrew of Massachusetts with regard to the *Peerless:*

" We have information that Steamer *Peerless* has been bought on Lake Ontario for the rebels. We rely upon you to take all possible steps to stop this piratical cruiser at the Canals or elsewhere." The Federal government apparently took notice of this ship and on May 1, 1861, Lord Lyons entered a protest against the orders given from Washington to naval officers authorizing the seizure and detention of the vessel " under whatever Flag or whatever Papers she may bear."

In his reply of May 1, 1861, Seward stated the reasons for these orders which Lyons had considered improper. As soon as the President had received information believed to be authentic that the *Peerless* was in the hands of the enemy

---

[1] Viscount Monck—Successor to Sir Edmund Head—In 1861, he was appointed Gov.-Gen. of Canada and British North America; in 1867 Gov.-Gen. of the Dominion of Canada; in 1868 he resigned office.

[2] *Despatch marked 11633,* Letter of Seward to J. H. Burnley, Jan. 14, 1865.

on her way out of Lake Ontario with British papers, Seward declared that he had sought an interview with Lord Lyons. In the course of this interview, he had suggested that it would be agreeable to the President if the Governor-General of Canada would order the detention of this vessel. In view of the uncertainty with regard to the whole matter, the British minister had replied that he did not think such directions could be given. Admitting that the United States had no right to require such an order, Seward declared that the United States would not tolerate the fitting-out and delivery of piratical vessels on the St. Lawrence. If, therefore, he received reliable information that the *Peerless* was to be used by the Confederates, he would direct it to be seized and detained by the United States forces, and the parties affected by such an action would be referred to the United States government. Disregarding both the spoken and written protests of the British minister, Seward gave conditional directions for the seizure of the *Peerless* in these words:

> To Commanders of Naval or other Forces of the United
>   States.
> If you have reliable information that the
> *Peerless* has been sold or contracted for,
> and has been delivered, or is to be de-
> livered to the insurgents to be used against
> the United States, seize and bring her into
> Port, and detain her there under whatever
> Flag, or whatever Papers she may bear, and
> refer the Parties to this Government."

He further added that it was hardly necessary to add that this order had not been prompted by any feeling of hostility toward Great Britain. He felt satisfied, moreover, that the British government would consider the seizure justifiable, if the information that had prompted it proved to be correct.

If, however, it was proved to be incorrect, the United States government would give full satisfaction to the British government and the parties aggrieved. The British government, he believed, would admit that such proceedings were sometimes " indispensable when a Flag [was] abused to cover aggressions upon a friendly nation."

Lord Lyons immediately transmitted the information contained in Seward's letter, together with his own opinion, as British Minister, of the course outlined, to Sir Edmund Head in the following telegram:

This Government suspects that the *Peerless* now at Toronto has been sold to become a Southern Privateer, and asked me to beg you to detain her. I expressed doubts whether you have legally power to do so if her Papers are in order. I solemnly protested against any vessel under British Flag and with regular Papers being interfered with by United States Navy. This Government has nevertheless ordered its naval officers to seize *Peerless* if they have reliable information that she has been sold to the South. I adhere to my protest.[1]

The following day Lord Lyons wrote a detailed account to Sir Edmund Head of his conversation with Seward on the subject of the detention of the *Peerless*. In the course of the conversation he repeated three times a solemn protest against the seizure of any vessel " under the British Flag and with regular British Papers." [2]

The documents in the Canadian Archives do not give the end of this incident. The concluding letter, however, intimated that Seward, upon the Governor-General not agreeing to detain the *Peerless* at Toronto, ordered its seizure provided the officers of the United States were reasonably sure that it was to be delivered to the insurgents.

[1] *Series G, 229*, Telegram to His Excellency, May 1, 1861.
[2] *Series G, 229*, May 2, 1861.

Throughout the entire period of the American Civil War, it was necessary for both governments to use the utmost vigilance in order to prevent the purchase by Southerners of Canadian vessels to be used against the North. On March 8, 1864, Secretary of War Stanton received information from Provost-Marshal Colonel Baker, of the United States War Department, that about seventeen miles from Chatham, Canada West, there was a steamer *Montreal* commanded by Captain Whitby, formerly a lieutenant in the Confederate Navy. This vessel was manned by rebel soldiers and well supplied with ammunition, including equipment for boarding other vessels. In the same despatch Colonel Baker mentioned the *Saratoga* lying in New Creek, Long Point Marsh, about fifteen miles from Port Stanley, Canada West. This vessel was, likewise, well supplied with ammunition. The fact that both vessels were kept ready for sailing at the season of the year when ordinarily Canadian vessels were dismantled, aroused the suspicions of the United States agent. In his conversation with the crew, he found his suspicions confirmed, for certain members of the crew avowed " their piratical intentions as soon as navigation is resumed in the spring." The information relative to the schooners, *Montreal* and *Saratoga,* was transmitted by Lord Lyons to Viscount Monck, the successor of Sir Edmund Head as Governor-General of Canada, who promptly replied: " I will take immediate measures to ascertain the accuracy of this information and to prevent any violation of the neutrality of Her Majesty's Canada." [1]   In his despatch of December 29, 1864, to J. Hume Burnley, British Chargé d'Affaires, Seward alluded to the measures adopted by the Canadian government in connection with the case of the steamer *Georgian.* He declared that the Canadian government, fully alive to the importance of preventing the formation of any

[1] *Series G, 232,* 1864, Lord Monck's reply to Lord Lyons, March 18, 1864.

plans hostile to the United States on British soil, had taken stringent measures to that end, both of a civil and military character. Further he added that he wished Burnley to convey to the Governor-General of Canada " an expression of the high appreciation entertained by this government of the friendly spirit which he [had] manifested " in " the judicious measures which he [had] adopted with a view to the preservation of the neutrality of Her Majesty's provinces." [1]

The intercepted correspondence received from Secretary Seward by J. H. Burnley, and forwarded to Viscount Monck, afforded additional evidence that an attempt was made by Southerners to purchase the *Georgian* to be used against the North. The Canadian government adopted the attitude that the purchase of ships in Canada by Southerners to be used against the United States involved a breach of neutrality. The devices, therefore, used by the Southerners to conceal the real purpose for which they planned to use a steamer were more or less ingenious, such for instance as the allegation that the *Georgian* was to be used in the Saginaw lumber trade.

Yielding to a natural desire to influence Canadian opinion, especially official opinion, the United States government sent Mr. Ashman as the unofficial agent of the government to Canada. Notices appeared in the *New York Herald* and other newspapers that Mr. Ashman was such an agent, and this publicity given by the press to his visit made it extremely difficult, Sir Edmund Head declared, " to communicate with him in any confidential manner." [2] In his letter of May 3, 1861, to Lord Lyons, Sir Edmund Head wrote an account of an interview with Mr. Ashman:

Mr. Ashman has this day visited me, and in the presence of

---

[1] *Cf. Series G, 234*, Despatch of Seward to J. Hume Burnley.

[2] *Series G, 229*, Sir Edmund Head to Mr. Ward, April 20, 1861.

Mr. Cartier and Mr. Vankoughnet—members of my Council—
he informed me that he was requested by the Secretary of State,
Mr. Seward, to visit Canada for the purpose of explaining the
true position of the United States in the present crisis of their
affairs.

I distinctly informed him that I have no authority to recog-
nize him or any other person as the Agent of the United States
Government or to communicate with him in that capacity—that
all the official intercourse between the Government of the United
States and that of a British Colony must pass through Her
Majesty's accredited representative at Washington.

Mr. Ashman replied that he was not accredited in any way to
this Government or authorized to make any communications to
me, but that it was supposed that good might be done by explaining the position of affairs, as Agents for the Southern
States were said to be lying up armed, etc.

I replied that I had no wish to fetter his intercourse with any
one, but that I might have a doubt in my mind whether it was
altogether a regular or usual mode of proceeding, on the part
of any Government to request a person to visit another country
on a mission of this kind. Nothing could be more candid or
straightforward than Mr. Ashman was. He said that he would
talk to no one and return at once if I desired him to do so. I
replied " No—I would make no such request." He could talk
to whom he pleased. We had nothing to conceal, nor any desire to impede his intercourse with anybody.[1]

The Governor-General had acted in strict accordance with
the obligations imposed upon him by the Queen's Proclamation of Neutrality. To Mr. Ashman had simply been
granted the same freedom of intercourse and freedom of
speech that the Canadian government had accorded to the
Southern refugees. The same rights of asylum and of
hospitality were extended to both the people of the North
and the people of the South. The preservation of strict

[1] *Series G, 229*, 1861.

neutrality in the British North American provinces did not
imply any limitation of speech, for freedom in this respect
was accorded to Northerner and to Southerner.

The arbitrary arrest of British subjects was another cause
of contention between the two countries. During the period
of the American Civil War, the American government contended that the condition of the country justified the arrest
and imprisonment of both citizens and aliens without legal
process. The British government protested against what
Britishers regarded as an arbitrary use of authority, that,
in its opinion, the national crisis failed to warrant. Lord
Lyons protested solemnly, but in vain. Through his efforts
to help individuals and the necessity thereby imposed upon
him to adduce reasons which the United States would accept
as legitimate reasons for their releases, Lord Lyons found
himself not a little embarrassed by the obligation imposed
upon him by his position as British minister to maintain the
position taken by Her Majesty's government that the arrest
of British subjects without legal process was unjustifiable.[1]

The Trent incident, as an examination of the government
correspondence will prove, was only one of a series which
threatened grave international complications; nevertheless it
is, perhaps, true to say that this single incident more than any
other aroused public opinion in the British North American
Provinces. The Canadian government, as well as those of
the mother land and the United States, was keenly aware of
the seriousness of the situation created by the removal of
the two Southern commissioners, Mason and Slidell, from
the British steamer.

The governments of the British North American Provinces, namely those of Canada, Nova Scotia, New Brunswick
and Prince Edward Island, were all conscious of the in-

[1] *Series G, 229*, Letter to His Excellency the Viscount Monck by
Lord Lyons, November 14, 1861.

adequacy of the military forces at their disposal in the event
of the actual outbreak of hostilities.   In a despatch addressed
to the Secretary of State for War, in London, from his headquarters in Halifax, General Hastings Doyle pointed out the
inadequate means at his disposal for the defence of Nova
Scotia, New Brunswick, Newfoundland and Prince Edward
Island.   To the British Fleet, Doyle declared, he must chiefly
look for the defence of the coast of New Brunswick.

This latter province in consequence of its contiguity to the
United States would be a source of great anxiety, and the result
of my reconnaissance leads me to conclude that the Harbour and
Town of St. John, with the adjacent harbour of St. Andrews are
vital points, the possession of which would place the whole
Province at the command of an enemy, and these must at
present be left entirely to the protection of the navy; the work
on Partridge Island, at the entrance of the harbour of St. John,
being almost utterly useless and the remaining defences of but
little avail.   The possession of the River St. John being of
essential importance to that Province, would naturally be coveted
by our neighbors in the United States.[1]

The War Office sent orders to Doyle, as General Officer in
Command, regarding the passage of troops through New
Brunswick to Canada.   In this despatch the statement is
made that Her Majesty's government has a full realization
that provision must be made for the safety of the Provinces.
Assurance is given that the need for reinforcements under
the existing relations between the United States and Great
Britain has already been anticipated.   " Two more Batteries
of Garrison Artillery have been placed under orders for
Nova Scotia and New Brunswick, and one for Newfoundland
—some heavy guns and a full supply of stores and ammunition are likewise to be sent to that Island for the purpose of
strengthening the armaments of the Works." [2]

[1] *File:* *CR/Q/408*, Part II, G. O. C. to S. S. W. d/28/11/61.
[2] *File:* *CR/Q/408*, Part II, 6, W. O. to G. O. C. d/21/12/61.

A despatch of Doyle to the Secretary of State for War, will serve as an illustration of the precautionary measures that were taken:

States that 62nd Regiment will proceed to Woodstock to cover advance of troops, and to watch American Post at Houlton, 12 miles distant. Has requested Lieutenant Governor of New Brunswick to call out volunteer cavalry (25 in no.) for scouting purposes; the services of such a corps, were, he says found very valuable in 1837 and 1838. Hears from a reliable source that at Augusta, the capital of Maine, there is one Regt. of Cavalry and one of Infy. These had been ordered South, but countermanded since the " Trent " difficulty. Has written to Governor of N. F. Land asking for the Detachment of the 62nd Regt. stationed there.[1]

The British government realized the difficulties that were involved in the transportation of troops through New Brunswick to Canada during the winter months.

If war actually breaks out all the reinforcements required in Canada will have to pass through New Brunswick during the winter and part of the spring and the defence of that Province and the duties connected with it are therefore in the opinion of Her Majesty's Government peculiarly important and responsible.[2]

A comprehensive report of actual conditions in the British North American Provinces, at the period of anxiety which arose out of the Trent incident, and a rather detailed account of the efforts which were put forth by the government to meet an unexpected situation, appeared in the *Times*, February 10, 1862:

[1] *Central Registry, Headquarter Office, Halifax, N.S. File*: CR/Q/408, Part II, G. O. C. to S. S. W. d/26/12/61.

[2] *Central Registry. File*: CR/Q/408, Part II, W. O. to G. O. C. d/21/12/61.

When the news of the "Trent" affair reached England, Canada, though it had been reinforced by two regiments of infantry last summer, had only a garrison throughout the entire colony of less than 5000 men of all arms and ranks. While the Prince of Wales was there there were only 3000. In simple truth, the garrison before Christmas only amounted to one field battery, two batteries of garrison artillery, six officers of engineers, four regiments of infantry. An army hospital corps of 12 men, a commissariat staff of one rank and file (!), and the Royal Canadian Rifles, 1050 strong. In Nova Scotia the force was equally low, for though divided between Halifax and New Brunswick, the total strength was only 2000 men—a garrison of, in all, only 7000 troops to defend the exposed frontier of a country as large as Europe. With the first news of the Trent outrage every effort was made by the War Department to strengthen the colony with men and munitions of war; but the attempt had to be made at the worst possible time of the year, and though the government took up at once and in rapid succession the finest and best found steamers in our merchant navy, only one—the Persia—succeeded in getting up the St. Lawrence as far as Bic, and her able commander could only manage to land the troops, and was obliged, after losing his boats among the ice and leaving part of his crew on shore, to return with the military stores to Halifax. In all eighteen powerful steamers were despatched—the Melbourne, Australasian, Persia, Niagara, Adriatic, Parana, Delta, Magdalene, Asia, Canada, Calcutta, Cleopatra, Mauritius, Hibernia, Arabia, Adelaide, Victoria and St. Andrew. The united freight of these vessels enabled the War office to send away a perfect corps d'armée of 12,000 men, complete in all save cavalry, even to the most minute working details of commissariat staff corps, military train, army hospital corps, military store department, and engineers with garrison and field artillery. By these reinforcements the garrison of Canada has been raised from 5000 to 13,000 men; that of Halifax to 3000; New Brunswick to 2500; and Newfoundland has 200 additional artillerymen to man the guns in the batteries at the mouth of the harbor of St. John. In all, therefore, there

is now a total force in Canada, and the provinces of 18,000 exclusive of the Militia and Volunteers. But to march down
regiments to certain ports and embark them on board steamers
is a comparatively easy business. It is the enormous quantities
of stores that accompany each departure that have given all the
trouble, and what is only trouble here becomes a formidable
difficulty in Canada and Nova Scotia where everything has to be
forwarded in sledges over the snow to Rivière du Loup.

To the energy and foresight of Lord Grey was attributed the
promptness with which troops and ammunition were despatched to Canada.

To Major General Doyle credit should also be given for
the difficulties which he surmounted, for his task was no
light one. Not only must the necessary arrangements be
made for the reception of the British troops, but also arrangements for their march to Canada. Major General
Doyle had just five days in which to prepare temporary huts
for the soldiers who arrived in the first ship and it was necessary for his small force to work day and night in order to be
ready to receive them. Lord Mulgrave and the civil authorities rendered every possible assistance. The task which
confronted Major General Doyle is thus described:

He had to provide accommodation for the men almost as fast
as each regiment came in, to manage the disembarkation of
stores when ropes were frozen and snowstorms incessant, to
chalk out the line of march along the frontier by the Madawaska
road at a time when war was imminent, and it was necessary to
make a route that would give protection to the left flank against
the " scouters " and Filibusters that would certainly have been
on the watch. At New Brunswick the personal exertions of the
Governor, Mr. Gordon, and of General Rumley provided accommodation for the troops; but from this point Colonel Doyle
had to make all the arrangements for the winter march over the
snow to Rivière du Loup. It was decided to forward the men

in batches of from 200 to 150, partly by snow sledges and partly by marching from St. John's to Woodstock, and so on, by Tobique, Grand Falls, Little Fall, Florenceville, Fort Ingall, to Rivière du Loup. In the first place, measures were taken to insure telegraphic communication at all points of arrival and departure in case of such unforseen accidents, as snow drifts blocking the roads, while at the midday halting places Indian runners were kept to forewarn the night stations in advance. Hospital accommodation was erected at all the halts with purveyors' and medical stores, while the Commissariat Department provided each detachment with means to clear the roads, and a contract was made with the lumberers in the woods to keep the route as clear as they possibly could. Billeting was avoided in nearly all cases by the erection of log huts. Before starting, each man received an extra ration of hot coffee, and all the men took cooked provisions with them for use at the midday halting place, where an allowance of rum was served out. A hot meal was ordered to be ready on the arrival at the night station, and at these points the Commissariat had extra comforts for all men fatigued or suffering much from cold.[1]

A memorandum of the reinforcement sent to the British Provinces shows:

    I " The force in Canada previous to ' Trent ' affair, 7000 men.

    II to VI. Force sent in consequence (10,000 men) and total force (17,000).

    VII Arms, accoutrements, etc.

    VIII Transports, with dates of sailing, cargoes, etc. . . ." [2]

Not only was the government concerned, but popular indignation, too, was aroused in Great Britain by the removal of the Southern Commissioners from a British ship. As usual the war-at-any-price party made itself heard. The

---

[1] *Central Registry, CR/Q/408,* Part III; the *Times,* February 10, 1862.

[2] *Central Registry, CR/Q/408,* Part III, p. 12; *Confidential Paper,* January 11, 1862, printed lists d/W.O./3/1/62.

despatch, however, sent by Earl Russell, the Foreign Minister, to Lord Lyons in connection with the Trent incident was a conciliatory one, and showed unmistakably the desire of the British government to avoid war. To the Prince Consort, Prince Albert, has been assigned the credit for the conciliatory tone of the despatch. The story is told that a severe despatch which would have made war almost inevitable was submitted to Queen Victoria for her signature. The Prince at once recognized the serious consequences that the sending of such a despatch would involve, and suggested various changes. The harsh language was softened, and the chance for a peaceful solution of the difficulty presented to the American government. The ministers agreed to the changes.[1] In the despatch that Earl Russell sent to Lord Lyons, November 30, 1861, he expressed the unwillingness of the British government, in view of the friendly relationship that had previously existed between the two countries, to believe that the act of aggression committed by Captain Wilkes had been authorized by his government. While the British government insisted upon full reparation for the affront, it was reluctant to think that the United States had deliberately offended. The British government trusted that now the matter had been submitted to the United States that government would offer of its own accord, such redress as alone would satisfy the British nation. This reparation would involve both the liberation of the four gentlemen to be placed again under British protection, and a suitable apology for the aggression that had been committed.[2] It has sometimes been claimed that the enthusiastic welcome accorded the Prince of Wales on his recent visit in 1860 by the American people helped to determine the attitude adopted

[1] *Cf.* Lytton Strachey, *Queen Victoria*, p. 293.

[2] *Cf. 2333, Correspondence on Trent Affair*, Earl Russell to Lord Lyons, November 30, 1861.

by Great Britain in this crisis, for it made Queen Victoria anxious to avert war.[1]

Naturally the Canadian government was aware that a serious situation would confront the British North American Provinces in the event of war. Anxious to secure more information regarding the official viewpoint, the Canadian government, using as a pretext the threatened withdrawal of reciprocity, sent A. T. Galt, finance minister of Canada, on a visit to Washington. He had an interview with President Lincoln in the course of which a reference was made to this matter. Mr. Ashman, the unofficial agent of Seward, who was also present, had remarked that there was a " possibility of grave difficulty arising out of the Mason and Slidell affair. To which the President replied to the effect that in any case the matter could be arranged, and intimated that no cause of quarrel would grow out of that." [2]

The impression left on my mind (Galt wrote afterwards) has been that the President sincerely deprecates any quarrel with England, and has no hostile designs upon Canada. His statement that his views were those of all his cabinet is partly corroborated by the statement made to me by Mr. Seward that he should be glad to see Canada placed in a position of defence. I cannot, however, divest my mind of the impression that the policy of the American government is so subject to popular impression that no assurance can be, or ought to be, relied on under present circumstances. The temper of the public mind toward England is certainly of doubtful character, and the idea is universal that Canada is most desirable for the North, while its unprepared state would make it an easy prey. The vast military preparations of the North must either be met by corresponding organization of the British provinces, or conflict, if it come, can have but one result.[3]

[1] Sidney Lee, *Edward VII*, p. 109.

[2] O. D. Skelton, *The Life and Times of Sir Alexander Tilloch Galt*, p. 316.

[3] O. D. Skelton, *Life and Times of A. T. Galt*, p. 316, Memorandum, Washington, December 5, 1861.

In connection with Lincoln a story is told which refers directly to the Trent affair. When the President was asked how he felt with regard to the surrender of Mason and Slidell, he is said to have replied:

I feel a good deal like a sick man in Illinois who was told he probably hadn't many days longer to live, and that he ought to make peace with any enemies he might have. He said the man he hated worst of all was a fellow named Brown, in the next village, and he guessed he had better begin on him. So Brown was sent for, and when he came, the sick man began to say, in a voice as meek as Moses', that he wanted to die at peace with all his fellow-creatures, and hoped he and Brown could now shake hands and bury all their enmity. The scene was becoming altogether too pathetic for Brown, who had to get out his handkerchief and wipe the gathering tears from his eyes. It wasn't long before he melted and gave his hand to his neighbor, and they had a regular love-feast. After a parting that would have softened the heart of a grindstone, Brown had about reached the door when the sick man rose up on his elbow and said, " but, see here, Brown, if I should happen to get well, mind, that old grudge stands." [2]

Notwithstanding the above story the temper which Lincoln displayed at all times towards the British North American Provinces was wholly conciliatory.

Seward's statement of the reason for the surrender of Mason and Slidell was in accord with American precedent. He said that the principles laid down in 1804 by James Madison, Secretary of State during the administration of Thomas Jefferson, had prompted the surrender. Whenever property suspected of being contraband of war, and therefore subject to capture and condemnation was found in a neutral ship, Madison had declared that the matter should be decided by a legal tribunal before which, the captor him-

[2] F. F. Browne, *The Everyday Life of Abraham Lincoln*, p. 344.

self should be answerable for any abuse of his power. It was hardly reasonable then, or just, that a belligerent commander, who was not permitted to decide in a case where property alone was involved, should be permitted without having recourse to a court, to examine the crew of a neutral ship, to determine the important question of their respective allegiances. Much less did he possess the right to carry that decision into execution by forcing individuals into the service.[1] Seward, therefore, decided that since the action of Commander Wilkes was irregular, it must be disavowed by the United States government, and restitution made.

A rather humorous situation arose on the arrival at Portland, Maine, January, 1862, of a British transport, too late to go to Canada by the St. Lawrence route. In a note dated January 13, 1862, John Henry Murray, the British Consul at Portland, informed Lord Lyons that the local authorities had received instructions from Mr. Secretary Seward to permit the landing of British soldiers enroute to Canada. A private company, Edmonston, Allen & Co., assumed the responsibility of transporting the officer's baggage which had been left on board the *Persia*. Lord Lyons did not wish to place any obstacles in the way of the transportation of British troops and supplies to Canada; yet he apparently could not determine whether he should avail himself of the generous offer of the American government. It does seem remarkable that British troops which, in view of the grave international crisis due to the Trent incident, had been despatched to the Colony for the express purpose of aiding British America in the event of the outbreak of hostilities against the United States, should have been permitted to land at an American port, and pass unmolested through American territory to their destination. Thus in spite of the popular excitement

[1] *Cf. 2333, Correspondence on Trent Affair*, Seward to Lyons, December 26, 1861.

prevalent in both countries, it looks as if the government at Washington believed that the differences between the two countries might be adjusted without having recourse to war; otherwise, this permission would hardly have been granted.

The Canadian government had certain definite plans for the naval defence of the Province. A report had been submitted to the government on November 29, 1861, by William Holt Noble, Captain of the Royal Engineers. The document was as follows:

CANADA LAKES

Memoranda on the assistance which can be rendered to the Province of Canada by Her Majesty's Navy in the event of War with the United States. . . . Absolutely necessary to seize the following American forts at the very outset of the war.

1st—Fort Champlain, at Rouses Point, at the northern end of Lake Champlain; this point is the key of Montreal.

2nd—Fort Niagara, at the mouth of the Niagara River, to obtain the command of the western end of that lake.

3rd—Fort Mackinaw, between Lakes Huron and Michigan; this is the key of those two lakes. Forces, Naval and Military, must defend the Beauharnais Canal which is on the southern or American side of the St. Lawrence River. Also the Cornwall Canal, which is much exposed from its proximity to the American city of Ogdensburg. Also the Welland Canal, in the Niagara peninsula, where all the fighting will in all probability take place.[1]

[1] *Central Registry, File: CR/Q/408*, Part III, p. 9.

The American government, likewise, was not wholly indifferent to the question of naval defence. Petitions received from the states of Michigan and Ohio were referred to Congress. In his despatch of March 24, 1862, to Viscount Monck, Lord Lyons enclosed a copy of the " Report of the Naval Committee of the Senate on the resolutions of State Legislatures requesting Congress to establish Naval Depots on the Lakes." The committee submitted its opinion that the establishment of such Depots would be in direct violation of the Rush-Bagot Treaty of 1817. Mr. Hale submitted on behalf of that Committee in the Senate of the United States, March 10, 1862, the following report :

> The Committee on Naval Affairs, to whom
> were referred the memorials of citizens of the State
> of Michigan, the memorial of the county officers of
> Saginaw County, Michigan, and the petition of citi-
> zens of the State of Michigan, praying the location
> of a naval depot on the Saginaw River in that State ;
> The resolutions of the legislature of Michigan in
> favor of the establishment of a naval station and dock-
> yard in the State of Michigan ; the resolutions of the
> State of Ohio, praying the establishment of a naval
> depot at some point on the western lakes, in the
> State of Ohio ; and the memorial of the mayor and
> city council of the city of Sandusky, Ohio, praying
> the establishment of a naval depot at Bull's Island,
> in Sandusky Bay, have had the same under consideration,
> and submit the following report :
>
> By an " arrangement " entered into and con-
> cluded between the United States and Great Britain
> in April, 1817, it was agreed that the naval forces
> to be maintained upon the American lakes by the two
> governments should henceforth be confined to the
> following vessels on each side, viz :

On Lake Ontario, to one vessel not exceeding one hundred tons burden, and armed with one
eighteen-pound cannon.

On the upper lakes, to two vessels not
exceeding like burden each, and armed with like
force.

On the waters of Lake Champlain, to one
vessel not exceeding like burden, and armed with
like force.

And that all other vessels on those
lakes should be forthwith dismantled *and no other
vessels of war should be there built or armed.*

It was then provided that this stipulation might be annulled
on six month's notice from either government to the other.

The establishment of a naval depot on either of these lakes,
or any river flowing into either of them could have no other
object than the building and equipment of vessels-of-war, and
would as the Committee conceive, to be in direct contravention
of the spirit of that convention, the stipulations of which have
never been annulled, and are now binding upon both the con-
tracting parties.

The Committee do not deem any breach of faith, or of its
treaty obligations on the part of the government, advisable under
and circumstances, and therefore recommend that they be discharged from the further consideration of the above-named
memorials, petitions and resolutions.[1]

The devices used by American recruiting officers to secure
the enlistment of Canadians in the Northern army had
aroused considerable irritation in the British Provinces.
The accusation was frequently made that Canadians were
enticed across the border on one pretext or another, only to
find themselves drafted for service in the field. In his
despatch of August 9, 1864, to Earl Russell, Lord Lyons

[1] *Series G, 230,* Accompanying Despatch, March 24, 1862.

drew the attention of the home government to the determined efforts made by American agents to secure recruits from the British Provinces. Realizing the difficulty of supplying proof in individual cases, he contended that a general system of kidnapping was in operation by means of which recruits in British America were obtained for the Northern army. Although not directly concerned in these practices, the federal government in its eagerness to receive reinforcement secretly if not openly connived in not pressing the investigation of such methods against those who were responsible with the vigor that would insure their discontinuance on the part of minor officials. Holding this opinion Lord Lyons felt that it was his duty to seek redress from Secretary Seward who in his reply stated that he had submitted the information to the Secretary of War for his consideration. Lack of any definite action on the part of the United States government greatly distressed Lord Lyons who was firmly convinced that the number of illegal enlistments of Canadians in the United States army was on the increase. Among the many cases brought to his attention, he declared the most pitiful were those of the French Canadians, often mere boys, "not speaking or understanding English, who had been enticed, deceived, and sometimes kidnapped in the most heartless manner."

Very difficult did he find it, in spite of a voluminous correspondence carried on with the United States Government in behalf of these individuals, to secure any special consideration for them, since there was the same routine for all. The Secretary of State referred them to the Secretary of War who ordered an investigation, or rather called upon the Recruiting Officers for a report. These officials protested that they never enlisted any one except in the most cautious and scrupulous manner; that the allegations in the individual cases were altogether false, and that the enlistments were perfectly legal. Since no other evidence except that of the recruits themselves was admitted, the United States government accepts the report of its own officers and keeps the men. In order that the British government might be in possession of all the information in connection with the illegal enlistment of British citizens, Lord Lyons transferred to Lord Russell copies of three despatches from Mr. Donohue, Her Majesty's Consul at Buffalo, which conveyed a general idea of the nature and extent of the devices used to secure soldiers for the North, and in addition copies of his own correspondence on the subject, both to the Governor-General of Canada and Secretary Seward. Feeling keenly his own powerlessness, Lord Lyons urged the former to suggest further steps that could be taken by him in order to induce the United States government " to cooperate with the Canadian authorities in efforts to put a stop to the nefarious practices." [1]

In his despatch of August 25, 1864, to Lord Lyons, Earl Russell expressed the confidence of the British government in the willingness of the United States government to prevent such illegal enlistments in the future, and in token thereof, expected a satisfactory answer from Seward to the remonstrances which Lord Lyons had addressed to him in behalf of the unfortunate victims. [2] In the meantime Lord Lyons was instructed to continue his protest in such cases.

The duties of a British minister were indeed manifold. The task of safeguarding Canadian interests without doing anything contrary to the wishes of the Home government was a delicate one, calling for the keenest vigilance. Some of the pretexts to entice the Canadians across the frontier were somewhat ingenious. For instance, F. Lousada, British Consul at Boston, reported to Lord Lyons, December

---

[1] *Series G, 233*, No. 568.

[2] *Ibid.*, No. 397.

5, 1863, that one of the agents, liberally supplied with funds, had visited him with the intention of finding out just " how far the recruiting law of Canada would touch him and his partner if he attempted to secure recruits there." To this question the British Consul replied that the practice was illegal. The agent then hazarded the statement that " he supposed it was no harm to invite men over the boundary line to have a good time at a farm on this side of it; and that they would be free to do as they pleased." [1] From these remarks, and others of a similar nature, the Consul was convinced that either the United States government or others with its connivance were attempting to secure the enlistment of British subjects by illegal means. High premiums were also offered as a further inducement to Canadians to enlist.

Recruiting agents, under the designation of a committee of the Stone Quarries of Vermont, induced one of their members to ask the Consul to sign a certificate under his consular seal that " aliens not naturalized [were] not compelled to serve in the armies of the United States." He presented the plea that the apprehension of military service in the United States stood in " the way of obtaining a very fair supply of laborers for the Welsh Quarries." [2] The request was refused. The two reasons assigned by Consul Lousada for his refusal to grant such a request were cited in a memorandum. Although he was aware that the law was as cited above, namely, that theoretically foreigners in the United States were not compelled to serve in the army, yet practically, under existing conditions by means almost amounting to compulsion, he was equally convinced that they were being forced into the service. Knowing therefore that his certificate might be a device to entice Canadians across the border, believing themselves secure from the draft, he declined to

[1] *Series G, 231,* p. 339.

[2] *Ibid.,* p. 343.

sign it. That his suspicion was correct is undoubtedly established by the applicant's admission that such use might be made of the document.[1] The memorandum was endorsed by Lord Lyons. Consul Lousada was instructed to forward any further information regarding names, dates, places, that he could procure with regard to the recruiting in order that the Canadian authorities might be assisted in the detection of persons who should be brought to justice.

The efforts made by the Canadian government through Lord Lyons to secure the release from the Northern army of Canadians who were minors were largely unavailing. In a letter to Viscount Monck, as early as January 13, 1862, Lord Lyons suggested that all applicants requesting the Canadian government to obtain the discharge of their sons from the Northern army should be informed that in all probability the American government would not comply with their requests. The repeal of the fifth section of the Act of September 28, 1850, which had provided for the discharge of minors who had enlisted in the United States Army without the consent of their parents or guardians, was approved by Congress, February 22, 1862. A provision was enacted that "hereafter no person under the age of eighteen shall be mustered into the United States Service and the oath of enlistment taken by the recruit shall be conclusive as to his age." Although Lord Lyons continued to present certain petitions relative to the discharge of minors, the passage of the above-mentioned provision rendered practically futile all his efforts. The petitions presented by well-nigh frantic parents undoubtedly evoked the sympathy of Lord Lyons, but sympathy was all he had to offer.

Taking advantage of the difficulties which confronted the American government, the Sioux Indians in Minnesota organized a rebellion. After committing the usual Indian

---

[1] *Series G, 231* p. 344, Memorandum.

barbarities upon the white people of that state, the Sioux Indians took refuge in British territory. The Canadian government was desirous of doing all in its power to prevent hostile Indians on either side of the line from being supplied with arms and other supplies to be used against the people of the United States. In accordance with the desire of the Canadian government, William McDougall, Superintendent General of Indian Affairs, sent his instructions to the officers of the Hudson Bay Territory, the British authorities in the West. The Sioux Indians who had murdered men, women and children in the state of Minnesota to the number, variously estimated, of eight hundred to a thousand, had sought refuge along the Red River of the North. Although the British government did not possess a police force sufficiently powerful in this region to prevent the Indians from committing further depredations, the request of the United States government for permission to pursue the hostile Indians across the border was refused. Major General Pope, Commander of the North West Department, forwarded to Washington a statement of his opinion that the Canadian government should either take action against the Indians or permit the American government to do so, for if the Indians were permitted to find a safe refuge on British soil, he feared that they would continue to make raids into Minnesota, and there murder helpless women and children. In view of the fact that within a few miles of British territory there was a sufficient force of United States soldiers to exterminate these Indians, it seemed unjust to him that they should be powerless to act.[1] Major General Pope contended that the suggestion which had been made to him to ask for their extradition was impracticable, since the Indians exceeded in num-

---

[1] *Series G, 232,* Letter of Major General Pope, Headquarters Department of the Northwest, to Col. T. C. Kelton, Headquarters of the Army, Washington, D. C., January 12, 1864.

ber and strength, the British settlers among whom they
dwelt.   Mr. Seward referred the matter to Lord Lyons, who
continued to refuse permission to the United States to pursue hostile Indians across the line.   Realizing that a grave
international crisis might arise as the result of further depredations planned on British soil, Lord Lyons forwarded a
despatch relative to the Indians to Viscount Monck.   The
Deputy Governor of the Hudson Bay Territory was urged
to take the necessary precautions in order to forestall any
plans of the Indians to injure citizens of the United States.
As there were no further American protests recorded, the
precautionary measures taken were evidently adequate.   In
spite of the efforts of the Americans to have the Indians
return to the United States, they remained in the North
West Territory.   In 1870 when the province of Manitoba
was established, these Indians asked to be allowed to settle
on a reserve in that province.   In 1873 the Canadian government permitted this settlement, but informed the Indians
that their case was exceptional; moreover, the reserve was
for themselves alone, and the Sioux in the United States
must remain there.   On April 20, 1873, an order in council,
Ottawa, authorized the continuance under the British flag
of a band of Sioux who immigrated into the North West.[2]

In March, 1864, the restrictions placed upon the exportation of live stock and anthracite coal from the United States
to the British North American Provinces threatened to be a
real hardship to the inhabitants of British North America.
In the imposition of this measure, Seward declared that the
United States government was not actuated by any un-
friendly spirit toward Great Britain, but by the exigencies
of the time.   The military and naval forces of the United

---

[1] *The Treaties of Canada with the Indians, of Manitoba the Northwest
Territories and Teewatin.*   The Hon. Alexander Norris, late Lieut.-Gov.
of Manitoba, the Northwest Territories and Teewatin.

States needed the meat.   With regard to the anthracite coal, there was a prevalent opinion that the Confederates in Canada were supplying themselves with that article needed for their blockade runners.   Motives of self-preservation, therefore, prompted the United States to place temporary restrictions upon the exportation of live stock and anthracite coal, even though this measure was a serious inconvenience to the trade of the British North American Provinces.   Probably realizing that any attempt to secure the removal of the restrictions upon live-stock would be futile, the Canadian government apparently made no such effort.   A committee of the Executive Council of Canada acting upon the advice of the Minister of Finance did, however, recommend that Lord Lyons again bring the matter of anthracite coal to the attention of the Secretary of State, pledging that in the event of the removal of restrictions, Canada would be prepared to prohibit its exportation from any Canadian port.   Thus a valuable trade might be preserved to the United States and Canada without involving any risk that the article in question might be used by the enemies of the United States.[1] Due to the action taken by the Canadian Government, August 17, 1864, the Treasury Department of the United States issued a statement that the restrictions on the exportation of anthracite coal into Canada, except by sea, had been removed.[2]

The conduct of the American authorities on the border in their efforts to enforce the draft, aroused the indignation of the Canadians.   Naturally the American officers on the border found the task of enforcing the draft complicated by their proximity to British territory, for the Northern draft-

[1] *Series G, 232*, p. 255, Copy of a Report of a Committee of the Hon. the Executive Council approved by His Excellency the Gov. Gen. on the 3rd of May, 1864.

[2] *Cf. Series G, 233*, p. 174, U. S. Treasury Department, August 17, 1864, signed by Geo. Harrington, Acting Secretary of the Treasury.

evader readily turned his face toward Canada. In a letter marked private and confidential, addressed to Secretary Seward, William Stuart, acting in the absence of Lord Lyons, drew the attention of the American government to the existence of a feeling of irritation in Canada which might be allayed by a timely warning from the administration in Washington to the American officers to discharge their duty in a conciliatory spirit, instead of needlessly antagonizing the Canadians. The complaint was made that Canadians in boats, and even soldiers in British uniform, had been fired upon by the United States sentries stationed at Niagara.[1] Gratefully acknowledging the friendly spirit that had prompted the letter, Secretary Seward assured Stuart that the civil authorities on the frontier would be " cautioned to practice the utmost justice, forbearance, moderation and courtesy toward British subjects " in the discharge of the duties which devolved upon them as American officials.[2]

Many were the stories that circulated with regard to the plots of the Confederate refugees in Canada. If the Canadian government had not shown conscientious vigilance in the transmission of information regarding suspicious circumstances, Confederate raids upon the Northern cities of the United States would undoubtedly have materialized. As the war progressed, the number of Confederate refugees in Canada increased. Escaped prisoners from the Northern prisons found their way northward to British territory. As was only natural, these Confederates, desirous of aiding the South, planned raids upon the cities of the North. Lieutenant Colonel Hill, who was stationed on the Northern frontier, with his headquarters at Detroit, estimated that there were nearly " 2000 rebel refugees, escaped prisoners, and active rebel sympathizers in Canada." [3]

[1] *Series G, 230*, p. 159.
[2] *Ibid.*, p. 164.
[3] *Series G, 230*, p. 279.

In November, 1863, rumors circulated that the Confederates were planning to cross the Canadian border into the United States to destroy the city of Buffalo. Furthermore, steamboats on Lake Erie, it was alleged, were to be seized, Johnson's Island surprised, and the Confederate prisoners there liberated. Information regarding these plans, corresponding very closely to that transmitted by Colonel Hill to the American government, was forwarded by Viscount Monck to Washington. The Canadian government took all the precautions in its power to frustrate the project.[1] Orders were issued that the Welland Canal should be watched very closely. Any steamboat which aroused suspicions as to its character was to be detained. Realizing that this information might be of grave import, the Canadian government lost no time in its transmission by telegram to Lord Lyons, and although the telegram was received at a late hour at night, the minister immediately communicated its contents to Secretary Seward. The War Department at once despatched the needed reinforcement; the guard on the island was increased by five hundred, and all necessary precautions were taken to insure its safety. A volunteer militia force of two thousand was ordered to assemble at Sandusky; and the volunteer forces at Cleveland and Toledo were ordered " to hold themselves in readiness to come out at a moment's warning." On November 15, 1863, the Secretary of War, Stanton, received a telegram from Brigadier General Cox, Commander of the Army of the Ohio, that a " Despatch from Detroit says, Rebels who left Windsor to join the raid, are returning, saying that the plans are frustrated for the present, and will have to be postponed for a time. I regard this as ending the immediate danger, but will keep the force here as it is, till the above is confirmed." [2]

[1] *Ibid.*, p. 268.
[2] *Ibid.*, p. 297.

Throughout the year 1864, stories continued to circulate regarding Confederate plots to invade the United States from Canada. The Canadian and American Governments worked in unison to frustrate these plans. Information each received, was exchanged for the guidance of the other. On May 26, 1864, the United States Consul, Howard, at St. John, New Brunswick, reported that " an unusually large number of disloyal citizens of the United States have recently passed through the city enroute for Canada via Fredericton, and Rivière du Loup. The greater part of these insurgents have been living for some months in Halifax, others have found their way north from Nassau and Bermuda. The rebel General Frost has also recently proceeded to Canada from St. John." [1] Consul Howard believed that this activity on the part of the Confederates indicated that they were planning a raid upon the Northern cities. On July 30, 1864, another alarm was raised. The American Government received information, similar in character to that reported by Consul Howard, from Colonel Hill.

Jacob Thompson arrived in Canada having in his possession credentials received from Jefferson Davis, April 27, 1864:

Confiding special trust in your zeal, discretion, and patriotism, I hereby direct you to proceed at once to Canada, there to carry out such instructions as you have received from me verbally in such manner as shall seem most likely to conduce to the furtherance of the interests of the Confederate States of America which have been entrusted to you.[2]

Under Thompson's leadership an attempt was made to carry out the plot which had for its object the seizure of the *Michigan,* the only American warship on the great lakes,

[1] *Series G, 232,* p. 283.
[2] James Ford Rhodes, *History of the United States,* vol. v, p. 330.

and the release of the Confederate prisoners on Johnson's Island.   The plot having been disclosed to the lieutenant-colonel commanding at Detroit, the necessary measures were taken to defeat it.   Various other schemes for which Thompson was largely responsible likewise failed; for instance, the plot to burn New York City was a disappointment because the Greek fire, upon which the Confederate agents had depended, failed to spread with the expected rapidity, and it was therefore possible to extinguish the fires.   Thompson's complaint, elsewhere noted, that "the bane and curse of carrying out anything in this country [Canada] is the surveillance under which we act," was a high tribute to the constant vigilance of the Canadian officials.[1]

In spite of the numerous reports of Confederate plans for the invasion of the United States from Canada, the St. Albans raid was the only one which was attempted.   About twenty-five Confederate soldiers, under the leadership of Lieutenant Bennett H. Young, attempted to burn the town of St. Albans, Vermont.   The failure of the chemicals to explode alone saved the town.   Before retreating to Canada, the Confederates robbed three banks.   The men of St. Albans who organized a party to pursue the Confederates, did not overtake them until British territory was reached. Upon their arrival in Montreal the Confederates were arrested.   Under the Extradition Treaty, existing between the two countries, the American government made an appeal for the surrender of the prisoners.   Undoubtedly Lieutenant Young was acting in accordance with his instructions from the Confederate government.   The Canadian government had in its possession intercepted correspondence addressed to J. P. Benjamin, the Confederate Secretary of State, which proved beyond a doubt that the Southern Confederacy was implicated in the raid, for Lieutenant Young's instructions

[1] *Ibid.*, vol. v, p. 337.

gave ample justification for the attack " in the way of retaliation." [1] The excitement did not subside with the failure
of the St. Albans raid. The Governor of Vermont, Mr.
Edmunds, stated that further raids were planned. The Confederate plans, as reported by him, included the destruction
of Burlington as well as St. Albans.[2] No part of this program was carried out, but some time elapsed before the excitement subsided. Major General Dix considered that further troops were needed to insure the safety of the Northern
cities. In spite of the efforts of the Canadian government
to preserve the neutrality of Her Majesty's domain, there
were many Americans, General Dix included, who blamed it
for the Confederate plots. A formal protest against the
use of British territory as a war base by the Confederates
was presented to Great Britain.[3] Certainly the measures
adopted by the Canadian government to preserve the peace,
were thought inadequate by large sections of the American
people; indeed there were some who even threatened a raid
upon Kingston, Canada, in retaliation for the St. Albans
raid. Acting in good faith, in accordance with the usual
government policy, the administration at Washington notified
the Canadian government of the threatened expedition, at
the same time assuring them that the United States officers
had received orders to prevent such a retaliatory act.

A few of the precautions which had been taken by
Canadian authorities to insure the safety of the frontier
were mentioned by Viscount Monck, in his despatch of
December 20, 1864. In response to the letter relative to the
apprehended attempts of persons hostile to the United States

[1] *Series G, 234*, Intercepted Correspondence received from the Secretary
of State by J. H. Burnley and forwarded to Viscount Monck, Dec. 21,
1864, p. 191.

[2] *Ibid.*, Extract sent by Mr. Seward to Lord Lyons, November 22, 1864.

[3] *M 11616*, Department of State, Washington, December 6, 1864.

from Canada, " he declared that as precautionary measures he had established a detective police force under stipendiary magistrates along the border, and had " called out for permanent duty a strong force of the volunteer militia " to be stationed on the frontier.[1] Furthermore the Canadian government considered that the clues afforded by the intercepted correspondence furnished sufficient evidence against the Confederates to warrant an investigation. This investigation was conducted under the leadership of John A. Macdonald, Attorney General for Canada West. Realizing that the surrender of General Lee at Appomattox, April 14, 1865, virtually ended the war, Macdonald suggested that no action should be taken on the written information unless new circumstances should arise calling for some proceeding therein.[2] The need for government action had passed.

To the political leaders on both sides throughout the period of the American Civil War, much of the credit for the preservation of peace between the United States and Great Britain must be given. The diplomatic history of this period is one of which an American and a Canadian may both be proud. In addressing the American Newspaper Publishers' Association, April 24, 1924, Sir Esme Howard, British Ambassador, thus defined the diplomat's creed, a creed which may well be said to have guided British and American diplomats throughout the period of the American Civil War:

To serve the country to the best of one's ability, more no one can do; carrying out instructions, but in such a way as not to give offense, keeping a cool head and an open mind, avoiding suspicion, irritation and distrust; dealing fairly, honestly and truthfully, and, last but not least, politely, and always giving a

[1] *Series G, 234*, Despatch, December 20, 1864, to J. H. Burnley from Viscount Monck.

[2] *Canadian Archives Paper*, 11750.

fair consideration to the point of view of others. The fact is that what are called diplomatic triumphs and successes are generally gained at too great a sacrifice, just as military victories are, and in most cases it is better to sacrifice the less in order to obtain a settlement of a dispute by consent than to make what is ultimately the greater sacrifice, that of mutual trust and good-will in order to secure an apparent success.[1]

As an illustration of the spirit of British diplomats in the sixties, an incident of the Civil War related by Sir Esme might well be considered. "Lyons received from London a note of protest against certain actions of the American government which he was instructed to deliver. It was so sharp in tone that he feared that if he delivered it, it might even result in a breach of diplomatic relations." He, therefore, went to President Lincoln and showed him the note privately, informing him that he had received instructions to deliver it, but that he feared the consequences of doing so, and asked the President to anticipate the delivery of the note by some friendly message which would enable him to inform his government that the note was no longer advisable. The President at once agreed, sent a message, the note was not delivered and a serious situation was averted.[2]

[1] The *New York Times*, April 25, 1924.
[2] *Cf. ibid.*

CHAPTER VII

The Triumph of the North

Hostility to Canada—How Far Justified by Facts? Repeal of the Reciprocity Treaty—Attempts to Renew it—Fenian Raids—A Closer Union of the Provinces—Confederation—The Treaty of Washington.

WAS the underlying Northern resentment that had smouldered fitfully throughout the Civil War against British North America, now the refuge of the Confederate, as it had once been of the slave, to blaze forth in hostility? Were the oft-repeated threats of the section of the northern press, hostile to Great Britain, notably the *New York Herald*, to be fulfilled? The British North American governments, as has been shown, had made every effort to prevent the violation of her Majesty's territory. Firmly believing in the righteousness of its cause, the North was displeased by the sympathy evidenced by many Canadians for the Confederates, if not for their cause. Then, as has ever been the case in disputes which have arisen between the United States and Great Britain, the lesser offender, Canada, not the greater offender, Great Britain, has borne the brunt of the resentment aroused in the United States. The American Civil War, undoubtedly, was fraught with momentous consequences to Canada, both from an economic and political standpoint.

The threat to repeal the Reciprocity Treaty, heard at intervals throughout the progress of the war, was fulfilled. As far back as March, 1861, a resolution of Congress accused the Canadian government of having violated the spirit of the treaty by the imposition of heavy duties on many

194   [482

articles which the United States had to sell, while nearly all
Canadian exports were admitted free of duty; and, further,
the accusation was made that Canadian legislation had imposed " discriminating tolls and duties in favor of an isolat
ing and exclusive policy " against American merchants and
forwarders, "meant and intended to destroy the natural
effect of the treaty and contrary to its spirit." [1]

The discussion on this subject also resulted in the passage
of a resolution by which the Senators and Representatives
from New York state in Congress were requested to take
the necessary measures for the appointment of commissioners
to confer with persons designated by the Canadian government with regard to "the unequal and unjust system of
commerce " which that state believed existed between the
two countries.   Since the prevailing opinion, especially in
New York, was that the interests of the United States were
not adequately protected in accordance with the terms of the
treaty, the commissioners should consider what further regulations were required.   At the time of its passage free trade
sentiment was at its height in both countries.   Shortly
afterwards there was a strong reaction in favor of protection; especially was that true in New York where the merchants wished to secure a monopoly of the western trade for
the Erie Canal.   Under the treaty the merchants of the West
had a choice between the Canadian route and the American
one.

The Montreal *Gazette* of March 13, 1861, in its comment,
expressed its surprise that resolutions of such a nature should
have been passed in the Senate of the United States.

Canada has more faithfully observed both the letter and spirit
of the Reciprocity Treaty than the United States.   The United
States never fulfilled all the conditions of the Treaty; not only

---

[1] The Montreal *Gazette*, March 13, 1861.

have they not done so, but they have hampered it with petty annoyances. The terms of the Treaty leave no room for quibbling about its " spirit ". For certain plainly mentioned conditions they agreed to grant certain other plainly mentioned conditions for a given number of years; and concluded a solemn contract.

And we are not to be bullied into concessions inimical to the true interests of Canada by the " tomtom " Chinese warfare of empty threats. We believe that it can be demonstrated that the United States, as a whole, have gained more than Canada; and if in the present situation of affairs at Washington, Mr. Seward and particular New York State interests, have been able to get such a resolution through the United States Senate, they may come to find that the general public interests of the whole country may have something to say in the matter before a final decision comes. After such a tariff [1] as that just passed by the Congress of the United States, it is not often one meets anything so refreshingly cool as this Senate resolution about the " spirit " of the Reciprocity Treaty.

The resolutions of the United States Senate were directed against the province of Canada, not the Maritime Provinces. Galt, Canadian Minister of Finance, as has been previously noted, ably answered all charges, claiming that any additional duties had been levied with the purpose of aiding Canada, not of injuring the United States.[2] It must not be forgotten that the Reciprocity Treaty had been ratified through the aid of the Southern Senators, influential in pre-war days. Throughout the war period their absence from Congress meant a reaction in favor of protection. Realizing full well the financial loss [3] to both countries, if the Reciprocity Treaty were repealed, Galt made his first diplomatic trip to Washing-

[1] Morrill Tariff.

[2] *Cf.* O. D. Skelton, *Life and Times of Sir Alexander Tilloch Galt*, p. 927.

[3] *Confederation Debates*, pp. 62-67.

ton, but all his efforts were in vain.   However unjustifiable
the resentment may have been, and unjustifiable it undoubtedly was as far as the Canadian government was concerned,
there nevertheless existed in the United States at the termination of the Civil War a bitter feeling of hostility toward
Canada.   To satisfy the popular demand, the American Government was prepared to wage trade warfare.   Formal notice
was given of the abrogation of the treaty in March, 1866.

Unwilling to relinquish the idea of a renewal of the
Reciprocity Treaty, Galt made another trip to Washington.
After a consultation with Sir Frederick Bruce, the British
Ambassador, he had several interviews with McCulloch, the
Secretary of the Treasury.   The latter refused to consider
a renewal of the treaty, but suggested reciprocal legislation.
Realizing the difficulties that would have to be confronted
in passing the necessary legislation through six legislatures,
Galt was loath to accept the suggestion.   In his opposition
to a renewal of the treaty, McCulloch received the support
of Seward.   Later Galt explained the attitude of Seward
toward the question of Reciprocity to a Canadian Cabinet, in
the course of which he explained that no new treaty could be
recommended by the United States government for reasons
which could not properly be made public.   Declaring himself
friendly to Canada, Seward advised Galt to see the Chairmen
of the Ways and Means Committee and the Finance Committee, as soon as the committees of Congress were organized, with the object of reaching a trade agreement satisfactory to both countries.[1]

Able financier that he was, Galt was at last convinced that
reciprocal legislation was at this time the only possible trade
concession that the United States would consider.   Upon
his return to Canada, therefore, he prepared a memorandum,
embodying a statement of his opinion, in which he urged

---

[1] *Cf.* O. D. Skelton, *Life and Times of A. T. Galt*, p. 392.

upon the Canadian legislature such a program in view of
the fact that the United States continued to refuse a renewal
of the treaty.   In the Cabinet, George Brown, the Liberal
leader, denounced the memorandum with its suggestion of
reciprocal legislation, which he said left Canada dependent
upon the whims of Congress.   The instability of such an
arrangement was apparent to all Canadians.   To the further
charge that the Maritime Provinces should have been consulted, Galt replied that his negotiations were not due to
any desire on his part that Canada should adopt a separate
policy, but to the emergency that did not justify the delay
involved in waiting for action by the British American
provinces as a whole.   With the exception of Brown, the
other members of the Cabinet approved the proposals and
appointed Galt and W. P. Howland,[1] as the Canadian delegates, to continue the negotiations with the United States
government.

On the next trip to Washington, Galt and Howland were
accompanied by two delegates from the Maritime Provinces.
This experience convined the Canadian delegates that
further efforts to secure concessions were vain, for Congress
was unwilling to pass the reciprocal legislation.   On March
31, 1866, the formal notice of the termination of the
Reciprocity Treaty took effect.   Although Galt had convinced the administration officials that such reciprocal legislation might be beneficial to both countries, he was unable
to convince Congress.   Sir Frederick Bruce, the British
Ambassador at Washington, in his letter of February 19,
1866, to Lord Monck, Governor of Canada, approved the

[1] *Cf.* edited by J. O. Coté, Notary Public and Clerk in the Executive
Council Office, *Political Appointments and Elections in the Provinces of
Canada*, 1841-1865.   Howland was not in office at this time.   From May
24, 1864, he was a member of the Executive Council; in addition, he held
other government offices.

services rendered by Galt, " Mr. Galt's knowledge, ability and fair spirit made a very favorable impression on the members of the Committee and the Secretary of the Treasury." [1]

In addition to the two reasons which have been cited for the American opposition to a renewal of the Reciprocity Treaty, namely, hostility to Canada, due in part to the Civil War, and the reaction in favor of high protection, there was a third reason based on a widely prevalent opinion throughout the United States that a refusal to continue the treaty would force the British North American Provinces into a political union with the neighboring Republic. This third reason, Howe declared at the Detroit Convention, July, 1865, resulted from a total misconception of opinion in these Provinces. Howe expressed himself thus:

I know that it has been asserted by some and I have heard it uttered since I came to the convention, that if the reciprocity treaty is annulled the British Provinces will be so cramped that they will be compelled to seek annexation to the United States. I beg to be allowed to say on that point that no man knows better the feeling in the Lower Provinces, and I believe I am well enough acquainted with the Canadians to speak for them all, with such exceptions as must be made when speaking for an entire population, when I make the assertion that no consideration of finance, no question of balance for or against them, upon interchange of commodities, can have any influence upon the loyalty of the inhabitants of the British Provinces, or tend in the slightest degree to alienate the affections of the people from their country, their institutions, their government, and their Queen. There is not a loyal man in the British American Provinces, not a man worthy of the name, who, whatever may happen to the treaty,—will be any the less loyal, any the less true to his country on that account. There is not a man who would dare, on the abrogation of the treaty, if such should be

[1] *Series G, 237.*

its fate, take the hustings and appeal to any constituency on annexation principles throughout the entire domain. The man who avows such a sentiment will be scouted from society by his best friends. . . .

In concluding his address, he told the Americans that he did not believe that there was a young Canadian in the American army who did not love his own flag as they loved theirs, and that if he did not, he ought to be despised. If any member of the Convention, therefore, harbored the idea that by refusing Reciprocity to British America, he was undermining the loyal feelings of these colonies, he was "laboring under a delusion and fostering an imputation upon the character and integrity of an honorable people of the most dastardly kind that can, by any possibility, receive a lodgment in his breast." [1]   Who was better qualified to be the spokesman of the British North American Provinces in the United States than Howe whose undoubted sympathy for the North had been strengthened by the fact that one of his sons had served in the Northern Army?

In its refusal to renew the Reciprocity Treaty the United States government was more influenced by the popular desire to penalize the British North American Provinces than by the commercial benefits derived by both countries. The refusal to renew the treaty was, therefore, not regarded as final. The Canadian viewpoint, voiced by George Brown, was that the practical good sense of the American people in view of the balance sheet resulting from the treaty of 1854 would not permit them to persist in their refusal to renew the treaty. Although the American statesmen in view of the anti-Canadian feeling aroused in the United States by the events of the late war did not deem it well to ignore popular opinion of the moment, Canada was determined to play " a

[1] The Halifax *Citizen*, July 29, 1865.

good neighbor's part, and incidentally serve her own ends by continuing to grant the United States most of the privileges which had been given under the treaty—free navigation and free goods, and subject to a license fee, access to the fisheries."[1]

The commercial warfare, of which the abrogation of the Reciprocity Treaty was the sign, did not wholly satisfy a certain anti-British element in the United States, namely, the Fenians, who demanded further acts of hostility, even invasion. The Fenians had a secret Irish organization, and to it quite naturally, belonged many of the Irish soldiers serving in the Northern army. As early as September 16, 1865, E. M. Archibald, British Consul at New York, forwarded to Lord Monck a confidential despatch, relative to the Fenians. This document reported "increasing activity on the part of the Fenians, who are using every effort to despatch both men and arms to Ireland with the view of aiding an insurrectionary movement which I have good reason to believe will be seriously attempted in the course of the autumn." The danger was, however, nearer the British North American Provinces for the writer continued thus:

I have at the same time, reason to suspect that an attempt will shortly be made to create disturbance on the Canadian frontier. From the reports which have been communicated to me and which are not very different I incline to believe that a number of outlaws, men who have been in the United States Military service and who are probably Fenians, will organize a raid or raids for the purpose of plundering Banks and committing outrages on Canadian towns near the frontier. Vague as is this information I deem it proper to communicate it, at once, to your Lordship, in order that the attention of the Police may be called to the matter.[2]

[1] *Memoir on Proposed Reciprocity Treaty*, 1874.

[2] *Series G, 236*, Confidential E. M. Archibald, British Consulate, to Lord Monck, September 16, 1865.

That the invasion of Canada by the Fenians was not merely the unpremeditated attack of a few lawless men may be proved by the fact that their plans were all carefully formulated in a committee meeting representing a considerable organization.   An extract of a secret despatch from Consul Archibald to Earl Russell, Her Majesty's Secretary of State for Foreign Affairs, revealed certain plans.   In the fall of 1865, a Fenian Convention was held in Philadelphia. Changes were made in the constitution of the organization. Colonel Omahony was elected President.   To one of the visitors at this convention, who later informed Consul Archibald of the conversation, the President of this society said that as yet the Fenians had determined upon no definite course of action, but that every effort was being made to secure money, arms and volunteers, in order to be ready for action at the proper time.   Referring to Ireland, he said that no direct aid for the present would be rendered that country, but that an attempt would be made to encourage their Irish fellow conspirators and thus prepare for future insurrection in that country by a raid into Canada where in cooperation with the Fenians there a provisional republican government, authorizing the seizure and destruction of British ships, would be established.   The press of Canada and the United States freely discussed the probability of a Fenian attack on the province.   Such a movement seemed all the more probable since Omahony had declared in his address at the Convention that the enemy against whom the first blow would fall would least expect it.   Those who were able to give information concurred in the opinion that an attack would be first made on Canada—adjoining British territory and hence most easily available—with the immediate object in view of causing a rupture between Great Britain and the United States.   Although convinced that the United States authorities would notice any movement in the direction of

Canada and would make every effort to repress it, Consul Archibald yet believed that the raid might be carried out in such a tumultuous manner that serious damage might be done to some Canadian towns. Firmly believing that the publicity given the Fenians was largely for political purposes, namely, to secure votes, the Consul said that after the State election in New York, which was to take place shortly, little would be seen in print concerning them. In view of the disclosures that had been made to him, he considered that he had reason for believing that the Fenians contemplated an invasion of Canada:

In confirmation of the apprehension of such a movement, I may add that an intelligent man who has for nine months been a member of the Fara Circle of Brooklyn, which meets near the City Hall, tells me that they have received an order from Omahony (which he believes has also been issued to other circles) for Volunteers to hold themselves in readiness at short notice, when required. He further informs me that this Circle has increased in number from thirty to three hundred and eighty members within a year;—that the members of it possess four hundred stand of arms, but no ammunition; and that the drilling of their number is regularly practiced once or twice a week.[1]

Furthermore, Consul Archibald's attempt to investigate the financial strength of the Fenian organization led to interesting revelations. The money collected from Irish sympathizers was kept in the safe of the organization, not in the banks. Consul Archibald reported that a personal friend, a prominent banker of New York, had told him that the officers of the Fenian Organization had called upon the head of a certain bank to ask that his institution take charge of their funds. In their possession they had a cheque for between five thousand and six thousand in gold contributed

[1] *Series G, 236*, enclosure in a despatch of Archibald to Sir John Michel, November 1, 1865.

by the Fenians in California, and to this sum they hoped to add from time to time the money collected. Their desire was to open a checking account from which money might be drawn if the cheques were endorsed by Omahony and two other members of the organization. Since the president of the bank was an Irishman by birth, Omahony had relied upon his sympathy with the Fenian organization. This expectation was unrealized. The banker, believing that the Fenians would by their course of action only increase the misery of the poor people in Ireland, refused to accept their deposits. Omahony replied that the Fenians had abandoned the idea of inciting insurrection in Ireland.

The banker then asked Omahony of what use was their plotting for the invasion of Canada;—that they could not carry out their project unless through a War between England and the United States,—and that, at the utmost it would be only a disgraceful plundering raid. Omahony replied that there was more in the matter than was generally supposed; and hinted that prominent parties in the United States government were encouraging the movement. The banker replied that some of the political leaders would, doubtless, cajole the Fenians so long as they could make them useful, but that he was sure the Government would interfere to repress any movement as soon as a demonstration were made.[1]

Undoubtedly the banker was correct in his diagnosis of the attitude frequently adopted by certain politicians, unwilling to lose the Irish vote. If, however, any hostile movement was undertaken against Canada as an outlet for the anti-British feeling, the United States government would strive to check it.

The Fenians had so often declared their purpose of invading Canada that many of the inhabitants of both the United States and Canada did not believe them. In spite,

[1] *Ibid.*, Letter of Consul Archibald to Lieut. General Sir John Michel.

therefore, of numerous warnings, their invasion of Canada found the United States government unprepared to prevent the violation of British territory. The telegram despatched by Consul Archibald to Governor Gordon of New Brunswick, June 2, 1866, gives an account of the invasion:

The following are the probable facts extracted from conflicting telegrams. About fifteen hundred Fenians crossed near Lake Erie early yesterday morning and moved toward Chippewa —well armed but without adequate supplies. The United States Forces are now patrolling river and prevent any others crossing. General Grant is at Buffalo and advises calling out Militia to prevent hostile expedition leaving New York side and plundering by mobs.

Volunteers and regulars from Toronto on the ground and forces rapidly increasing.

An engagement with Fenians by Volunteer regiment, Queen's Own, at Ridgeway seven miles above Fort Erie reported from Toronto as a rout of the Fenians, but from Buffalo the reverse. Fenians are moving from different cities towards northern frontier, but the Canadians will give good account of them all.

About four or five hundred Fenians are at St. Albans and more moving thither.

U. S. Regular troops are also proceeding to St. Albans.

The invasion will be a complete failure.[1]

The Candians drove back the Fenians, but not without bloodshed. Later the Canadian government presented a claim to the United States government for damages inflicted by the Fenian raid of 1866. The Fenians captured in Canada were sentenced to death. Later their sentences were commuted to imprisonment for a certain term of years, the maximum penalty being twenty years' imprisonment. The two reasons for the commutation of the death penalty, as stated by Lord Monck, were: first, that representation on behalf of the convicted Fenians had been made by the United

---

[1] C 1864 Fenian Raid, pp. 443-5.

States Secretary of State to the British Ambassador at Washington, and transmitted by him to the British Secretary of State for Foreign Affairs; and second, that the unanimous opinion of his Canadian Council in which he entirely concurred was that the death sentence in these cases should not be enforced.

In view of the fact, however, that the Fenian Society in the United States was still in existence and showed no abatement of its sentiments of hostility to Canada, his opinion was that the convicts " should not be allowed to escape without the infliction of some adequate punishment." [1]

For a number of years there were successive rumors of further Fenian raids. Realizing the military advantage to be derived if their request were granted, the Ottawa authorities applied to those in Washington for permission, in case of need, " to British armed vessels, or vessels carrying troops, or military stores to pass through certain waters of Lake Champlain without delay from the Customs' Authorities of the United States." This request made with the purpose in mind of pursuing the Fenians if necessary, somewhat similar in nature to that made by the United States government to pursue the hostile Sioux Indians on British soil, was, likewise, refused.

In his refusal of the request, Seward stated that he could not recommend to the President that such permission should be granted; moreover, he doubted whether the government had the power to concede it, for the jurisdiction of such internal waters as those of Lake Champlain did not belong to the federal government, but to the states in which they were situated. Since he thought the mere suggestion that United States waters might be used for hostile purposes against the Fenians would be very unpopular in the United

---

[1] *Series G, 466*, To Secretary of State 1866, vol. xii, no. 183, Despatch to the Right Honorable, The Earl of Carnarvon.

States, he urged that this proposal of the Canadian government be kept a secret. Then he added that the information which he had recently received led him to believe that the Fenians " neither had the power nor intended to attempt any aggression upon Canada for the present." [1]

The American Civil War with its aftermath of American hostility toward the British North American Provinces, of which the repeal of the Reciprocity Treaty and the Fenian raids were the outward and visible expression, undoubtedly hastened the federation of these British provinces. The friction, the danger of war with the United States, impressed anew upon the provinces the need of a closer union than that which consisted in a common loyalty to the British Crown. There had been, however, a number of earlier proposals for a British North American union. In 1858, Galt illustrated the need of union thus: " It is the old story of the bundle of sticks, the provinces now are liable to be every one of them broken in detail by the United States, while united they could withstand any power on this continent." [2] In the same year, Galt put forward a practicable scheme for a federal union of the provinces in a confidential note to Sir Edward Lytton, Secretary of State for the colonies. The British government had given careful consideration to the Order-in-Council submitted by the Canadian government September 4, 1858, on the subject of a union of the British North American Colonies, and to the request therein that the Secretary of State for the Colonies should authorize a meeting of delegates from the respective provinces to consider the question. Duly impressed with the difficulties attendant upon the administration of public affairs in Canada, the British government was prepared to do

[1] *Series G, 239.* Confidential No. 24, pp. 185-7.
[2] O. D. Skelton, *Life and Times of Sir Alexander Tilloch Galt*, p. 220.

all in its power to remove them, in conjunction with the provincial legislatures in so far as " the maintenance of the Queen's authority and of constitutional government permitted." [1]   Since, however, the question of union involved not only the province of Canada and its relations to the Empire, but also the other British provinces, the suggestion was made that before the meeting was called the British government should communicate directly with these provinces in order to find out if such a convention would be in accordance with their wishes.   The British government, realizing " the importance of promoting the consolidation and strength of the Crown in North America," was prepared to promote any plan which had such an object in so far as compatible with the maintenance of the British connection.

Galt regretted that the British government did not more enthusiastically endorse a union of the provinces, and begged that it should at least refrain from any expression of opinion hostile to confederation.   Since the plan would assuredly be discussed in the colonies, he did not consider it advisable that such discussion should take place " in the face of an adverse decision from the Home government."   In the conclusion of his letter Galt stated that he felt it his duty to express his firm conviction that the question was " simply one of the confederation of the provinces with each other or of ultimate absorption in the United States, and every difficulty placed in the way of the former is an argument in favor of those who desire the latter." [2]

In his early advocacy of Confederation, in 1858, Galt had received very little support from the other political leaders in British America who were to share with him the honor of

[1] *Ibid.*, p. 251.
[2] *Ibid.*, p. 252.

being counted among the Fathers of Confederation. He rendered valuable service, indeed almost inestimable service, in making possible a united Canada, and not the least of his services as representative of the English-speaking minority of Canada East was his winning over to the cause of Confederation, Cartier, the representative of the French speaking majority. An incorporation of the West was included in Galt's conception of federation, and owing to his railway experience, he was able to visualize the linking of all the Provinces by means of railway connection. One of the ablest of Canadian financiers, he naturally presented to the British North Americans the business phase of Confederation, namely, the commercial advantages which would accrue to all the provinces.

If Galt, as early as 1858, was thoroughly convinced that federation was the only possible alternative to annexation with the United States, not so the other political leaders of British North America. It took the events of the American Civil War to impress upon them the need of presenting a united British America to the American people. Macdonald, the Conservative leader, for instance recognized the fact that throughout the Civil War, the possibility of a war with Great Britain had frequently arisen, and might at any time in the future, again arise. If Great Britain were at war with the United States, it would then be too late to consider measures for strengthening the provinces, or to begin negotiations for a union. He recognized, as did the other leaders in British America, that ill feeling existed between the two countries, in consequence of which the Reciprocity Treaty between Canada and the United States was to be repealed. Reasons of trade, therefore, as well as military reasons, prompted a careful consideration of Confederation.[1] Cartier believed that the American Civil

[1] *Debates on Confederation*, Macdonald, p. 32.

War had demonstrated that the only alternative to absorption in the United States was a British North American Confederation, for had not the Northern press repeatedly threatened the forcible annexation of the British provinces upon the conclusion of the war? He recognized that these provinces separated as they were, could not be easily defended. The absorption of British America had long been contemplated, as article seven of the original draft of the American Constitution proved.[1] The articles in favor of confederation which appeared in *La Minerve* were inspired by Cartier, who declared that the province of Canada East had

> not the right to put itself in the path of the political march of the times and arrest a great idea. If it does so, it will be the end for it. It will fall back to the fights of 1837, with this difference, that it will be no longer the English with which it will have to deal, but its own compatriots of other races who will never pardon its action.[2]

Sir Wilfred Laurier, toward the close of the nineteenth century, claimed that in the advocacy of confederation, no one risked more than Cartier, " whose chief reliance against the rising tide of hostile sentiment in Quebec was in the Catholic clergy. These were distinctly favorable to the scheme of union and the fact had profound significance in the making of confederated Canada. Without Cartier and the Catholic ecclesiastics of Quebec, the union of 1867 could not have been accomplished." [3] Sir Richard Cartwright, the Liberal leader in Ontario, thus assigned the credit to the men who brought about confederation:

> In sporting phrase, if Mr. Brown [were] first, Galt and Cartier

---

[1] *Debates on Confederation*, Cartier, pp. 55-56.

[2] *La Minerve*, September 22, 1864.

[3] John Willison, *Sir Wilfred Laurier and the Liberal Party*, quoted by John Boyd, *Sir Georges Etienne Cartier*, p. 280.

came in as very good seconds. All three took heavy risks and heavy responsibilities, and in one way or the other all three suffered more or less for their action. There is Galt forced to resign in 1866 because he was unable to obtain quite as ample concessions for the Protestant minority in Quebec, whom he represented, as they thought he ought to have secured; and as for Sir George Cartier, his hold on his fellow countrymen was a good deal shaken and his position in their eyes was considerably lessened by the place Quebec had to assume under the British North America Act. I do not deny that there were others who did good work in the business, but none who could compare, in any way with these three.[1]

Perhaps it was natural that Sir Richard Cartwright, who had the reputation of being the war horse of the Liberal Party, should refuse to recognize the signal service rendered by Macdonald, the Conservative leader. Neither political party, however, can claim a monopoly of the credit for bringing about Confederation, for only through a coalition was that successfully consummated. The times of crises that had arisen throughout the American Civil War had convinced the political leaders of Canada that union was necessary for defensive purposes. Whatever the causes of jealousy which separated French Canada from the British Provinces, the incidents of the American Civil War had at least demonstrated that the French Province was not one whit behind the British Provinces in its loyalty to Great Britain. For instance at the time of the Trent affair, the insult to the British flag was apparently just as keenly resented by the French Canadian as by the British Canadian. In the words of Cartier the attitude of his constituents is defined: " We French Canadians are British subjects like the others, but British subjects speaking French." [2]

[1] Richard J. Cartwright, *Reminiscences*, Interview Number Eight, p. 45.
[2] Alfred D. DeCelles, *The Makers of Canada Series*, Cartier, chap. vii, p. 69.

Throughout the period of the American Civil War, the people of British America were constantly congratulating themselves upon their enjoyment of a monarchical system of government. Looking upon the Republic, rent asunder by bitter internal strife, the British in North America attributed all the ills which afflicted the Americans to their Republican form of government. In a speech delivered at Picton, June 17, 1861, John A. Macdonald in his laudation of the monarchical system was simply giving expression to the conviction of the vast majority of the British in North America.

If we wished to be equally happy, we must follow England's example, and certainly not look for our model to the neighboring democracy. He spoke with every respect of his brethren in blood, in literature, in feeling. He deeply deplored and re gretted the unhappy events which were occurring there. But the reason they did not occur here was that we had a monarchical government, which a French writer had well said was the principle of honor, and because we had a strong central government, not one like the United States so weak that at the first trouble it threatened to tumble to pieces. We were happily free from democratic institutions which had led every republic of which we read in history, first into anarchy and then into military despotism. The whole policy of his [Mr. Macdonald's] life had been directed to one course, to preserve in its integrity the constitution of Great Britain which we enjoyed here, and under which we were blessed with order and with liberty without licentiousness.[1]

Still firmly believing that the United States presented a warning to British North America, Macdonald, two years later, thus declared: " On the part of the Conservative party, I may say we will adhere to the principles for which we have so long contended. We cling to the British crown. We

[1] The Montreal *Gazette*, July 8, 1861.

will take warning by the awful breakdown of Democratic institutions in the neighboring country. We will adhere to the principles of monarchical and liberal institutions." [1]

The argument urged by the opponents of confederation in British America, namely, that the federal principle had proved a failure in the United States was declared unsound by *La Minerve* in its issue of September 6, 1864: " The Civil War among our neighbors is evidently not the result of the federal system but of the persistent efforts of the Northern States to infringe upon the independence of other States." Realizing that they would form a minority in a federation, the French Canadians were naturally zealous upholders of the States Rights' theory which would insure for them within the federation their French customs and institutions. *L'Union Nationale* thus described the only form of federation which could win the support of the French Canadian population :

We can only desire a system of confederation in which the federal government will have the control of general legislation, and the local governments the initiative and control of local legislation—in one word, we wish that the two governments should be each in its sphere, completely independent one of the other.[2]

The American Civil War with the evidence which it presented of the lack of a strong central government in the United States, powerful enough to restrain the states, helped to determine the form of Canadian government which was incorporated in the British North America Act of 1867. As early as 1858, Galt, a keen observer of political affairs in the neighboring Republic, had attributed the differences which had arisen between the federal and the state governments to the lack of a sovereign power. In the document

[1] The *Globe*, April 10, 1863.

[2] The Montreal *Gazette*, September 8, 1864.

which he prepared in that year, Galt, therefore, urged that this source of danger be avoided in the Canadian scheme of Confederation.

It will be observed that the basis of Confederation now proposed differs from that of the United States in several important particulars. It does not profess to be derived from the people but would be the constitution provided by the imperial parliament, thus affording the means of remedying any defect, which is now practically impossible under the American constitution. The local legislature would not be in a position to claim the exercise of the same sovereign powers which have frequently been the cause of difference between the American states and their general government. To this may be added that by the proposed distribution of the revenue each province would have a direct pecuniary interest in the preservation of the authority of the Federal Government. In these respects it is conceived that the proposed Confederation would possess greater inherent strength than that of the United States, and would combine the advantage of the unity for general purposes of a legislative union with so much of the Federation principle as would join all the benefits of local government and legislation upon questions of provincial interest.[1]

Since the inability of the central government to control the state government in the United States was generally conceded to be the cause of the American Civil War, the Canadian "Fathers of Confederation" were convinced of the necessity of strengthening the central government of Canada. In the British North America Act of 1867, twenty-nine different powers of the Federal or Dominion Parliament of Canada are enumerated. In addition all power not specifically granted to the Provincial Parliaments is reserved for the Dominion Parliament. In order to safeguard further the Dominion Parliament, there is a provision in-

[1] O. D. Skelton, *Life and Times of A. T. Galt*, pp. 243-4.

serted that any provincial act may be disallowed by the
Governor-General and Council within one year of their receiving a copy of the law.[1] This provision is for the purpose of safeguarding the common good of all. The
Dominion is greater than the Province, as the whole must
ever be greater than the part; if the interests of the whole
country can be best served by disallowing the provincial act,
the Governor-General and Council should consider the
country, not the province. In assigning all power to the
Federal or Dominion Parliament, not specifically granted to
the Provincial Parliaments, the Canadian Fathers of Confederation were reversing the order found in the United
States. Under the monarchical form of government to
which they adhered, the executive power was vested in the
sovereign of Great Britain or his representative who under
responsible government could act only on the advice of his
ministers responsible to the people through Parliament.
Thus they thought they were avoiding another weakness in
the republican form which had for its executive a president,
a party leader, often ambitious for reelection, who was under
no obligation to consult the members of his cabinet, often
merely departmental chiefs, in no sense responsible to Congress. To the sovereign or representative of the sovereign,
a non-partisan head, they believed the people would render
an undivided allegiance which no party leader could hope to
command. Too much power, the Canadians believed, had
been entrusted to the President of the United States in his
rôle as Commander in Chief of the army and navy. The
amount of patronage at his disposal, and his veto power were
also regarded as dangerous. As the king of Great Britain
had not exercised the veto since the eighteenth century, the

---

[1] Under section 90 and 56 of the British North America Act the Governor-General and Council may disallow provincial acts. Practically this
means the Governor-General and Minister of Justice.

British people did not regard this power as a prerogative of their sovereign.   Indeed throughout the period of the sixties, the Canadians were more impressed with the weakness than with the strength of the United States government.   In framing the British North America Act the Canadian leaders were, therefore, anxious to avoid the provisions which they considered a source of weakness, and not of strength in the Constitution of the United States.   Like the Constitution of the mother-land, the Canadian Constitution is partly unwritten, and hence capable of progressive interpretation.

With the exception of Howe, all the ablest political leaders of the British North American Provinces were advocates of Confederation.   The Fenian Raids that followed the American Civil War quickened the desire of the leaders for a closer union in order to make the country more compact for defensive purposes.   Unfortunately Howe, the popular hero of Nova Scotia, became the leader of the Anti-Confederation party of Nova Scotia.   It seems hardly necessary to impute unworthy motives to him, or to doubt the sincerity of his conviction that the interests of the people of the Maritime Provinces were not sufficiently safeguarded by the British North America Act.   Howe himself stated that he opposed confederation not because he had " an invincible objection to becoming a unionist," but because he believed the Quebec plan sacrificed the interests of the Maritime Provinces; moreover, he thought the people of the provinces should have the opportunity, after the terms of union had been published and duly considered, either to accept or reject it.   He announced his opposition: " My course is clear, old opinions have nothing to do with the matter.   I resist the Quebec scheme of government because I do not like it, and the plan for sweeping away the institutions of my country without the consent of its people — because it is an atrocious violation of legal rights, never abused or abandoned." [1]

[1] J. W. Longley, *Life of Joseph Howe*, pp. 190-1.

Not only did Howe lead the anti-confederation party prior to the passage of the British North America Act, but he also led the party which sought its repeal.   In the spring of 1868, a delegation from Nova Scotia, under the leadership of Howe, sailed for England to seek a repeal.   Dr. Tupper, likewise of Nova Scotia, was chosen as the delegate of the Dominion Parliament, to oppose the repeal.   Upon meeting Howe in England, Tupper frankly addressed him thus: " Mr. Howe, you are here seeking a repeal of this union. You are commissioned for that purpose and bound to exert your utmost efforts. You will fail. What then?"   Realizing the importance of securing Howe as a supporter if the people of Nova Soctia were to be reconciled to the union, Macdonald proposed a conference with Howe for the discussion of better terms for the Maritime Provinces.   Before agreeing to meet Sir John, Howe had an interview with his co-laborer for repeal, Annand, in which he revealed very clearly that they were limits to his advocacy of repeal. In the words of Howe the interview is described thus: " I said, ' If I put this by for six months and let you send a delegation and the answer is unfavorable — what then?' Mr. Annand replied, ' Then I will go for annexation ' "— that is, of course, to the United States. To this Mr. Howe answered, " In that case we should have to part, and we may as well part now and save six months' time." [1]   The better terms which Howe secured for Nova Scotia were that the sum of $1,188,750.00 was to be added to the debt to be credited Nova Scotia on entering confederation, and an annual payment of $800,000.00 for ten years. As a guarantee of good faith, Macdonald insisted that Howe enter his government.   This he did, and the repeal movement came to an end. [2]

[1] *Ibid.*, p. 215.

[2] *Ibid.*, p. 225.   " Sir John Macdonald stated that it involved great diffi-

Not only did the United States help to determine the form of the Canadian government, but also indirectly to determine the name applied to the British North American union. The title of " Kingdom of Canada," a title which would have contained a clear recognition of the national status of Canada was proposed by the delegates from British America. In the Canadian draft of union, the united provinces were proclaimed an auxiliary kingdom of Great Britain. The change of title from Kingdom to Dominion " was made at the instance of Lord Derby, then Foreign Minister, who feared the first name would wound the sensibilities of the Yankees." [1]

Until 1871, the United States claims for damages inflicted by the Alabama and other Confederate vessels built in England were still unsatisfied. The Canadian government, likewise, had a counter claim for damages inflicted by the Fenian Raid of 1866. In addition to these claims there were other issues still unsettled. Since a renewal of the Reciprocity Treaty was still refused by the United States, the Canadian government, hoping thereby to force certain trade concessions, was insisting upon the strict enforcement of her inshore fishery rights. Prior to the decision of the United States and Great Britain to submit the points at issue to arbitration, the Dominion Parliament had suggested the appointment of a Commission to settle the fishery dispute. For the first time in Canadian history the British government had appointed a Canadian on an international commission, Sir John A. Macdonald. When the differences came up for general consideration, foreseeing full well the difficulties

culty and risk to agree to these large concessions to Nova Scotia and that his only hope of being able to carry such a measure through the House of Commons was by the assurance that the repeal movement would cease, and that the only substantial guarantee he could give to his colleagues and supporters was the presence of Mr. Howe himself in his cabinet helping to carry out the great work of confederation."

[1] Joseph Pope, *Memoirs of Sir John A. Macdonald*, vol. i, pp. 312-3.

which would confront him in his efforts to safeguard Canadian interests, Macdonald very reluctantly agreed to act. The Canadians were very loath to see the linking up of the purely Canadian issues with the Alabama claims.

Canadian opinion found expression in a series of resolutions presented by Galt in the Canadian House of Commons, February 24, 1871. Realizing fully the importance of the settlement of all disputes between Great Britain and the United States, the Canadians declared that they would rejoice if the task entrusted to the Joint High Commission could be so accomplished that it would be productive of cordial and permanent friendship between the two countries. Any attempt, however, on the part of the Commission to regulate the inshore fisheries and the inland waters, powers specifically granted the Canadian Parliament under the British North America Act, would arouse its apprehension. Willing as ever, to grant the United States the free and unrestricted use of the fisheries and inland navigation upon receiving its equivalent from that country, the Dominion Parliament believed that concessions granted by the Commission without such compensation would place Canada in a disadvantageous position in all future negotiations by " depriving her of the means of offering any adequate equivalent for those concessions she was desirous of obtaining from the nation." The Canadian government expressed its willingness to submit to the Joint High Commission for consideration all subjects of mutual interest, and to abide by the decisions unless they interfered with Canadian national interests, and tended " to their subordination to the United States in the future." Referring to the claims of Canada upon the United States in consequence of the Fenian raids, the Canadian Parliament desired that they might be " so dealt with by the Joint Commission as to afford indemnity for the past and security against similar outrages in the future." [1]

[1] O. D. Skelton, *Life and Times of A. T. Galt*, p. 459.

Strongly impressed with the necessity of upholding Canadian interests, Galt declared his viewpoint of the situation thus:

We must guard our rights and not be in a position of inferiority to the United States. I wholly repudiate the idea that this country is in any way subordinate or ought to be subordinate to the policy of the United States. I desire to retain our connection with Great Britain so long as it can be maintained in the interest of both countries, but if the time ever comes that that connection will cease, I desire that the people of Canada should not be in a position of inferiority to the great republic. We must preserve in our hands the great interests which would go hereafter to build up a great Empire on this continent and keep it intact for our posterity.[1]

Convinced that Canadian interests would not be served by the passage of such a resolution, since it might be considered by Americans indicative of a lack of harmony in purpose between Canada and Great Britain—traceable to an insufficient confidence in the latter country's power or ability to safeguard Canadian interests, Macdonald, Blake and Mackenzie the three leading Canadian statesmen, persuaded Galt to withdraw the resolution without putting it to the test of a vote.

The proceedings of the Washington Commission justified every fear to which Galt had given expression. Owing to the oversight of the British minister in framing the issues for settlement, the Canadian claim for damages as a result of the Fenian raid was not even considered. If the British Government were to be held responsible for the building of Confederate ships in English waters, then surely the United States government should have been held responsible for the damage inflicted upon Canadians by the Fenians who were, moreover, citizens of the United States.

[1] *Ibid.*, p. 460.

Macdonald found that he had not over-estimated the difficulty of his task. Keenly disappointed by the conduct of his British colleagues on the commission, Macdonald wrote thus: " I must say that I am greatly disappointed at the course taken by the British Commissioners. They seem to have only one thing in their minds—that is, to go home to England with a treaty in their pockets, settling everything, no matter at what cost to Canada." [1] His firm and resolute opposition alone prevented the granting of inshore fishing rights in perpetuity to the United States in return for a million dollars. To his fellow commissioner, Lord de Grey, he stated that this right was one that could not be surrendered " for any compensation whatever; that we had no right to injure posterity by depriving Canada *either as a dependency or as a nation* of her fisheries." [2] Disheartened with his vain attempt to serve Canadian interests, Macdonald at one time thought seriously of withdrawing from the Commission. That he did not withdraw was due to the fear that such a move on his part with issues still unsettled between Great Britain and the United States might involve the two countries in war. In exchange for the free admission of Canadian fish products into the United States, the American fishermen were to be given free access to Canadian waters. The additional compensation that should be made by the United States for fishing privileges was referred to arbitration. The Halifax Commission of 1877 secured for Canada $5,500,000.00 of which $1,000,000.00 was paid to Newfoundland.

Dissatisfied as he was with the Washington Treaty of 1871, Macdonald was yet confident that greater evil would result from its rejection by the Canadian Parliament than

[1] Joseph Pope, *Memoirs of Sir John A. Macdonald*, vol. ii, Correspondence with Dr. Tupper, chap. xx, p. 91.

[2] *Ibid.*, p. 105.

by its acceptance. In his defence, therefore, of the treaty in the House of Commons, Macdonald urged the people of Canada to "accept this treaty, to accept it with all its imperfections; to accept it for the sake of peace and for the sake of the great Empire of which we form a part." Few Canadians today will doubt the sincerity of Macdonald's statement in the House of Commons with regard to his participation in framing the Treaty of Washington. "When some one writes my biography—if I am ever thought worthy of having such an interesting document prepared— and when as a matter of History, the questions connected with this treaty are upheld, it will be found that, upon this, as well as upon every other point, I did all I could to protect the rights and claims of the Dominion."[1] With the signing of the Treaty of Washington, the final score of the American Civil War, as it affected Great Britain and the United States, was settled.

Thus the American Civil War was not without significance to the people of the British North American Provinces. Many were the causes for friction, elsewhere enumerated in these pages, that the Civil War afforded. To the wisdom of the statesmen of both countries, much of the credit for the avoidance of war must be given. Canada must ever be the country through which the United States will give expression to its resentment or approval of Great Britain's policy. Two countries with a frontier of three thousand miles practically unguarded should and do present to the world an example of international good-will. The frontier, as far as intercourse between the two countries is concerned, is merely a line on a map. Sympathy between nations, as well as individuals, must be based upon understanding. Throughout the period of the American Civil War, how-

[1] Joseph Pope, *Memoirs of Sir John A. Macdonald*, Speech of Sir John, House of Commons, May 3, 1872, vol. ii, chap. xxi, p. 140.

ever, the easy approach across the frontier to British territory was often a source of international complication.   As
the years go by, the American and Canadian, who necessarily
must have much in common, should do much toward bringing
into being an era of international good-will.   Over a hundred years of peace in which all difficulties have been solved
by means of arbitration should be indicative of what the
future may hold in store for all nations.   Loyal to Great
Britain, proud of being a part of the British Empire, Canada
yet is well qualified to act as the interpreter of Great Britain
to the United States, for Canadians possess an understanding of both the American and British.   Great Britain and
the United States with Canada as the middle link uniting
them, may, if they will, preserve the peace of the world.
May Canada unite Great Britian and the United States in a
firm and lasting friendship for the good of all mankind!

BIBLIOGRAPHY

CANADIAN ARCHIVES, GOVERNMENT CORRESPONDENCE

Guide to the Documents in the Manuscript Room at the Public Archives,
Ottawa, Canada, vol. i (by David W. Parker).

Correspondence Relative to the Affairs of Canada—No. 33, 1839, P. F.
73, vol. x.

Series G—229 to 239 Inclusive—Correspondence with the British Minister
at Washington. Not indexed.

Series G—321 to 328—Despatches from Lieutenant Governors: George
Dundas, R. Hodgson, W. Robinson, to Secretary of State. Prince
Edward Island—May 1868 to March 1873.

Series G—184-221—1835-1867—Drafts of despatches from the Governor-
General to the Colonial Secretary. (Incomplete.)

Series G 466—To Secretary of State, 1866, vol. xii, no. 183.

Canadian Archives *M 11616, Department of State, Washington, December 6, 1864.*

2333 Correspondence on Trent Affairs 1861. Received from the State
Department of United States.

Head Quarters Office—Halifax, N. S. Central Registry
File: *C. R.*

$$\frac{Q}{408}$$ Part I, Part II, Part III. Cited as CR/Q/408

Subject: Trent Affair

G. O. C's. Telegrams

C 186 A Fenian Raid — January to November 1866. Telegrams from
Lord Monck, Gen. Williams, Gen. Doyle, The British Ambassador
U. S., The Consul General at New York and others to Lieut. Gov-
ernor Gordon of New Brunswick.

Canadian Archives—*State K*

State Q

Despatch Marked 11633—Letter of Seward to J. H. Burnley, January
14, 1865.

Canadian Archives, *Paper 11750.*

DOCUMENTS

Documents printed in the *Annual Register (British)* for 1861.
Census of 1851 and 1861, Canada West.
Census of 1851 and 1861, Canada East.
Census of Nova Scotia, 1861.

Nova Scotia Journal 1852, Appendix 94.
Journal of the House of Assembly of the Province of New Brunswick, 1862.
United States Presidents — Messages and Papers 1789–1897, vol. v, 1849–1861. Washington, 1895.

PARLIAMENTARY DEBATES

Hansard Parliamentary Debates, 3rd ser., vols. 86, 87, 88, 105, 108, 124, 156.
Parliamentary Debates on the Subject of the Confederation of the British North American Provinces.

NEWSPAPERS

Newspaper files : Canada West
The Toronto *Globe*, March, 1850, 1857 to 1867 inclusive and 1871.
The Toronto *Leader*, November, 1858, 1859 to 1867 inclusive and 1871.
The *British Colonist*, Toronto, 1849-1850 semi-weekly.
The *Patriot*, Toronto, October, 1849, 1861 to 1862 inclusive.
The Ottawa *Tribune*, 1861 to 1862 inclusive.
The Ottawa *Times*, 1861 to 1862 inclusive.
The Huron *Signal*, 1861 to 1865 inclusive.

Newspaper files : Canada East
Le *Canadien*, 1849–1850, vol. xix.
Le *Pays*, August 1862.
Le *Journal de Quebec*, 1861–1863, inclusive, October 20, 1864.
L'*Avenir*, October 1849.
La *Minerve*, 1849.
The Quebec *Chronicle*, 1861.
The Montreal *Pilot*, October 1849 to October 1850, May 3, 1853 to April 29, 1854, November 1856 to May 1857, October 1857.
The Quebec *Mercury*, 1850, 1854, 1856, 1857, 1861, 1864.
The Quebec *Gazette*, 1849, 1850.
The Montreal *Transcript and Commercial Advertiser*, October 1849.
The Montreal *Gazette*, October 1849; July 1 to Dec. 30, 1850; 1861 to 1865 inclusive.
The Montreal *Witness*, 1861.
The Montreal *Herald*, 1849 to 1850, 1861.
The Montreal *Courier*, 1849.

Newspaper files : Maritime Provinces
Acadian Recorder, January 1855 to August 1859 weekly; 1862 to 1864 inclusive.
The *Islander* or *Prince Edward Island Weekly Intelligencer and Advertiser*, August 16, 1861.

The *Casket*, February 1, 1861. Published weekly at Halifax and Antigonish.

The Halifax *Morning Chronicle*, 1861 to 1864 inclusive.

The Halifax *Citizen*, July 29, 1865.

Newspaper files: New York

The *New York Times*, 1863, April 25, 1924.

The *New York Herald*, 1860-1862 inclusive.

The *New York Tribune*, 1860-1861 inclusive.

The Utica *Morning Herald* and *Daily Gazette*, 1861.

See also *A History of Canadian Journalism, 1859-1908*, edited by a Committee of the Press Association (Toronto, 1908).

HISTORICAL PUBLICATIONS RELATING TO CANADA

Review of Historical Publications Relating to Canada, 20 vols., edited by G. M. Wrong, H. H. Langton, W. S. Wallace.

Canadian Magazine, vol. x, March, 1898, Hodgins, Thomas, " British and American Diplomacy affecting Canada "; vol. xi, Bourinot, Sir John G., " The Makers of the Dominion of Canada "; vol. xi, 1898, September, 1898, Tupper, Sir Charles, " Canada's International Status"; vol. xviii, 1901, Grant, W. L., " Cape Breton, Past and Present."

The World's Work, October, 1904, Turnbull, George, " The Progress of Canada."

Quarterly Review, vol. 191, January–April, 1900, Contents of no. 382, art. iv, p. 337, " Canada and Sir John Macdonald."

The Canadian Historical Review 1920–1925, New Series of

The Review of Historical Publications relating to Canada (founded 1898).

    Vol. I, 1920, No. 3, Sept., 1920, Landon, Fred, " Canadian Opinion of Southern Secession, 1860."

    Vol. II, March, 1921, Bovey, Wilfred, " Confederate Agents in Canada during the American Civil War."

    Vol. III, March, 1922, Landon, Fred, " The Trent Affair of 1861."

    Vol. V, Sept., 1924, Trotter, Reginald G., " Some American Influences upon the Canadian Federation Movement"; Penny, Arthur G., " The Annexation Movement 1849-1850 "; March, 1925, Wrong, George M., " The Evolution of the Foreign Relations of Canada "; June, 1925, Trotter, Reginald G., "An Early Proposal for the Federation of British North America."

Annual Report of the American Historical Association, 1892 to 1919 (inclusive).

    1893, Woodburn, James A., " The Historical Significance of the Missouri Compromise."

    1895, Siebert, W. H., " The Underground Railroad."

1895, Callahan, J. M., "Agreement of 1817—Reduction of Naval Forces upon the American Lakes."

1896, Callahan, J. M., "The Northern Lake Frontier during the Civil War."

1898, Callahan, J. M., "Diplomatic Relations of the Confederate States with England."

1906, Beer, George Louis, "The Colonial Policy of Great Britain."

1911, Allin, Cephas D., "The Genesis of the Confederation of Canada."

Ontario Historical Society—Papers and Records 1899 to 1921 inclusive.

Vol. II, Tasker, L. H., "The United Empire Loyalist Settlement at Long Pt., Lake Erie."

Vol. XII, Burpee, Lawrence J., "Influence of the War of 1812."

Vol. XIII, Allin, Cephas D., "The British North American League 1849."

Vol. XVII, Landon, Fred, "Canada's Part in Freeing the Slave."

Vol. XIX, Riddell, W. R., "Some References to Negroes in Upper Canada."

Collections of the Nova Scotia Historical Society, 20 vols.

Vol. VII, "Story of Deportation of Negroes from Nova Scotia to Sierra Leone"—Read by Ex-Governor Archibald, 12th March, 1885.

Vol. X, Smith, T. Watson, "The Slave in Canada."

Vol. XIV, Graham, Wallace, "The Fisheries of British North America and the United States Fishermen."

Political Science Quarterly, vol. xxxii, 1917, Schuyler, R. L., "Preference and Sir Robert Peel"; vol. xxxiii, 1918, Schuyler, R. L., "The Abolition of British Imperial Preference."

Smith College Studies in History, vol. iii, no. 4, July 1918, Lowrey, Lawrence Tyndale, "Northern Opinion of Approaching Secession, October 1859–November 1860."

Johns Hopkins University Studies, 1922, Tansill, Charles C., "The Canadian Reciprocity Treaty of 1854."

Journal of Negro History

Vol. III, Landon, Fred, "The Buxton Settlement in Canada."

Vol. IV, Landon, Fred, "The Anti-Slavery Society of Canada."

Vol. V, Riddell, Wm. Renwick, "Slavery in Canada."

Vol. V, Landon, Fred, "The Negro Migration to Canada after 1850."

July 1921, Riddell, Wm. Renwick, "The Baptism of Slaves in Prince Edward Island."

PAMPHLETS AND CONTEMPORARY WORKS

Canadian Pamphlets 21

Earl Grey, *The Commercial Policy of the British Colonies and the McKinley Tariff.*

Pamphlets in the Canadian Archives

2324, Ferguson, James, *Notes of a Tour in North America in 1861,* Wm. Blackwood and Son.

2331, Denison, Captain George T., *The National Defences* (Toronto, 1861).

2332, By a Native Canadian, *Canada: Is she prepared for War?* (Toronto, 1861).

2333, *Correspondence relative to the case of Messrs. Mason & Slidell* (Washington, 1861).

2352, *Report of the Select Committee of the Legislative Assembly* (Quebec, 1861).

2366, Booty, James Horatio, *Three Months in Canada and the United States* (London, 1862).

2382, By an Upper Canadian, *The Military Defences of Canada, considered in respect to our Colonial Relations with Great Britain, in a series of letters in the Quebec Morning Chronicle.* Revised and corrected with notes and additions (Quebec, 1862).

2388, Somerville, Alexander, *Canada, A Battle Ground,* 1862, Hamilton, Donnelley & Lawson.

2457, Russell, William Howard, *My Diary North and South* (New York, 1863).

2461, T. D. L., *A Peep at the Western World* (London, 1863).

2534, Crichton, Viscount, *A Tour in British North America and the United States 1862* (Dublin, 1864).

2628, Alison, A., *Independence of Canada* (London, 1865).

2639, Cordner, John, *The American Conflict, 1865* (Montreal, 1865).

2657, Norton, Robert, *Maple Leaves from Canada for the Grave of Abraham Lincoln* (St. Catherines, 1865).

2683, Porter, Jane, *A Six Weeks' Tour in Western Canada.*

1239 C., vol. 44, Dawson Pamphlet 1862.

The editor of *Life in Normandy, A Short American Tramp in the Fall of 1864* (Edinburgh, 1865).

Kohl, J. G., *Travels in Canada and the States,* 2 vols. (London, 1861).

Day, Samuel Phillips, *English America,* 2 vols. (London, 1864).

Borrett, George Tuthill, *Out West, A Series of Letters from Canada and the United States* (London, 1866).

Watkins, Sir E. W., *Canada and the United States* (London, 1887).

Russell, W. H., *Canada: Its Defence, Condition and Resources, being a Second and Concluding Volume of "My Diary North and South"* (Boston, 1865).

Woods, N. A., *The Prince of Wales in Canada and the United States* (London, 1861).

MacGregor, John, *Our Brothers and Cousins, Summer Tour in Canada and the United States* (London, 1859).

Trollope, Anthony, *North America* (New York, 1862).

United States and Canada 1858-1861 as seen by Two Brothers (London, 1869).

Spedon, Andrew Learmont, *Rambles Among the Blue Noses during the Summer of 1862* (Montreal, 1863).

Geikie, John C., *Adventures in Canada or Life in the Woods*, 1864 (Boston, 1865).

By a Soldier of the Regiment, *Voyage and Journey of the Second Battalion Scots Fusilier guard from Southampton to Montreal during the Winter of 1861-1862* (Montreal, 1862).

Duncan, Francis, *Our Garrisons in the West or Sketches in British North America* (London, 1863).

Barrett-Lennard, Capt. C. E., *Travels in British Columbia with the Narrative of a Yacht Voyage around Vancouver Island* (London, 1862).

BIOGRAPHIES

Statesmen of Canada West

Cartwright, Sir Richard, *Reminiscences* (Toronto, 1912).

Mackenzie, Alexander, *The Life and Speeches of Hon. George Brown* (Toronto, 1882).

Pope, Joseph, *Memoirs of Sir John A. Macdonald*, 2 vols. (Ottawa, 1894).

Statesmen of Canada East

Boyd, John, *Sir Georges Etienne Cartier, His Life and Times, A Political History of Canada from 1814 until 1873* (Toronto, 1914).

Skelton, O. D., *The Life and Times of Sir Alexander Tilloch Galt* (Toronto, 1920).

Statesmen of the Maritime Provinces

Chisholm, J. A., *The Speeches and Public Letters of Joseph Howe*, 2 vols (Halifax, 1909).

Joseph Howe Papers, vol. viii, Letters from Howe 1861-1865; vol. ix, Letters from Howe 1866-1872. (Canadian Archives—Unpublished Letters.)

Saunders, Edward, Manning, *Three Premiers of Nova Scotia—The Hon. J. W. Johnstone, The Hon. Joseph Howe, The Hon. Chas. Tupper* (Toronto, 1909).

Saunders, Edward Manning, *The Life and Letters of the Rt. Hon. Sir Chas. Tupper* (London, 1916).

Tupper, Sir Charles, *Recollections of Sixty Years* (London and New York, 1914).

Other Biographical Series

   The Makers of Canada (Toronto, 1903-1911).

     Vol. VI, De Celles, A. D., *Louis Joseph Papineau*, 1904.

     Vol. VII, Longley, J. W., *Joseph Howe*, 1904.

       Hannay, James, *Lemuel Allan Wilmot*, 1907.

     Vol. VIII, Leacock, Stephen, *Baldwin, La Fontaine, Hincks*, 1907.

     Vol. IX, Parkin, G. R., *Sir John A. Macdonald*, 1908.

       De Celles, A. D., *Sir Georges Cartier*, 1904.

     Vol. X, Lewis, John, *George Brown*, 1906.

       Hannay, James, *Sir Leonard Tilley*, 1907.

     Supplement—*Index and Dictionary of Canadian History*, 1911.

Chronicles of Canada Series

   Grant, W. L., *The Tribune of Nova Scotia* (Toronto, 1915).

   Colquhoun, A. H. U., *The Fathers of Confederation* (Toronto, 1916).

Other Biographical Material

   Browne, F. F., *The Everyday Life of Abraham Lincoln* (New York, 1915).

   Curtis, G. Ticknor, *Life of James Buchanan*, vol. ii (New York, 1883).

   Goldwin Smith, *Letters* (Boston, 1864).

   Lee, Sidney, *Edward VII* (New York, 1925).

   Newton, Lord, *Lord Lyons, A Record of British Diplomacy*, 2 vols. (London, 1913).

   Nicolay and Hay, *Abraham Lincoln* (New York, 1914).

   Oliphant, Laurence, *Episodes in a Life of Adventure*, 1887.

   Oliphant, Margaret, *Memoirs of the Life of Laurence, and of Alice Oliphant, his wife*, 2 vols. (New York, 1891).

   Strachey, Lytton, *Queen Victoria* (New York, 1921).

   Walrond, Theodore, *Letters and Journals of Lord Elgin* (London, 1872).

BRITISH COLONIAL POLICY

Beer, George Louis, *British Colonial Policy*, 1754-1765 (New York, 1907).

Beer, George Louis, *The Old Colonial System* (New York, 1912).

Durham, Earl, *The Report of the Earl of Durham, Her Majesty's High Commissioner and Governor-General of British North America*, 2nd edition (London, 1905).

Egerton, H. E., *A Short History of British Colonial Policy*, 4th edition (London, 1913).

Egerton, H. E., *Historical Geography of the British Colonies*, vol. v, pt. ii (Oxford, 1908).

Egerton, H. E. and Grant, W. L., *Canadian Constitutional Development* (London, 1907).

Morison, J. L., *British Supremacy and Canadian Self-Government, 1839-1854* (Toronto, 1919).

Osgood, Herbert L., *The American Colonies in the Seventeenth Century,* vol. iii, New York, 1907).

RECIPROCITY AND TRADE

Allin, Cephas D. and Jones, G. M., *Annexation, Preferential Trade and Reciprocity* (Toronto, 1912).

Maclean, John, *The Tariff Hand-Book* (Toronto, 1878).

CONFEDERATION

Cauchon, Joseph, *L'Union des Provinces de l'Amérique Britannique du Nord* (Quebec, 1865).

Gray, John Hamilton, *Confederation* (Toronto, 1872).

Hammond, M. O., *Canadian Confederation and Its Leaders* (New York, 1917).

Skelton, O. D., *The Canadian Dominion* (New Haven, 1919).

Trotter, Reginald G., *Canadian Federation* (Toronto, 1924).

CANADIAN HISTORIES DEALING WITH THE VARIOUS SECTIONS OF BRITISH NORTH AMERICA

Brown, Richard, *A History of the Island of Cape Breton* (London, 1869).

Dent, John C., *The Last Forty Years: Canada Since the Union of 1841* (Toronto, 1881).

Haliburton, Thomas C., *An Historical and Statistical Account of Nova Scotia,* 2 vols. (Halifax, 1829).

Hopkins, Castell, *Canada, an Encyclopaedia of the Country,* vol. iv (Toronto, 1898).

Montreal History and Gazetter, 1892 (Montreal, 1892).

Shortt, Adam and Doughty, A. G., *Canada and Its Provinces,* vol. xiii (Toronto, 1914) ; vol. xv (Toronto, 1917).

Siegfried, André, *The Race Question in Canada* (London, 1917).

OTHER WORKS

Benjamin, L. N., *The St. Albans, Vt., Raid, or Investigations into the Charges Against Lieut. Bennett H. Young and Command for their Acts at St. Albans, Vt., on the 19th October, 1864* (Montreal, 1865).

Bernard, Montague, *Notes on Some Questions Suggested by the Case of the Trent.*

Channing, Edward, *A History of the United States,* vol. vi (New York, 1925).

Civil War—*Diplomatic History*—Correspondence respecting the *Alabama* also respecting the *Maury* at New York (Washington, 1861-1869).

Greeley, Horace, *The American Conflict, a History of the Great Rebellion in the United States of America* (Hartford, 1864-1866).

Rhodes, James Ford, *The History of the United States,* vol. v (New York, 1919).

Siebert, Wilbur H., *The Underground Railroad* (New York, 1898).

Smith, Edward C., *A Dictionary of American Politics* (New York, 1924).

Stanwood, Edward, *History of the Presidency,* 2 vols. (Boston, 1912).

Woodburn, James Albert, *Political Parties and Party Problems in the United States* (New York, 1914).

INDEX

STUDIES IN HISTORY ECONOMICS AND PUBLIC LAW

EDITED BY
THE FACULTY OF POLITICAL SCIENCE
OF COLUMBIA UNIVERSITY

VOLUME ONE HUNDRED AND TWENTY-FOUR

New York
COLUMBIA UNIVERSITY
LONGMANS, GREEN & CO., AGENTS
LONDON: P. S. KING & SON, LTD.
1926

CONTENTS

Columbia University
in the City of New York

The University includes the following:

Columbia College, founded in 1754, and **Barnard College,** founded in 1889, offering to men and women, respectively, programs of study which may be begun either in September or February and which lead normally in from three to four years to the degree of Bachelor of Arts. The program of study in Columbia College makes it possible for a qualified student to satisfy the requirements for both the bachelor's degree and a professional degree in law, medicine, mining, engineering, chemistry, or architecture in six years.

The non-professional graduate Faculties of **Political Science, Philosophy** and **Pure Science,** offering advanced programs of study and investigation leading to the degrees of Master of Arts and Doctor of Philosophy.

The Professional Schools of:

Law, established in 1858, offering courses leading to the degrees of Bachelor of Laws, Master of Laws and Doctor of Law.

Medicine. The College of Physicians and Surgeons, established in 1807, offering courses leading to the degree of Doctor of Medicine.

Mines, founded in 1863, offering courses leading to the degrees of Engineer of Mines and Metallurgical Engineer.

Chemistry and Engineering, set apart from School of Mines in 1896, offering courses leading to degrees in Civil, Electrical, Mechanical, Chemical and Industrial Engineering.

Teachers College, founded in 1888, offering through the School of Education and the School of Practical Arts courses leading to the degrees of Bachelor of Science, Master of Arts and Master of Science, and to appropriate Teachers College diplomas. Teachers College also conducts graduate work in education, under the Department of Educational Research of the Faculty of Philosophy, leading to the degree of Doctor of Philosophy.

Architecture, offering a program of indeterminate length leading to the degrees of Bachelor of Architecture and Master of Science.

Journalism, founded in 1912, offering courses leading to the degrees of Bachelor of Literature in Journalism and Master of Science.

Business, founded in 1916, offering courses in business training leading to the degrees of Bachelor of Science and Master of Science.

Dentistry, founded in 1917, offering courses leading to the degrees of Doctor of Dental Surgery.

Pharmacy. The New York College of Pharmacy, founded in 1831, offering courses leading to the degrees of Pharmaceutical Chemist, Bachelor of Science in Pharmacy and Doctor of Pharmacy.

In the **Summer Session** the University offers courses giving both general and professional training which may be taken either with or without regard to an academic degree or diploma.

Through its system of **University Extension** the University offers many courses of study to persons unable otherwise to receive academic training.

Home Study courses carrying no academic credit are offered to persons unable to attend courses conducted at the University.

The Institute of Arts and Sciences provides lectures, concerts, readings and recitals—approximately two hundred and fifty in number—in a single season.

The price of the University Catalogue is twenty-five cents postpaid. Detailed information regarding the work in any department will be furnished without charge upon application to the *Secretary of Columbia University,* New York, N. Y.

The Albert Shaw Lectures on Diplomatic History

LATIN AMERICA AND THE WAR

BY

PERCY ALVIN MARTIN, Ph. D.

Professor of History, Stanford University

594 pages.   *1925.*   *Cloth $3.50*

Professor Martin is a well-known student and writer in the Latin-American field, and he has had access to a vast number of contemporary documents, journals and newspapers published in the various states included within the scope of the volume. Of the twenty Latin-American republics, eight declared war on Germany, five severed relations without declaring war, and seven remained neutral. Pan-Hispanism and Yankeephobia each played its part in preventing a realization of that solidarity which has been the aim of Pan-Americanism. The author describes in some detail the reactions to the World War in each of the American republics, and draws a number of interesting conclusions in the final chapter. Among them may be mentioned the increased dependence on their own resources and initiative, the development of trade between the different republics, and the extension of financial and commercial relations with the United States.

Eleven Latin-American states affixed their signatures to the Treaty of Versailles, and that Treaty was ratified by all these states with the exception of Ecuador. These states became members of the League of Nations, and most of the other Latin American states have since joined. At the present time Mexico, Ecuador and the Dominican Republic are the only Latin-American republics outside the League. Brazil has been a member of the Council of the League ever since it came into existence, and three judges of the Permanent Court of International Justice have been chosen from Latin-American countries. In theory, Latin America would seem to be confronted with the dilemma of choosing between the League of Nations and the Monroe Doctrine. These and other problems are discussed in an authoritative way by Professor Martin.

THE JOHNS HOPKINS PRESS
Baltimore, Maryland, U. S. A.

The Johns Hopkins University Studies

in

Historical and Political Science

The Johns Hopkins Press

Baltimore, Maryland

COLUMBIA UNIVERSITY PRESS BOOKS

LAW AND ITS ADMINISTRATION. By HARLAN F. STONE, Justice of the United States Supreme Court. Pp. vii+232. $2.50.

CONSTITUTIONAL GOVERNMENT IN THE UNITED STATES. By WOODROW WILSON, late President of the United States. Pp. vii + 236. $2.50.

OUR CHIEF MAGISTRATE AND HIS POWERS. By WILLIAM HOWARD TAFT, Chief Justice of the Supreme Court. Pp. vii + 165. $2.50.

CONSTITUTIONAL POWER AND WORLD AFFAIRS. By GEORGE SUTHERLAND, Justice of the United States Supreme Court. Pp. vii + 202. $2.50.

THE EQUALITY OF STATES. By JULIUS GOEBEL, Jr., Associate in International Law in Columbia University. Pp. viii + 89. $2.00.

THE GENIUS OF THE COMMON LAW. By SIR FREDERICK POLLOCK. Pp. vii + 141. $2.50.

THE MECHANICS OF LAW MAKING. By COURTENAY ILBERT, formerly Clerk of the House of Commons. Pp. viii + 209. $2.50.

AMERICAN CITY PROGRESS AND THE LAW. By HOWARD LEE McBAIN, Eaton Professor of Municipal Science and Administration in Columbia University. Pp. viii+269. $2.25.

THE CANADIAN CONSTITUTION IN FORM AND IN FACT. By WILLIAM RENWICK RIDDELL, Chief Justice of the Supreme Court of Ontario. Pp. ix + 77. $1.60.

THE AMERICAN COLONIES IN THE EIGHTEENTH CENTURY. By HERBERT LEVI OSGOOD, late Professor of History in Columbia University. In four volumes, 8vo, cloth. 550 pages each. $5.50 per volume; $20.00 per set.

THE PURPOSE OF HISTORY. By FREDERICK J. E. WOODBRIDGE, Dean of the Graduate Faculties in Columbia University. Pp. 89. $1.50.

RECENT CHANGES IN AMERICAN CONSTITUTIONAL THEORY. By JOHN W. BURGESS, Emeritus Professor of Political Science and Constitutional Law in Columbia University. Pp. xi + 115. $1.75.

BISMARK AND GERMAN UNITY. By MUNROE SMITH, Emeritus Bryce Professor of European History in Columbia University. Pp. xiv + 188. Third revised edition. $2.75.

THE LEAGUE OF NATIONS AND MISCELLANEOUS ADDRESSES. By WILLIAM D. GUTHRIE, Member of the New York Bar. Pp. ix + 383. $2.50.

MARXISM VERSUS SOCIALISM. By VLADIMIR G. SIMKHOVITCH, Professor of Economic History in Columbia University. Pp. xvi + 298. $2.50.

THE ECONOMIC INTERPRETATION OF HISTORY. By EDWIN R. A. SELIGMAN, McVikar Professor of Political Economy in Columbia University. Pp. ix + 166. Second edition, revised. $2.50.

THE SHIFTING AND INCIDENCE OF TAXATION. By EDWIN R. A. SELIGMAN. Pp. xii + 431. Fourth edition. $4.50.

THE FEDERAL INCOME TAX. Edited by ROBERT HAIG, Professor of Business Organization in Columbia University. Pp. xii + 271. $3.25.

THE HISTORICAL FOUNDATIONS OF THE LAW RELATING TO TRADE-MARKS. By Frank I. Schechter, of the New York Bar. Pp. xviii + 211. Illustrated. $6.00.

Records of Civilization : Sources and Studies

HELLENIC CIVILIZATION. By G. W. BOTSFORD and E. G. SIHLER. Pp. xiii+719. $4.50.

THE HISTORY OF THE FRANKS. By GREGORY, Bishop of Tours. Translated by ERNEST BREHAUT. Pp. xxv + 283. Map. $3.50.

THE BOOK OF THE POPES (Liber Pontificalis). Translated by LOUISE ROPES LOOMIS. Pp. xxii + 169. $2.85.

AN INTRODUCTION TO THE HISTORY OF HISTORY. By JAMES T. SHOTWELL, Professor of History in Columbia University. Pp. xii + 339. $4.50.

THE LITERATURE OF THE OLD TESTAMENT IN ITS HISTORICAL DEVELOPMENT. By JULIUS A. BEWER, Professor in Union Theological Seminary. Pp. xiv+452. $3.00.

A GUIDE TO THE PRINTED MATERIALS FOR ENGLISH SOCIAL AND ECONOMIC HISTORY, 1750-1850. By JUDITH B. WILLIAMS, Assistant Professor in the Department of History in Wells College. Two volumes. $10.00.

THE SEE OF PETER. By JAMES T. SHOTWELL, Professor of History in Columbia University, and LOUISE R. LOOMIS, Professor of History in Wells College. In press.

COLUMBIA UNIVERSITY PRESS

Columbia University   **New York**

P. S. KING & SON, Ltd.

WEALTH AND TAXABLE CAPACITY

By Sir JOSIAH STAMP, G.B.E., D.Sc. Being the Newmarch Lectures of 1920–21. *Second Edition.* 7s. 6d.

In the House of Commons during the Debate on the Budget, April, 1922, these Lectures were referred to.

Morning Post: "The book should be read, and read carefully, by all who are concerned in post-war financial problems. . . . When the book has been mastered the reader will be able to consider most of the current financial problems without being taken in by the many specious and ingenious remedies which are put forward."

ESSAYS IN APPLIED ECONOMICS

By A. C. PIGOU, M.A. Professor of Political Economy in the University of Cambridge. 10s. 6d.

Nation.—"Professor Pigou has done well to collect his occasional articles into a single volume; for it will be convenient both to the economic student and to the intelligent layman to find easy access even to the more *obiter dicta* of so eminent an authority."

CURRENT PROBLEMS IN FINANCE AND GOVERNMENT

Addresses and Papers. By SIR JOSIAH C. STAMP, G.B.E., D.Sc. 10s. 6d.

Author's Preface.—"The studies included in this volume have one feature in common—they deal with subjects which remain alive in public interest. . . . Some, by which I set little store, have been included because of repeated requests from correspondents; to these I accede on condition that other studies, whose message I imagine an unobservant public still needs without knowing it, are also accepted by them."

CO-OPERATION AT HOME AND ABROAD

By C. R. FAY, M.A., D.Sc., Late Fellow of Christ's College, Cambridge; Professor of Economic History, University of Toronto. Third Edition with Supplementary Chapters dealing with the Progress of Co-operation in the United Kingdom to 1918, Agricultural Co-operation in the Canadian West and the Canadian Wheat Pools. Demy 8vo. 480 pp. Cloth, 15s.

Economist: "This is a really useful book which should hold the ground for some time as a standard work on its subject."

HISTORY OF THE BANK OF ENGLAND

By A. ANDRÉADÈS, Professor of Public Finance in the University of Athens. With a Preface by Professor H. S. Foxwell, M.A. *Second Edition.* 15s.

Times.—"A work of high merit. . . . We are not disposed to quarrel with Prof. Foxwell's pronouncement that it is 'the most comprehensive and most readable account of the Bank yet published.'"

Orchard House, 14 Great Smith Street,
Westminster, England

The Academy of Political Science in the City of New York

The Academy of Political Science, founded in 1880, is composed of men and women interested in political, economic and social questions. Members receive the Political Science Quarterly, the Proceedings of the Academy, the Annual Record of Political Events and invitations to meetings. The annual dues are five dollars. Address: The Academy of Political Science, Columbia University, New York.

PUBLICATIONS

Managing Editor

PARKER T. MOON

POLITICAL SCIENCE QUARTERLY

The Political Science Quarterly is the official organ of the Academy and is devoted to politics, economics and public law. It follows the most important movements of foreign politics, international relations and questions of present interest in the United States. Its attitude is non-partisan, every article is signed and expresses simply the personal view of the writer.

The Record of Political Events, published annually, is a concisely arranged summary of the year's events throughout the entire world.

PROCEEDINGS OF THE ACADEMY

The Proceedings are issued semi-annually by the Academy as a record of its activities and as a means of giving detailed treatment to special subjects of importance. Recent issues are: Wealth and Taxation, Future of Prices at Home and Abroad, Popular Ownership of Property: Its Newer Forms and Social Consequences.* Trade Associations and Business Combinations.* Price $1.50 each in paper covers. A full list of the forty-three issues to date will be sent on request. Address: Academy of Political Science, Columbia University, New York.

* Price $2.50.

Studies in History, Economics and Public Law

edited by

Faculty of Political Science of Columbia University

VOLUME I, 1891-92. 2nd Ed., 1897. 396 pp. Price, cloth, $3.50.

1. **The Divorce Problem. A Study in Statistics.**
   By WALTER F. WILLCOX, Ph.D. (*Not sold separately.*)
2. **The History of Tariff Administration in the United States, from Colonial Times to the McKinley Administrative Bill.**
   By JOHN DEAN GOSS, Ph.D. Price, $1.00.
3. **History of Municipal Land Ownership on Manhattan Island.**
   By GEORGE ASHTON BLACK, Ph.D. Price, $1.00.
4. **Financial History of Massachusetts.**
   By CHARLES H. J. DOUGLAS, Ph.D. Price, $1.00.

VOLUME II, 1892-93. (See note on last page.)

1. [5] **The Economics of the Russian Village.**
   By ISAAC A. HOURWICH, Ph.D. (*Out of print*).
2. [6] **Bankruptcy. A Study in Comparative Legislation.**
   By SAMUEL W. DUNSCOMB, Jr., Ph.D. (*Out of print.*)
3. [7] **Special Assessments; A Study in Municipal Finance.**
   By VICTOR ROSEWATER, Ph.D. Second Edition, 1898. (*Out of print*)

VOLUME III, 1893. 465 pp. (See note on last page.)

1. [8] *History of Elections in American Colonies.
   By CORTLAND F. BISHOP, Ph.D. (*Out of print.*)
2. [9] **The Commercial Policy of England toward the American Colonies.**
   By GEORGE L. BEER, A. M. (*Out of print.*)

VOLUME IV, 1893-94. 438 pp. (See note on last page.)

1. [10] Financial History of Virginia. By WILLIAM Z. RIPLEY, Ph.D. (*Out of print.*)
2. [11] *The Inheritance Tax. By MAX WEST, Ph.D. (*Out of print.*)
3. [12] History of Taxation in Vermont. By FREDERICK A. WOOD, Ph.D. (*Out of print.*)

VOLUME V, 1895-96. 498 pp. Price, cloth, $3.50.

1. [13] **Double Taxation in the United States.**
   By FRANCIS WALKER, Ph.D. Price, $1.00.
2. [14] **The Separation of Governmental Powers.**
   By WILLIAM BONDY, LL.B., Ph.D. Price, $1.00.
3. [15] **Municipal Government in Michigan and Ohio.**
   By DELOS F. WILCOX, Ph.D. Price, $1.00.

VOLUME VI, 1896. 601 pp. Price, cloth, $4.50 ; Paper covers, $4.00.

[16] **History of Proprietary Government in Pennsylvania.**
   By WILLIAM ROBERT SHEPHERD, Ph.D.

VOLUME VII, 1896. 512 pp. Price, cloth, $3.50.

1. [17] **History of the Transition from Provincial to Commonwealth Government in Massachusetts.** By HARRY A. CUSHING, Ph.D. Price, $2.00.
2. [18] *Speculation on the Stock and Produce Exchanges of the United States
   By HENRY CROSBY EMERY, Ph.D. (*Out of print.*)

VOLUME VIII, 1896-98. 551 pp. Price, cloth, $4.00.

1. [19] **The Struggle between President Johnson and Congress over Reconstruction.** By CHARLES ERNEST CHADSEY, Ph.D. Price, $1.00.
2. [20] **Recent Centralizing Tendencies in State Educational Administration.** By WILLIAM CLARENCE WEBSTER, Ph.D. Price, 75 cents.
3. [21] **The Abolition of Privateering and the Declaration of Paris.**
   By FRANCIS R. STARK, LL.B., Ph.D. Price, $1 00.
4. [22] **Public Administration in Massachusetts. The Relation of Central to Local Activity.** By ROBERT HARVEY WHITTEN, Ph.D. Price, $1.00.

VOLUME IX, 1897-98. 617 pp. Price, cloth, $4.00.

1. [23] *English Local Government of To-day. A Study of the Relations of Central and Local Government. By MILO ROY MALTBIE, Ph.D. Price, $2.00.
2. [24] German Wage Theories. A History of their Development.
   By JAMES W. CROOK, Ph.D. Price, $1.00.
3. [25] The Centralization of Administration in New York State.
   By JOHN ARCHIBALD FAIRLIE, Ph.D. Price, $1.00.

VOLUME XXXIV, 1909. 628 pp. Price, cloth, $4.50.

1. [89] **Transportation and Industrial Development in the Middle West.**
By WILLIAM F. GEPHART, Ph.D. Price, $2.00.
2. [90] **Social Reform and the Reformation.**
By JACOB SALWYN SCHAPIRO, Ph.D. Price, $1.25.
3. [91] **Responsibility for Crime.** By PHILIP A. PARSONS, Ph.D. (*Out of print.*)

VOLUME XXXV, 1909. 568 pp. Price, cloth, $4.50.

1. [92] **The Conflict over the Judicial Powers in the United States to 1870.**
By CHARLES GROVE HAINES, Ph.D. Price, $1.50.
2. [93] **A Study of the Population of Manhattanville.**
By HOWARD BROWN WOOLSTON, Ph.D. Price, $1.25.
3. [94] *Divorce: A Study in Social Causation.**
By JAMES P. LICHTENBERGER, Ph.D. Price, $1.50.

VOLUME XXXVI, 1910. 542 pp. Price, cloth, $4.00.

1. [95] *Reconstruction in Texas. By CHARLES WILLIAM RAMSDELL, Ph.D. Price, $2.50.
2. [96] * The Transition in Virginia from Colony to Commonwealth.
By CHARLES RAMSDELL LINGLEY, Ph.D. Price, $1.50.

VOLUME XXXVII, 1910. 606 pp. Price, cloth, $4.50.

1. [97] **Standards of Reasonableness in Local Freight Discriminations.**
By JOHN MAURICE CLARK, Ph.D. Price, $1.25.
2. [98] **Legal Development in Colonial Massachusetts.**
By CHARLES J. HILKEY, Ph.D. Price, $1.25.
3. [99] *Social and Mental Traits of the Negro.
By HOWARD W. ODUM, Ph.D. Price, $2.00.

VOLUME XXXVIII, 1910. 463 pp. Price, cloth, $3.50.

1. [100] **The Public Domain and Democracy.**
By ROBERT TUDOR HILL, Ph.D. Price, $2.00.
2. [101] **Organismic Theories of the State.**
By FRANCIS W. COKER, Ph.D. Price, $1.50.

VOLUME XXXIX, 1910-1911. 651 pp. Price, cloth, $4.50.

1. [102] **The Making of the Balkan States.**
By WILLIAM SMITH MURRAY, Ph.D. Price, $1.50.
2. [103] **Political History of New York State during the Period of the Civil War.** By SIDNEY DAVID BRUMMER, Ph. D. Price, $3.00.

VOLUME XL, 1911. 633 pp. Price, cloth, $4.50.

1. [104] **A Survey of Constitutional Development in China.**
By HAWKLING L. YEN, Ph.D. Price, $1.00.
2. [105] **Ohio Politics during the Civil War Period.**
By GEORGE H. PORTER, Ph.D. Price, $1.75.
3. [106] **The Territorial Basis of Government under the State Constitutions.**
By ALFRED ZANTZINGER REED, Ph.D. Price, $1.75.

VOLUME XLI, 1911. 514 pp. Price, cloth, $3.50; paper covers, $3.00.

[107] New Jersey as a Royal Province. By EDGAR JACOB FISHER, Ph. D.

VOLUME XLII, 1911. 400 pp. Price, cloth, $3.00; paper covers, $2.50.

[108] Attitude of American Courts in Labor Cases.
By GEORGE GORHAM GROAT, Ph.D.

VOLUME XLIII, 1911. 633 pp. Price, cloth, $4.50.

1. [109] *Industrial Causes of Congestion of Population in New York City.
By EDWARD EWING PRATT, Ph.D. Price, $2.00.
2. [110] **Education and the Mores.** By F. STUART CHAPIN, Ph.D. Price, 75 cents.
3. [111] **The British Consuls in the Confederacy.**
By MILLEDGE L. BONHAM, JR., Ph.D. Price, $2.00.

VOLUMES XLIV and XLV, 1911. 745 pp.

Price for the two volumes, cloth, $6.00 ; paper covers, $5.00.
[112 and 113] The Economic Principles of Confucius and his School.
By CHEN HUAN-CHANG, Ph.D.

VOLUME XLVI, 1911-1912. 323 pp. Price, cloth, $4.50.

1. [114] The Ricardian Socialists. BY ESTHER LOWENTHAL, Ph.D. (*Out of print.*)
2. [115] Ibrahim Pasha, Grand Vizier of Suleiman, the Magnificent.
BY HESTER DONALDSON JENKINS, Ph.D. Price, $1.00.
3. [116] *Syndicalism in France.
BY LOUIS LEVINE, Ph.D. Second edition, 1914. Price, $1.50.
4. [117] A Hoosier Village. BY NEWELL LEROY SIMS, Ph.D. Price. $1.50.

VOLUME XLVII, 1912. 544 pp. Price, cloth, $4.00.

1. [118] The Politics of Michigan, 1865-1878.
By HARRIETTE M. DILLA, Ph.D. Price, $2.00.
2. [119] *The United States Beet Sugar Industry and the Tariff.
By ROY G. BLAKEY, Ph.D. Price, $2.00.

VOLUME XLVIII, 1912. 493 pp. Price, cloth, $4.00.

1. [120] Isidor of Seville. By ERNEST BREHAUT, Ph. D. Price, $2.00.
2. [121] Progress and Uniformity in Child-Labor Legislation.
By WILLIAM FIELDING OGBURN, Ph.D. Price, $1.75.

VOLUME XLIX, 1912. 592 pp. Price, cloth, $4.50.

1. [122] British Radicalism 1791-1797. By WALTER PHELPS HALL. Price, $2.00.
2. [123] A Comparative Study of the Law of Corporations.
By ARTHUR K. KUHN, Ph.D. Price, $1.50.
3. [124] *The Negro at Work in New York City.
By GEORGE E. HAYNES, Ph.D. Price, $1.25.

VOLUME L, 1911. 481 pp. Price, cloth, $4.00.

1. [125] *The Spirit of Chinese Philanthropy. [By YAI YUE TSU, Ph.D. Price, $1.00.
2. [126] *The Alien in China. By VI. KYUIN WELLINGTON KOO, Ph.D. Price, $2.50.

VOLUME LI, 1912. 4to. Atlas. Price: cloth, $1.50; paper covers, $1.00.

1. [127] The Sale of Liquor in the South.
By LEONARD S. BLAKEY, Ph.D.

VOLUME LII, 1912. 489 pp. Price, cloth, $4.00.

1. [128] *Provincial and Local Taxation in Canada.
By SOLOMON VINEBERG, Ph.D. Price, $1.50.
2. [129] *The Distribution of Income.
By FRANK HATCH STREIGHTOFF, Ph.D. Price, $1.50.
3. [130] *The Finances of Vermont. By FREDERICK A. WOOD, Ph.D. Price, $1.00.

VOLUME LIII, 1913. 789 pp. Price, cloth, $4.50; paper, $4.00.

[131] The Civil War and Reconstruction in Florida. By W. W. DAVIS, Ph.D.

VOLUME LIV, 1913. 604 pp. Price, cloth, $4.50.

1. [132] *Privileges and Immunities of Citizens of the United States.
By ARNOLD JOHNSON LIEN, Ph.D Price, 75 cents
2. [133] The Supreme Court and Unconstitutional Legislation.
By BLAINE FREE MOORE, Ph.D. Price, $1.00.
3. [134] *Indian Slavery in Colonial Times within the Present Limits of the
United States. By ALMON WHEELER LAUBER, Ph.D. Price, $3.00.

VOLUME LV, 1913. 665 pp. Price, cloth, $4.50.

1. [135] *A Political History of the State of New York.
By HOMER A. STEBBINS, Ph.D. Price, $4.00.
2. [136] *The Early Persecutions of the Christians.
By LEON H. CANFIELD, Ph.D. Price, $1.50.

VOLUME LVI, 1913. 406 pp. Price, cloth, $3.50.

1. [137] Speculation on the New York Stock Exchange, 1904-1907.
By ALGERNON ASHBURNER OSBORNE. Price, $1.50.
2. [138] The Policy of the United States towards Industrial Monopoly.
By OSWALD WHITMAN KNAUTH, Ph.D. Price, $2.00.

VOLUME LVII, 1914. 670 pp. Price, cloth, $4.50.

1. [139] *The Civil Service of Great Britain.
By ROBERT MOSES, Ph.D. Price, $2.00.
2. [140] The Financial History of New York State.
By DON C. SOWERS. Price, $2.50.

VOLUME LVIII, 1914. 684 pp. Price, cloth, $4.50; paper, $4.00.

[141] Reconstruction in North Carolina.
By J. G. DE ROULHAC HAMILTON, Ph.D.

VOLUME LIX, 1914. 625 pp. Price, cloth, $4.50.

1. [142] The Development of Modern Turkey by means of its Press.
By AHMED EMIN, Ph.D. Price, $1.00.
2. [143] The System of Taxation in China, 1614-1911.
By SHAO-KWAN CHEN, Ph. D. Price, $1.00.
3. [144] The Currency Problem in China. By WEN PIN WEI, Ph.D. (Out of print.
4. [145] *Jewish Immigration to the United States.
By SAMUEL JOSEPH, Ph.D. Price, $1.50)

29
(4)